Rightward Bound

Rightward Bound

MAKING AMERICA CONSERVATIVE
IN THE 1970s

Edited by

Bruce J. Schulman
Julian E. Zelizer

HARVARD UNIVERSITY PRESS
Cambridge, Massachusetts
London, England
2008

Copyright © 2008 by the President and
Fellows of Harvard College
All rights reserved
Printed in the United States of America

Library of Congress Cataloging-in-Publication Data

Rightward bound : making America conservative in the 1970s /
edited by Bruce J. Schulman and Julian E. Zelizer.
p. cm.
Includes bibliographical references and index.
ISBN-13: 978-0-674-02757-2 (hardcover : alk. paper)
ISBN-13: 978-0-674-02758-9 (pbk. : alk. paper)
1. Conservatism—United States—History—20th century.
2. Nineteen seventies.   3. United States—Politics and
government—1969–1974.   4. United States—Politics and
government—1974–1977.   5. United States—Politics and
government—1977–1981.   I. Schulman, Bruce J.
II. Zelizer, Julian E.
JC573.2.U6R54   2008
320.520973'09047—dc22   2007043107

*For all the undergraduates who have inspired us
to explain how history matters
and helped us bring to life
the colors and sounds of the past*

Contents

Acknowledgments

This book has been a pleasure to assemble. Though the job of editing is often difficult, as the editors need to move the book along and round up essays, the contributors to this book have made our lives easy. Delightful to work with, they produced wonderful essays, always on schedule, and responded well to our suggestions as the book evolved. The authors have been willing to step out of their own intellectual worlds to connect their essays to the broader theme that has developed out of this publication. The quality of this volume is a testament to their skill.

We would also like to thank Joyce Seltzer at Harvard University Press. Since our breakfast at Henrietta's Table in Cambridge, Joyce has been invariably enthusiastic and supportive. Throughout the past year, she has pushed us to keep our eye on the main theme of the book. In doing so, she has helped us make sure that the essays read as a whole rather than as separate pieces. The rest of the team at Harvard has been first-rate.

Finally, we would like to thank our colleague Charles Dellheim, chairman of the History Department at Boston University. Charles has offered unfailing support—moral and material—for the collaboration of which this book is a major part, and he made completing this project a pleasure.

Introduction

BRUCE J. SCHULMAN

JULIAN E. ZELIZER

Today's newspapers scream with positively puzzling headlines. In many ways, Americans seem to be living in an age of conservatism. The nation battles over stem cell research and creationism in the public schools, testifying to the potency of evangelical Christian groups in contemporary public life. The United States scorns international law and collective security, flouting the United Nations and mounting an ambitious effort to "end tyranny" across the globe. Although gas prices fluctuate wildly, the government resists energy conservation or regulatory measures that might ease the crunch. Social Security and Medicare require reform, but market-based approaches remain the only proposals on the table. Conservative politicians seem as comfortable navigating the hostile waters of *The Daily Show* on Comedy Central as they do in the friendly confines of the Fox television network.

Yet at the very same time, conservatives seem unable to vanquish their worst enemies. The federal government remains extremely large and keeps growing. In fact, the federal government is larger today than when President George W. Bush took office. "If Bill Clinton had tolerated this," the editors of the *Wall Street Journal* said of domestic

1

spending, "Republicans would be shouting from the rooftops."[1] Popular culture seems immune from conservative attack. Athletes doped up on steroids take over the sports pages, teenagers make fine-haired distinctions about physical acts that justify their overall comfort with sexuality, and *Desperate Housewives* becomes a pop culture phenomenon, its combination of scurrilous sexuality and campy self-parody revealing deep uncertainties about gender roles in an ambivalent "post-feminist" era. Americans in the "red" part of the country seem as enthralled with these seductive entertainers as do those living in the "blue states." The once omnipotent House Majority Leader, Tom "the Hammer" DeLay of Texas, landed on the ethical hot seat and was forced to resign, one in a long line of lobbying and sex scandals in 2006 that helped bring to an end Republican rule on Capitol Hill. Democrats regained control of Congress, but only by relying on a group of new legislators from the South and Midwest who sounded more like Ronald Reagan than Lyndon Johnson.

Often mysterious, sometimes bizarre, contemporary public life reveals a series of seeming paradoxes that Americans can understand only by seeking their origin. For the United States of George W. Bush—with its brash, unilateral approach to the world, devotion to the seemingly incompatible ideals of Christian piety and free market economy, its Sunbelt style and freewheeling interweaving of politics and entertainment—emerged from the Big Bang of the 1970s. The 1970s unlock the mysteries of today because the decade constituted a critical turning point in American history that established the foundation for current public debates. The policies, social movements, leaders, and institutional changes that emerged out of this decade fundamentally reshaped America by moving the nation out of the New Deal and Cold War period into a new era defined by the conservative movement, and its persistent failures, at home and abroad.

Why did America move to the Right, and how far did the nation go? According to the conventional wisdom, the United States experienced a conservative turn as a result of the national trauma over

Vietnam, racial conflict, and the rampant liberalization of American culture. Others argue that economic decline combined with the uncertainties of international relations fueled backlash against liberalism, initiating a wholesale shift in how Americans thought about politics.

The authors in this book conclude that the embrace of conservatism was fiercely contested—that it involved hard-fought battles as well as crucial compromises in which the accomplishments of twentieth-century liberalism remained very strong. At the heart of the 1970s was a massive mobilization by activists, organizations, and political elites associated with the conservative movement. Without any question, the forces that fueled conservatism had been expanding for several decades. An impressive body of new scholarship has charted the persistence of conservative impulses throughout the "New Deal order"—the heyday of national liberalism that ran from the presidency of Franklin Roosevelt through the 1960s. Throughout the era, potent forces, such as the deindustrialization of northern cities, the rise of the suburbs, and the migration of people and dollars toward the Sunbelt, created a more hospitable national environment for conservatives. At the same time, struggles over jobs, taxes, and neighborhoods revealed powerful strains even at the heart of the liberal coalition.[2] Toiling in the political wilderness, an incipient New Right took shape, organizing suburban housewives, small businessmen, crew-cut collegians, even the 1964 presidential campaign of Senator Barry Goldwater.[3]

But though modern conservatism did not emerge out of nowhere, as a sudden backlash against the alleged excesses of the "sixties," the Right coalesced into a full-scale political movement and forged durable connections between state and society only in the 1970s. A series of important developments transformed the conservative movement into a dominant political force. The rise of conservatism was not inevitable nor was it automatic. It resulted from a concerted institutional and grassroots struggle to reshape the rhetoric and policies of America. During the 1970s, the conservative move-ment experienced a series of triumphs and setbacks that influenced the nation for the next three decades. These struggles produced a political system that empowered conservative politicians and elites, a popular culture that felt immense pressure to display conservative social values, and an economy that bucked regulatory oversight.

Yet conservatives failed to remake the nation. Rather, they layered themselves over the accumulated changes of the twentieth century. Liberalism remained deeply embedded in national politics, popular culture retained the impulses of the 1960s, and social movements op-posing conservative values flourished. Much more than a leftward cycle in American political history, the liberal ascendancy of the postwar era had refashioned national politics, firmly rooting a set of institutions and policies, as well as a series of public expectations about what government could and should accomplish. Politics and law reflected more informal shifts in sexual mores, language, dress, food, living arrangements, and social behavior. The triumphs of the Right, at the ballot box and broadly across American society, would take place against a backdrop where the achievements of liberalism still mattered.

Most Americans have failed to recognize the importance of the 1970s to today's confusing political universe. They regard the decade as a national joke—an era of outrageous fashions, vapid music, and cultural excess. Iconic images of the period—a paralyzed Jimmy Carter unable to resolve the crisis in Iran while TV newsmen counted the days of "America Held Hostage," the deranged veteran-turned-vigilante Travis Bickle stalking the menacing streets of New York in Martin Scorsese's *Taxi Driver,* glittering disco balls and yellow smi-ley faces—capture the conventional portrait of the 1970s as a decade when the country was frozen between the 1960s and 1980s, waiting to find itself and reestablish a national direction.

This book corrects that mistaken impression by showing that the seventies constituted a turning point. The 1970s transformed

American politics as much as the more famous 1960s. In race, ethnic, and gender relations, political economy, international relations, moral and cultural politics, and much more, America changed in the 1970s. A quarter century after the fact, historians have finally, albeit slowly, started to recognize the centrality of the 1970s to modern U.S. history.[4] By assembling the most innovative new scholarship about this decade, these essays unearth the sources of the nation's present dilemmas and advance bold scholarly reinterpretations of the lost decade in America's recent past.

Remarkably, despite the varied topics and approaches of the new scholarship, there have emerged areas of consensus that highlight crucial shifts in the 1970s that have exerted enduring impact on contemporary American life. Although modern American conservatism took shape in the 1950s and 1960s, it never cohered as a full-scale political movement. After 1970, the conservative movement completed its organizational infrastructure—the political action committees, the volunteer operations, the radio talk shows, the think tanks, and the direct mail network. The movement developed a post-Vietnam foreign policy agenda that would define America's position through the end of the Cold War and after, establishing the foundation for the war against terrorism. Mobilizing previously quiescent evangelical Christians, the conservative movement also framed a new domestic agenda around cultural issues that would attract millions of voters into a reconstructed Republican Party. The conservative movement of the 1970s would become the motive force driving American politics for the next three decades.

During the seventies, the United States also experienced a regional shift as national power drifted south and west. Drawing strength from its burgeoning population and booming economy, the South and Southwest wrested control of national politics. Since the mid-1960s, Sunbelt candidates have won every presidential election, sending to the White House residents of Georgia, Southern California,

Texas, and Arkansas. More important, Sunbelt power extended far beyond the White House. The South's historic policy prescriptions—low taxes and scant public services, deference to religious sensibilities, military preparedness and an inconsistent preference for state and local government over federal supremacy—came to define the national agenda during the seventies and have remained potent ever since.

A wave of government reform also crested in the 1970s when established political institutions, many of them in place since the Progressive Era, became the targets of change. Reformers overhauled the nomination procedures for presidential candidates to break the remaining hold of party elites. The political process opened to public view as access to information became easier to obtain in every arm of the government. Reformers also secured permanent rights for public interest groups in the administrative process, and the federal government embraced a proactive role in protecting the voting rights of citizens. At the same time, a series of independent counsels, grand juries, and the Federal Bureau of Investigation (FBI) institutionalized the investigation of political corruption. These developments produced a new era in American public life, defined by strong partisanship without secure party leaders, a television-centered media with a 24-hour news cycle, scandal warfare and the criminalization of politics, a dependence on polling, and codified rules of ethics.

Finally, in the 1970s the federal government underwent a dramatic expansion, after the age of liberalism had allegedly ended. When Congress raised benefits and indexed Social Security to the rate of inflation in 1972, for example, it launched a period of massive growth that turned the program into what House Speaker Tip O'Neill called the "third rail" of American politics. "You touch it," O'Neill explained, "and you die."

At the same time, a welfare rights movement persuaded the federal courts to guarantee the poor the right to all sorts of economic assistance. An environmental movement pushed Congress and the presidents to adopt bold regulations protecting the land and its species. Popular culture also liberalized dramatically in ways that made the 1960s counterculture seem tame. During the 1970s, Hollywood experimented with directors who depicted explicit sexuality and violence while television producers moved far away from the era of *Leave it to Beaver* with culturally edgy shows such as *All in the Family*. Popular musicians like David Bowie flaunted their androgynous sexuality without reservation while heavy metal and punk singers popularized aggressively anti-authoritarian lyrics among America's youth.

The contributors to this book crystallize a new portrait of this decade—with politics the locus of change that drives a wide variety of cultural, economic, and social transformations. The book examines three major realms of politics—domestic government, international relations, and political culture—to better understand the persistent tensions in the late twentieth century between conservative political power and liberal change that emerged in this decade. Although the contributors do not attempt to cover every issue from this decade, they provide a fascinating look at the triumphs of conservatism as the movement took form and achieved a series of important victories.

Part I examines the development of a conservative movement, focusing on the question of how such large numbers of Americans came to perceive themselves as sympathetic to political conservatism. In most cases, the contributors find that these shifts in political identity did not flow naturally out of long-term demographic and economic shifts, or in reaction to dramatic events, but were the product of political organization by energetic activists. The contributors also examine how conservatism gained organizational strength and entrenched itself in the nation's political institutions. Matthew Lassiter (Chapter 1) claims that conservative activists seized political advantage by emphasizing the cultural factors behind the breakdown of the nuclear family in the 1970s, submerging powerful economic forces that were at work. Placing more emphasis on activism from below rather than above, Paul Boyer (Chapter 2) traces a vast and energetic network of religious leaders, authors, and entertainers who nurtured grassroots enthusiasm for evangelical religion and political activism. Turning to the intersection of business and the university campus, Bethany Moreton (Chapter 3) reveals an enormous campaign conducted by major corporations to promote free-market values and business education to America's college-age youth. Marjorie Spruill (Chapter 4) shows that conservative women developed their organizational muscle and experience in response to the Equal Rights Amendment and the 1977 state and national International Women's Year Conferences, while Joseph Crespino (Chapter 5) discovers that the political mobilization of evangelical Christians resulted from struggles in the 1970s over the tax treatment of religious schools. Alice O'Connor (Chapter 8) argues that conservative foundations provided neoconservative policymakers and movement activists with the "venture capital" that they needed to mobilize politically and spread the ideas of the Right.

Capturing the importance of contingency that historians bring to the table, this book will also demonstrate that several developments in the decade that had little to do with the conservative mobilization and often sprang from very different political impulses eventually lent support to right-wing politics. Suleiman Osman (Chapter 6) shows how a new localism that was unconnected to Great Society liberalism or the conservative movement brought the middle class back to the cities in search of a new approach to governance. But that movement opened the way for a market-oriented approach to urban development that had little to do with the people who originally migrated back into the cities. Focusing on singer/songwriters in popular culture, Bradford Martin (Chapter 7) traces how artists such as Jackson Browne developed a social ethic and an oppositional politics, particularly a critique of institutional reform, that unintentionally lent support to a culture that blended easily with the market-centered, anti-government ethos promoted by movement conservatives. In many cases, conservative activists succeeded because liberal organizations encountered huge challenges and stumbled politically.

Part II turns to the battles that occurred in the 1970s over policy and politics, where the conservative movement scored important victories that established the Right as a serious force in American politics, as well as to the compromises the movement made along the way to achieve success. Thomas Sugrue and John Skrentny (Chapter 9) show how a small circle of advisers working in Richard Nixon's White House capitalized on the ethnic revival of the 1970s and harnessed it toward conservative electoral objectives. In the realm of energy crisis, Meg Jacobs (Chapter 10) explains, conservative elites institutionalized themselves in the executive branch so that they could promote a vision of energy policy that depicted big government rather than big oil as the main problem. According to Joseph McCartin (Chapter 11), conservatives benefited when the severe fiscal crisis that took place mid-decade crushed a real opportunity that had emerged for flourishing public sector unions to forge a powerful alliance with the Democratic Party. Jeremi Suri (Chapter 12) finds that conservative activists, most notably the former actor and California governor Ronald Reagan, started to break into the foreign policy community through attacks on détente. In the realm of foreign policy, Derek Buckaloo (Chapter 13) argues that the inability of Democratic leaders to respond to the challenges raised by Vietnam created a huge vacuum that conservatives exploited. Finally, Julian Zelizer (Chapter 14) ends the volume with an examination of how politicians affiliated with the movement were able to defeat President Jimmy Carter's effort to define a centrist national security agenda.

Together, the contributors make clear that the 1970s witnessed transformations that established the tenor of American political history in the last quarter of the twentieth century and the start of the twenty-first. The decade was not a pause in between two great periods, but itself marked an era that witnessed the emergence of trends, contests, and conflicts that have defined the public realm ever since.

PART ONE

MOBILIZING THE MOVEMENT

CHAPTER 1

Inventing Family Values

MATTHEW D. LASSITER

During the 1980 presidential contest, the Moral Majority launched a media campaign headlined "America: You're Too Young to Die." The new political organization, led by Virginia televangelist Jerry Falwell, claimed to represent more than 50 million social conservatives and evangelical Christians mobilized under the banner of the "pro-family movement." Because the nation had turned away from God, according to the Moral Majority's presentation, "the great American dream has become the hideous American nightmare." A placid image of a middle-class suburban home abruptly gave way to a montage of headlines about divorce and child abuse, photographs of aborted fetuses and feminists with placards proclaiming "Keep Your Laws and Your Morality off *My* Body," pornographic scenes from strip clubs and the red-light district of Times Square, and demonstrators with signs reading "Thank God I'm Gay" and "Lesbian Mothers." This fusion of traditional religious values and New Right politics reached a climax at a summer rally held in Dallas for evangelical ministers from across the nation. Reverend Falwell informed the gathering: "We have a three-fold primary responsibility. Number one, get people saved. Number two, get them baptized. Number three, get them registered to vote." Texas televangelist

James Robison followed by blasting "pro-family" conservatives for avoiding politics: "I'm sick and tired of hearing about all of the radicals, and the perverts, and the liberals, and the leftists, and the communists coming out of the closet. It's time for God's people to come out of the closet, out of the churches, and change America." Watching from the stage, presidential candidate Ronald Reagan then delivered the message that cemented the alliance between conservative Christian activists and the Republican Party: "I and many others have felt a new vitality in American politics . . . I endorse you and what you are doing."[1]

Looking back at the 1970s and early 1980s, it is common to reduce the politics of family values to the polarization of the "culture wars" that culminated in the rise of the religious Right. But the sense of a crisis of the American family emerged as a mainstream feature of the decade between Woodstock and Reagan's election, as voices from across the political spectrum expressed deep anxieties about a culture of moral permissiveness, the consequences of the sexual revolution, and the nation's uncertain economic future. The postwar embodiment of the American Dream—a heterosexual nuclear family with a working father and stay-at-home mother living in an upwardly mobile suburban neighborhood—appeared on the verge of collapse during the seventies. By the middle of the decade, fewer than half of married two-parent households, and fewer than one-fourth of all American households, conformed to the nuclear family ideal of a breadwinner father and a stay-at-home mother. Economic recession and runaway inflation squeezed standards of living for working-class and middle-class households alike, while the decline of the family wage combined with a substantial increase in divorce rates to push a large majority of mothers into the paid workforce. Social movements such as feminism and gay rights simultaneously challenged the boundaries of the traditional domestic ideology, and countercultural forms of sexual expression and illegal drug use filtered down from the college campuses into suburban high schools throughout the nation. These developments set the stage for a national "family values" panic over youth delinquency, a perceived epidemic hyped in countless news stories and widely attributed to an atmosphere of permissive parenting made worse by the spread of no-fault divorce and the inability of working mothers to supervise children at home.[2]

Although a broad public consensus in the 1970s highlighted the endangered status of the nuclear family, profound and lasting divisions emerged over the causes and therefore the solutions for the disintegration of the American Dream. The mainstream news media consistently elevated cultural over economic analysis in exploring the "crisis of the American family," and mass culture played a central role in popularizing the "moral permissiveness" critique that soon became a mainstay of the religious Right. Conservative Christian activists agreed that cultural forces were primarily responsible for the decline of traditional values, meaning that the intertwined fate of the family and the nation depended on a spiritual revival that would begin in the home. During the first half of the decade, future organizers of the religious Right expended much of their energy on an inwardly focused campaign against permissive parenting and juvenile delinquency. The mass movement of social conservatives into electoral politics represented the failure of this internal reform agenda, which led to a search for external answers that ultimately blamed feminists and gay rights advocates for a conspiracy to subvert traditional family values. On the other side of the political divide, the women's movement and other progressive groups interpreted the crisis of the American Dream primarily in economic terms and advocated public policies such as federally funded day care, flexible family-friendly employment practices, and equal rights protections under the law. Conservative leaders of the religious Right occasionally acknowledged the destabilizing effects of market capitalism and mass consumer culture, but they strenuously denounced government interference in the domestic sphere as a liberal scheme to empower alternative family arrangements. The key to understanding the political fallout of this pivotal era is not simply that conservatives defeated liberals in the electoral arena, but that cultural explanations triumphed over economic ones in setting the terms of public debate and determining the direction of public policies.

In 1968, Richard Nixon won the presidential election by appealing to "the great majority of Americans, the forgotten Americans," defined as the decent and hard-working people whose traditional moral values sustained the nation by giving "lift to the American Dream." By the end of 1969, when *Time* magazine recognized the besieged Silent Majority as "Man and Woman of the Year," the celebration of Middle American values had turned into the perception that the American Dream was slipping away from millions of families. After citing the economic uncertainty caused by inflation and indicting permissive parenting for the defection of middle-class youth to the counterculture, the article concluded that "a surprisingly large number of Middle Americans attribute the weakening of the family structures to the fact that so many mothers have gone to work." A 1970 report by the White House Conference on Children reinforced this diagnosis, warning that "America's families are in trouble—trouble so deep and pervasive as to threaten the future of our nation." *Time* quickly responded with another cover story headlined "The U.S. Family: 'Help!'" The article linked the implosion of the American Dream to the isolation of the nuclear family in the suburbs, a situation intensified by skyrocketing divorce rates and the mass entry of married women into the workforce. Mother blaming infused this analysis regardless of whether women pursued careers or stayed at home, as the essay attributed the epidemic of youth rebellion to the "benevolent permissiveness" practiced by "many American mothers." Although *Time* mentioned experts who advocated universal day care and mandatory maternity leave policies, the accompanying photographs played directly into the tropes of suburban panic by contrasting the "conventional" happiness of a white middle-class family of four with a group of hippies at a countercultural commune and an interracial day care center presided over by a black man with an Afro.[3]

For feminist groups and their political allies, government-subsidized child care represented the obvious solution to the challenge of balancing work and family obligations, especially for the vast majority of American women who did not enjoy the freedom to choose to stay out of the wage labor force. But in late 1970, after Congress passed legislation to establish a national day care system, President Nixon vetoed the measure on the grounds that it would undermine parental authority by favoring "communal approaches to childrearing over against the family-centered approach." The national panic over the morals of youth—so closely linked to this increasingly elusive suburban ideal of children supervised by stay-at-home mothers—continued to escalate in the aftermath of the day care showdown. In 1972, a *Time* cover story on "Sex and the Teenager" began with a female high school senior boasting of going "to bed with nine boys in the past two years" and a sixteen-year-old portrayed as the lonely virgin on her campus. Because of the "almost unlimited new sexual license," sexually transmitted diseases were reaching "epidemic proportions in high schools and colleges," and teenagers were responsible for one-third of the 1.5 million abortions performed the previous year in the United States. Summing up the conventional wisdom, *Time* ascribed the destigmatization of premarital sex to the birth control pill, peer pressure, the drug culture, the compromised moral authority of divorced parents, and the women's liberation movement. The article also placed responsibility for "the origins of homosexuality" on child rearing practices within the home and reported a parental consensus that the decline in sexual propriety resulted from the widespread "permissiveness" of American culture and family life.[4]

Popular culture in the early 1970s played directly into the discourse of family crisis, especially as the portrayals of suburban dysfunction that had long been a staple of Hollywood films began to appear during the previously sanitized family-friendly hours of network television. The sitcom *All in the Family* (1971–1979) addressed political conflict through the generation gap within the Bunkers' Middle American household, while *The Mary Tyler Moore Show* (1970–1977) portrayed a working woman making it on her own, and *Maude* (1972–1978) dealt with controversial issues such as abortion and divorce. But perhaps the most extraordinary television event came in 1973, when an estimated weekly audience of 10 million watched the twelve episodes of *An American Family*, a PBS documentary series featuring Bill and Pat Loud and their five children trying to live the California version of the suburban dream. By tapping into hot-button themes of divorce, homosexuality, and permissive parenting, this "real-life" odyssey became a popular benchmark of the changing family values of the upper-middle class and the subterranean traumas of the suburban landscape. The Louds' twenty-year marriage disintegrated during the filming of the series, culminating in Pat's demand in the ninth episode that her unfaithful and absentee husband move out of the house. The eldest son, twenty-year-old Lance, lived an openly gay lifestyle in New York City, leading his mother to admit that she knew "something was wrong, . . . but you just don't do anything about it—let him do his own thing." With Bill exiled to an apartment, the final episode of *An American Family* captured a poignant family meeting called by Pat, a suburban matriarch in pearls and knee-high boots, to confront her children for leaving the house a mess, breaking into her liquor cabinet, and taking sexual partners to the loft. In this era of trickle-down countercultural rebellion, Pat could do little but laugh as her long-haired and apparently stoned sons gently mocked her pretense of discipline and authority.[5]

An unexpected cultural phenomenon, *An American Family* elicited an avalanche of commentary that emphasized the exposed pathologies of suburban family life and especially the repercussions of no-fault divorce for the children caught in the middle. *Newsweek* described the "private civil war" within this seemingly normal middle-class household as a "scathing commentary on the American domestic dream," while the *Atlantic Monthly* attributed public fascination to the Louds' function as "a symbol of disintegration and purposelessness in American life." Writing in the *New York Times Magazine,* the feminist novelist Anne Roiphe condemned the "flamboyant, . . . camping and queening" lifestyle of Lance Loud and criticized his permissive mother for trying to "pretend everything is all right" with her lost gay son. *Newsweek*'s exhaustive coverage of *An American Family* included a cover story about the Louds and an investigative report on the "culture of divorce . . . in the permissive '70s." The magazine reported Pat Loud's insistence that their experience "demonstrated that divorce is not a tragic failure," as well as her older daughter's belief that the separation was "a relief." But the accompanying story on the "the American domestic dream and its dissolution" featured anecdotes of teenagers falling victim to sex and drugs without "a father's influence," ex-wives struggling to keep children in line without "a man to fall back on," and self-absorbed career women "running away from the carports, the barbeque pits and the washer-driers." In its own feature on "throwaway marriages," *U.S. News and World Report* blamed "diminished parental guidance and discipline" for much of the "nation's rising juvenile delinquency." Capturing the consensus among many experts, *Reader's Digest* warned that "we are now raising a generation of children from broken homes—and creating a social time bomb."[6]

A year before the filming of *An American Family,* during the period when the national media repeatedly linked permissive parenting to moral breakdown and youth crisis, child psychologist James Dobson published an instructional manual that sold more than 1 million copies by the end of the decade. A faculty member at the University of Southern California and a resident of suburban Los

Angeles, Dobson would later gain fame as the founder of two of the most influential organizations of the religious Right, the Christian media empire Focus on the Family and the political lobbying group Family Research Council. In 1970, when his book *Dare to Discipline* indicted permissiveness in child rearing as the fundamental source of the nation's problems, Dobson was operating well within the mainstream currents of America's ongoing family values debate, albeit with the moral certainty of a self-help message ultimately anchored in the Bible. According to Dobson's analysis, the pervasive disrespect for all forms of authority by American youth, whether unruly toddlers or wayward adolescents or campus radicals, could be traced back to the child-rearing philosophy that had "sacrificed this generation on the altar of overindulgence, permissiveness, and smother-love." While many other social critics were blaming lax disciplinary standards in the affluent suburbs for the political turmoil of the sixties, Dobson's best-selling book brought everything together under the permissiveness thesis, including immorality, civil disobedience, vandalism, violence, illegal drugs, illegitimate pregnancies, venereal diseases, antiwar protests, teenage delinquency, divorce, broken families, and more. He advised parents to spank their children judiciously during the preadolescent years, to teach abstinence-based sex education at home, and to curb exposure to the immorality promoted by Hollywood and network television. While acknowledging the economic strains facing many dual-income families, Dobson also urged sacrifice because "children need their mothers [at home] more than they do a newer car or a larger house."[7]

In the early 1970s, the anti-permissiveness campaign promoted by James Dobson and other traditionalists revolved primarily around an internal rather than an external agenda: reforming child-rearing practices within the nuclear family, rather than transforming public policies or moving directly into electoral politics. Religious conservatives still believed that, with the proper combination of moral authority and maternal supervision, the private family sphere could serve as a refuge against the secularization of American culture and the ramifications of the sexual revolution. Dobson's second book, *Hide or Seek* (1974), proclaimed that "we have met the enemy and it is *us!* Often the greatest damage is unintentionally inflicted right in the home, which should be the child's sanctuary and fortress." After reiterating his spanking recommendation, the psychologist urged parents to replace rock music and sexually explicit television programming with outdoor family activities and Disney productions. Dobson also addressed the "homosexual epidemic," which he attributed primarily to "an unhappy home life" marked by overbearing mothers and unloving fathers who failed to teach clear gender roles in the early childhood years. Neither feminism nor the gay rights movement yet registered as formal enemies in Dobson's public pronouncements, though in a passage that foreshadowed the culture wars on the horizon, he did conclude that "America's future is at stake" in the parental responsibility to prevent homosexuality through a "healthy, stable home environment." In a subsequent book, *The Strong-Willed Child* (1978), Dobson continued to emphasize his familiar message about the need for strict discipline to regulate adolescent behavior, but for the first time he also announced a public stance of opposition to legalized abortion. Catholic groups had been far more active than evangelical Protestants in the growing anti-abortion movement, and Dobson declared that "it is time that the Christian church found its tongue and spoke in defense of the unborn children who are unable to plead for their own lives."[8]

Over the course of the 1970s, future leaders of the religious Right gradually but inexorably came to believe that the internal focus on protecting traditional nuclear families from the sexual revolution was not enough, that instead they would have to go on the political offensive in order to win their defensive battles against the external threats of feminism, gay rights, and governmental interference in the domestic sphere. A key turning point came during the lengthy struggle over the Equal Rights Amendment (ERA), which the feminist movement considered essential to the realization of first-class citizenship and economic justice for working women and homemakers alike (for more on the ERA and the conservative movement, see Chapter 4 in this volume). The ERA galvanized an unanticipated but powerful antifeminist backlash led by Republican activist Phyllis Schlafly and her Eagle Forum organization, a grassroots mobilization of conservative religious women and other traditionalists who embraced an exclusionary identity as the "pro-family movement." Anti-ERA forces charged that a "tiny minority of dissatisfied, highly vocal, militant" feminists were conspiring to abolish the right to "stay at home, to rear your children, to be supported by your husband." Schlafly's 1977 manifesto, *The Power of the Positive Woman,* contended that the feminist "war on the family . . . deliberately degrades the homemaker" and that policies such as universal day care would "offer financial inducements to promote an exodus of mothers and babies from the home." She called instead for the repeal of no-fault divorce laws that encouraged husbands to abandon their wives, the defeat of the ERA in order to preserve legislation that required men to provide for their families, and even for affirmative action for primary wage earners to prevent childless workers (and mothers from dual-income families) from taking the jobs needed by heads of households.[9]

The confrontation between feminist and antifeminist forces reached a climax at the 1977 National Women's Conference in Houston, which brought the competition to define "family values" and "women's rights" into sharp relief. *Time* magazine's sympathetic cover story described the collective excitement as delegates discovered that "many other middle-of-the-road, American-as-Mom's-apple-pie women shared with them a sense of second-class citizenship and a craving for greater social and economic equality." With a heavy emphasis on economic rights, the convention endorsed a National Plan of Action that included ratification of the

ERA, national health insurance and universal day care, the extension of Social Security to homemakers, rape prevention and domestic abuse shelters, Medicaid funding for abortions, and nondiscrimination against lesbians. Phyllis Schlafly and other conservative activists organized a counterdemonstration under the umbrella of the new Pro-Family Coalition, which denounced the Houston conference agenda as an assault on mainstream American values, from the immorality of legalized abortion and gay rights to the weakening of the nuclear family by policies promoting day care and working mothers. Although the "pro-family movement" targeted feminism as the primary enemy and succeeded in its campaign to derail the ERA, a deeper appreciation of the forces reshaping American society in the 1970s reveals underlying anxieties about unregulated male behavior and the dislocations of free-market capitalism. Antifeminist activists at the grassroots level expressed concern that "the women's movement is turning into men's liberation," with no-fault divorce allowing husbands to "run off with their secretaries" and fathers in two-income families showing little inclination to help out with housework and childcare. Televangelist Pat Robertson, the future founder of the Christian Coalition, conceded that economic pressures had made it "necessary for women to enter the work force," which he blamed for the acceleration of teenage delinquency, promiscuity, and homosexuality.[10]

In the second half of the 1970s, the increasing visibility of the gay rights movement galvanized a fierce backlash among conservative religious activists, who began to portray homosexuality as an external political threat to the traditional family rather than their earlier characterization as a psychological disorder caused by bad parenting. "Gays on the March," a 1975 cover story in *Time* magazine, introduced many readers to the "spread of unabashed homosexuality once thought to be confined to the worlds of theater, dance, fashion." The grassroots counterattack gathered steam in Miami, where popular singer Anita Bryant formed an organization called Save Our Children to overturn the passage of a local gay rights ordinance. Reframing the debate as a homosexual demand for special rights rather than for equal rights, Bryant declared that gays who refused to stay in the closet were "asking to be blessed in their abnormal lifestyle" through protective legislation that "discriminates against my children's rights to grow up in a healthy, decent community." After voters in Miami repealed the ordinance, gay rights groups staged protests in cities across the country, making deliberate efforts to counter the restrictive politicization of the "family" label with slogans such as "We Are Your Children" and "I Am a Proud Gay Parent." Phyllis Schlafly responded by portraying the gay rights agenda to legalize same-sex marriage and adoption as "an assault on our right to have a country in which the family is recognized, protected, and encouraged as the basic unit of society." Jerry Falwell, the Southern Baptist pastor who had denounced political activism by ministers in a widely circulated 1965 critique of the civil rights movement, continued his reversal of course by organizing a "Clean Up America" rally outside the Capitol in 1979. The televangelist labeled homosexuality an "outright assault on the family," condemned the gay themes in television shows such as *Soap* (1977–1981) and *Three's Company* (1977–1984), and endorsed Anita Bryant's inflammatory allegation that "homosexuals cannot reproduce themselves, so they must recruit."[11]

The culture wars over who should have the power to define family values, and in what ways government policies should influence the domestic sphere, boiled over during the 1980 White House Conference on Families. President Jimmy Carter, a Southern Baptist who initially enjoyed the support of many evangelical leaders, proposed the initiative in order to achieve a broad consensus on public policies that would "reverse the trend . . . that has destroyed the American family." The politicization of this mission began almost immediately, as feminist and gay rights groups pushed for an expansive definition of families that included single parents and unmarried or same-sex couples, while conservatives defended an exclusionary vision restricted to people related by blood, marriage, or adoption. Although interest groups engineered clashes over abortion, gay rights, and the ERA, a large majority of the 125,000 participants in the White House Conference's state forums and regional hearings agreed that economic pressures posed the most urgent challenge for American families. The most popular recommendations equated family values with government intervention in both economic and moral affairs, including family-friendly employment policies, the extension of Social Security to homemakers, controls on sex and violence in the media, and drug and alcohol prevention campaigns. Connie Marshner, a leader of the Pro-Family Coalition forces, responded that "the best way to help the family is to get the government out of family life." Jim Guy Tucker, the chair of the proceedings, lamented that the economic focus had been eclipsed by "a denial of the realities of family life today, in a nostalgic search for easy answers, . . . a bitter partisan and ideological conflict over families." According to James Dobson, who authored the dissenting report, the White House Conference proved to be "a disaster . . . Massive governmental programs were requested . . . [that] would have brought the federal government into the family through the front door, which is what we *least* need at this time."[12]

The leaders of the religious Right movement that seemed to explode onto the American political scene in the late 1970s insisted that they were not seeking to impose a theocracy on a pluralist nation, but instead only trying to defend their own families and communities against the external threat of the sexual revolution and the unsolicited interference of the federal government. "The bottom line of the pro-family people," Phyllis Schlafly announced at the American Family Forum's inaugural convention in the summer of 1980, "is get the federal government off our backs." On NBC's *Meet the Press,* Moral Majority cofounder Jerry Falwell assured a national television audience that "we're not trying to jam our moral philosophy down the throats of others. We're simply trying to keep others from jamming their amoral philosophies down our throats." In his 1980 manifesto *Listen, America!*, Falwell portrayed a "vicious assault on the American family" by feminists who damaged the self-esteem of stay-at-home mothers, homosexuals seeking to sway impressionable children, immoral prime-time television shows, the removal of prayer from public schools, and federally funded day care centers. During the 1980 presidential campaign, Falwell emerged as the ambassador for an ecumenical coalition of social conservatives eager to exert their influence in electoral politics, a movement he defined as all those "opposed to abortion, pornography, the drug epidemic, the breakdown of the traditional family, the establishment of homosexuality as an accepted alternative life-style, and other moral cancers that are causing our society to rot from within." Merging spiritual renewal with political mobilization, Falwell proclaimed that "God is calling millions of Americans in the so-often silent majority to join in the moral-majority crusade to turn America around." At his convention speech, Ronald Reagan warmed their hearts with his promise that the Republican Party would "build a new consensus with all those across the land who share a community of values embodied in these words: family, work, neighborhood, peace and freedom."[13]

In the long run, the electoral alliance forged between social conservatives and the Republican Party has done little to resolve the fundamental economic causes of the crisis of the American Dream that emerged during the 1970s. The ritualistic standoffs of the culture wars have established a template for polarized and distorted debates that pit working women against stay-at-home mothers, moral traditionalism against cultural permissiveness, religious conservatism against secular liberalism. The seemingly permanent politicization of family values has obscured the evidence that a substantial majority of Americans, in the ill-fated findings of the 1980 White House Conference on Families, support government programs to provide economic assistance for full-time homemakers and child care for working mothers, while simultaneously worrying about moral decline and endorsing corporate regulations that mandate family-sensitive work policies. But the political defense of the traditional family ideal continues to be defined more by nostalgia and wishful thinking than by sociological reality, and public policies have barely begun to address the fact that a large majority of American households do not reflect the suburban mythology of a working father supporting a stay-at-home mother and their children. At the same time, the evolution of the religious Right from a grass-roots social movement to a powerful interest group within the Republican coalition has not succeeded in reversing the cultural trends of secularization and sexualization targeted by evangelical activists in the 1980 presidential contest and revisited during every subsequent election cycle. In 1999, twenty years after the formation of the Moral Majority, two of the group's original strategists concluded that "the moral landscape of America has become worse . . . In hopes of transforming the culture through political power, it must now be acknowledged that we have failed."[14]

The ideological contradiction at the core of the conservative "pro-family movement" has always revolved around the inherent tension between the enthusiastic celebration of free-market capitalism and the simultaneous defense of traditional family values. "Many women today say they must work for economic reasons," Jerry Falwell observed in 1980. "Although inflation has placed a financial burden on the family, . . . many Americans consider it more important to have several cars in the driveway, a beautiful house, and two color television sets than to have a stable home environment for their children." Asked in 1982 to describe the primary threat facing the American family, James Dobson singled out "overcommitment, time pressure. There is nothing that will destroy family life more insidiously than hectic schedules and busy lives," with mothers isolated in the suburbs and fathers driven to achieve success in the corporate world. But in the political arena, the key leaders of the religious Right could not follow the logical implications of this analysis, that many of the forces buffeting American families flowed from the anti-government agenda that they demanded and the hedonistic consumer society in which they participated. After a quarter century of the culture wars, surveys reveal that evangelical Christians get divorced, consume pornography, and engage in premarital and extramarital sex at about the same rates as their nonevangelical counterparts. Yet today, according to James Dobson of Focus on the Family, the push to legalize same-sex marriage by "the homosexual activist movement" represents the greatest threat to the nation's welfare, the latest step in a "master plan that has had as its centerpiece the utter destruction of the family." For the conservative champions of family values, it has often seemed easier to find external scapegoats—most notably, feminists, gays, and lesbians—than to come to terms with the creative destruction of a capitalist economy or to look for explanations in the mirror instead of on the television screen.[15]

CHAPTER 2

The Evangelical Resurgence in 1970s American Protestantism

PAUL BOYER

One cannot begin to understand the sea change in American political culture in the 1970s without grasping the centrality of religion to that transformation. In this decade, the nation's evangelical subculture emerged from self-imposed isolation to become a powerful force in mainstream culture and politics—a process that would accelerate in succeeding decades. When *Newsweek* magazine proclaimed 1976 as "The Year of the Evangelical," the editors underscored a phenomenon that was already well under way.[1]

This development caught many observers off guard. Throughout much of the twentieth century, America had seemingly grown more secular while mainstream Protestantism had grown more liberal. Herbert Croly in *The Promise of American Life* (1909) foresaw an enlightened commitment to social betterment replacing supernatural religion. Walter Lippmann in *Drift and Mastery* (1914) predicted that the sectarian village spirit would give way to a cosmopolitan, scientifically grounded culture. The assumption of inevitable secularization and religious liberalization long persisted. Will Herberg's 1955 survey of U.S. religion, *Protestant, Catholic, Jew,* ignored fundamentalism and devoted just two lines in the book to the

Southern Baptists while giving Pentecostalism four. Harvey Cox in *The Secular City* (1965) simply assumed secularization as a given. The sociologist Robert Bellah in 1967 found the nation's spiritual core in a generic "civil religion" more than in evangelical orthodoxy, which he largely ignored.[2]

Much evidence supported such assertions. In the Progressive Era, reform-minded Protestant ministers and Social Gospel theologians had advised Christians to focus less on the hereafter and more on uplifting the laboring masses. During the early years of the Cold War, the theologian Reinhold Niebuhr formulated a tough-minded anti-Communist ideology, while the Reverend Norman Vincent Peale in *The Power of Positive Thinking* (1952) offered therapeutic bromides to Americans worried about nuclear threats and superpower saber rattling.

In the later 1950s and the 1960s, Protestant leaders again emerged as social activists. Mainstream denominations and the National Council of Churches, the voice of liberal Protestantism, condemned racism and the Vietnam War. Yale chaplain William Sloane Coffin joined the Jesuit Berrigan brothers and Jewish leaders like Rabbi Arthur Lelyveld in calling for peace, racial equality, and social justice.

However, the predictions of inevitable secularization and liberalization in fact overlooked much contradictory evidence. In the Progressive Era, conservative Protestants opposed to theological modernism had produced *The Fundamentals* (1910–1915), a series of treatises affirming biblical inerrancy, Jesus' virgin birth and resurrection, and other bedrock doctrines. The grandly named World's Christian Fundamentals Association (1919) defended these core beliefs against modernist challenges. The Pentecostal movement, meanwhile, dedicated to recovering early Christianity's spirit-filled fervor, spread rapidly from a 1906 revival in Los Angeles.[3]

The Reverend Cyrus Scofield's annotated Reference Bible (1909) and other writings attracted many evangelical readers. Asserting that Bible prophecies reveal specific future events, Scofield explained *dispensationalism,* an interpretive system first formulated by the British churchman John Darby (1800–1882), a founder of the dissenting Plymouth Brethren sect. In Darby's scheme, buttressed with an array of ingeniously interwoven biblical texts, human history consists of a series of epochs, or dispensations, in each of which the means of salvation has differed, with a separate plan for Jews and Gentiles. According to the Darby–Scofield scenario, a series of developments foretold in the Bible make clear that the present dispensation, the Church Age, will soon end. These end-time signs include growing wickedness, a quickening pace of wars and natural calamities, and—most important—the rise of Zionism, the stirring of interest in the return of the Jews to the land God promised to Abraham, with its capacious boundaries from the Euphrates River to "the river of Egypt" (Genesis 15:18). For dispensationalists, the cosmic event marking the transition to the next dispensation will be the Rapture, when true believers will be snatched away, after which the Antichrist will rule for seven horrendous years before Christ returns to vanquish the Antichrist's armies at Armageddon and establish the millennial kingdom of peace and justice foretold in the Book of Revelation.[4]

From the 1920s through the 1960s, defying its predicted demise, evangelical Protestantism, increasingly gripped by end-time speculations, tenaciously survived at the grassroots level. Evangelical colleges, Bible schools, and seminaries like Wheaton College in Illinois, Chicago's Moody Bible Institute, William Bell Riley's Northwestern Bible and Missionary Training School in Minneapolis, Lewis Sperry Chafer's Evangelical Theological College in Dallas, and the Bible Institute of Los Angeles graduated countless ministers, missionaries, educators, and civic leaders. Wheaton's enrollment surged from 400 in 1925 to more than 2,000 by 1970. Wheaton graduates in these years included the future evangelist Billy Graham (1943); a future Indiana senator, Daniel Coats (1965);

a future justice of the Illinois Supreme Court, S. Louis Rathje (1961); and a future Speaker of the U.S. House of Representatives, J. Dennis Hastert (1964).[5]

Post–World War II Protestant leaders included not only Niebuhr and Peale, but also Billy Graham, with his apocalyptic message: humanity is doomed; only Christ offers hope. Rocketing to fame after a Los Angeles tent revival in 1949, Graham recorded thousands of "decisions for Christ" throughout the 1950s and 1960s.[6]

"Youth for Christ," an evangelical initiative launched in 1945, drew young people to Saturday night rallies. The National Association of Evangelicals (NAE), founded in 1942, though initially small compared with the liberal National Council of Churches, nevertheless provided evangelicals a forum through its conferences and publications. *Christianity Today* magazine, founded by Carl F.H. Henry in 1956, offered an evangelical alternative to both Protestant liberalism and the more extreme forms of fundamentalism.[7]

The InterVarsity Christian Fellowship (IVCF), a British movement imported to America in the 1930s, championed evangelicalism on college campuses. John Stott, an Anglican clergyman influential in IVCF circles, marshaled his formidable intellectual powers in defense of evangelicalism in *Basic Christianity* (1958) and other works.[8]

Christian bookstores, mostly evangelical in focus, proliferated. The Christian Booksellers Association, founded in 1950, informed members of marketing ideas and products targeting evangelical consumers. Local evangelical radio programs and national ones like the Reverend Charles E. Fuller's *Old Fashioned Revival Hour,* aired by the Mutual Broadcasting System, drew many listeners. Other religious bodies outside the liberal Protestant mainstream, such as the Church of Jesus Christ of Latter-day Saints (i.e., the Mormons), the Seventh-day Adventist Church, and the Watchtower Bible and Tract Society (i.e., Jehovah's Witnesses), grew steadily thanks to door-to-door evangelism, extensive publication programs, and close-knit congregational structures.

Pre-1970s evangelicals, focused on evangelism and denominational concerns, generally avoided overt political involvement. Post–World War II evangelical leaders were, however, staunchly anti-Communist and supported Washington's militant Cold War foreign policy. Billy Graham's denunciations of "godless Communism" caught the attention of William Randolph Hearst, who famously telegraphed his editors, "Puff Graham." The Christian Anti-Communism Crusade, founded in Iowa in 1953 by the Australian evangelist Fred C. Schwarz, and the Christian Crusade, launched by Tulsa's Billy James Hargis, made anti-Communism central to their ministries. Anticipating evangelicalism's later exploitation of mass-market paperbacks, Schwarz's *You Can Trust the Communists (to Be Communists)* and Hargis's *Communist America—Must It Be?* sold briskly in the 1960s.[9]

Except for the Graham revivals, these developments fell below the radar of most cultural observers. But cumulatively they laid the groundwork for the 1970s' evangelical renaissance. A dense web of institutions was in place to undergird a resurgence of conservative Protestantism if favorable circumstances arose. As the 1960s ended, the circumstances became favorable.

Denominational membership statistics document the momentous shift. From 1970 to 1985, as the liberal Episcopal, Presbyterian, Methodist, and Congregational churches suffered membership losses of around 15 percent, evangelical churches grew explosively. America's largest Protestant denomination, the evangelical Southern Baptist Convention, grew by 23 percent in 1970–1985. In a 1976 Gallup Poll, 34 percent of Americans answered yes when asked, "Would you describe yourself as a 'born again' or evangelical Christian?"[10] Pentecostal churches, black and white, favoring demonstrative worship services and viewing glossolalia (speaking in tongues) and divine healing as "gifts of the spirit" heralding Christ's imminent return, helped fuel this boom. The Assemblies of God Church, a major Pentecostal body, grew by a whopping 300 percent from 1970 to 1985.[11] By 2005, some 90 million Americans belonged to "conservative, evangelical" denominations—almost twice the membership in the liberal "mainstream" churches.[12] The roots of this turnaround lie in the 1970s.

The preexisting evangelical network readily accommodated this shift. Christian bookstore sales burgeoned. The NAE gained visibility. Campus Crusade for Christ, founded by the Oklahoma-born evangelist Bill Bright in 1951, grew dramatically in the 1970s. John Stott's many books and U.S. tours sponsored by the IVCF reinforced evangelicalism's claims among the intellectually inclined.[13]

As Billy Graham's crusades continued, his magazine *Decision* as well as numerous books, films, and recordings (including *Rap Session: Billy Graham and Students Rap on Questions of Today's Youth* [1974]) extended his reach.[14] Graham typically ended his worldwide *Hour of Decision* radio broadcasts with the line "Just write to me, Billy Graham, Minneapolis, Minnesota," and thousands did. (One envelope from Africa reached its destination bearing the address: "Billy Graham, Many Applause, Many Sorrows.")[15]

Why this 1970s upsurge of conservative religion? Most broadly, it was, of course, part of a larger reaction against the social upheavals, radical politics, and counterculture of the 1960s. Media coverage during the 1960s had focused more on radical protests and counterculture provocations than on the conservative reaction, and early histories of the decade (often written by former activists) generally followed that emphasis. Today, the 1960s seem less a radical decade than a polarizing one.[16] The liberal clergy who marched for civil rights and against the war drew attention, but their activism also stirred a powerful reaction. In 1965, the young Lynchburg, Virginia, minister Jerry Falwell implored the ministers marching for civil rights to concentrate instead on "the pure saving gospel of Jesus Christ." Declared this future leader of the intensely political Moral Majority organization, "Preachers are not called to be politicians but to be soul winners."[17] The evangelical reaction against liberal Protestantism's social activism intensified a broader conservative turn in the nation—a shift exploited by presidential candidate Richard Nixon in his 1968 appeal to the "Silent Majority" repelled by marches and demonstrations.

Among religious folk, this reaction unquestionably fueled the evangelical upsurge of the 1970s. As early as 1972, in *Why Conservative Churches Are Growing,* Methodist minister Dean C. Kelley, an official of the National Council of Churches, cited churchgoers' frustration with pastors and denominational leaders who embraced social issues and neglected parishioners' spiritual needs. Such disaffected Christians, Kelley argued, were turning to evangelical churches that offered emotionally fulfilling worship services, a supportive congregational life, and a personalistic theology of conversion and righteous living.[18] Deepening their appeal for many anxious Americans, the evangelical churches took unambiguous stands on contentious moral issues, in contrast to the liberal churches' openness to diverse viewpoints, particularly on sensitive matters relating to sex and gender, including homosexuality, abortion, sex education, pornography, "radical feminism," and teenage sexuality.

Much of the conservative reaction to shifting mores flowed into a "pro-family" movement spearheaded by conservative Catholics and evangelical Protestants. Responding to intensifying pressures, presidential candidate Jimmy Carter in 1976 pledged to try to strengthen families. At eight White-House-sponsored hearings and conferences on family issues late in Carter's term, newly energized religious conservatives often dominated. As a journalist described one of these gatherings, "During the first three hours . . , divorce, homosexuality, violence on television, sex education in public schools, welfare and prayer . . . fell into the boiling pot of controversy."[19]

The writer Francis Schaeffer stiffened evangelicals' backbone on moral and cultural issues. An American Presbyterian minister, Schaeffer founded a retreat center in Switzerland called *L'Abri* (the Shelter). In *How Shall We Then Live: The Rise and Decline of Western Thought and Culture* (1976) and other works, Schaeffer inveighed against "secular humanism." Tracing this evil to such diverse sources as Pablo Picasso and James Joyce, Schaeffer found its poison pervading contemporary America. Publicized by such evangelical leaders as Falwell, Tim LaHaye, and Charles Colson (after his Watergate-related prison term), Schaeffer gave evangelicals an ideological framework for challenging the decadence and immorality allegedly pervading American life.[20]

Roe v. Wade, the 1973 Supreme Court decision upholding women's right to abortion in early pregnancy, intensified the reaction. Following the high court's 1962 finding in *Engel v. Vitale* that officially sponsored public-school prayers violated the First Amendment, *Roe* deepened evangelical suspicions that the federal government, once a force for good, had turned to the dark side. The Internal Revenue Service's 1978 challenge to the tax-exempt status of many private Christian schools, alleging racial discrimination, strengthened these suspicions.[21]

In the wake of *Roe,* many evangelical Protestants overcame their suspicions of Rome to unite with Catholics in opposition. (Protestants and Catholics had earlier found common ground, of course, in a shared anti-Communism.) The Catholic–evangelical rapprochement represents a crucial development in the post-1970 reorientation of American religion. As James Davison Hunter has noted, waning denominational loyalties and the emergence of special-interest religious lobbies, plus Pope John XXIII's liberalizing innovations, encouraged a new ecumenism built around shared cultural values and objectives. This, in turn, eroded anti-Catholic prejudices dating to the earliest English settlements in North America and later reinforced by heavy Catholic immigration. Paul Blanshard's 1949 polemic *American Freedom and Catholic Power* summed up the suspicions of many evangelicals of that era. As Richard Mouw, president of Fuller Theological Seminary, has written of his youth in the 1950s, "I was exposed to the worst of evangelical anti-Catholicism . . . I regularly heard evangelical preachers proclaim . . . that the Pope was the Antichrist." Doctrinal differences persisted after 1970, and evangelical and Pentecostal proselytizing among Hispanic Catholics continued to irritate Catholic leaders. But overall, evangelical–Catholic relations improved dramatically after 1970.[22]

The quest for certitude underlying the 1970s evangelical resurgence found expression, too, in growing interest in Bible prophecy, as evidenced by Hal Lindsey's bestseller *The Late Great Planet Earth* (1970). Born in 1929, Lindsey found God in his late twenties and attended Dallas Theological Seminary, a dispensationalist bastion. Joining Campus Crusade for Christ, he was preaching on the UCLA campus in 1969 when his prophecy lectures drew capacity crowds. *The Late Great Planet Earth,* a slangy popularization of John Darby's century-old dispensationalist scheme of prophecy interpretation, cited prophecies allegedly foretelling European unification, America's moral decline, nuclear war with Russia, and Israel's 1948 founding and post-1967 occupation of the West Bank and Gaza—all signs of the approaching End. Lindsey's book and other prophecy popularizations diffused more widely the end-time scenario of Darby and Scofield, adding a note of apocalyptic urgency to the 1970s religious revival.[23]

The movement's leaders enthusiastically appropriated the era's mass media even as they criticized its degradation by the secular culture. In a sense, this was nothing new. The American Tract Society (1825) had flooded the cities and the frontier with mass-produced evangelical tracts. The followers of William Miller, who predicted Christ's return in 1844, had used high-speed steam printing presses to produce periodicals and colorful charts explaining their teachings. In the 1920s, evangelist Paul Rader's Chicago-based *National Radio Chapel* had featured jaunty music and children's segments.[24]

But most earlier evangelicals, while appropriating new technologies, had maintained firm cultural boundaries and resisted the lure of "worldliness." Evangelical leaders of the 1970s still criticized the secular culture, but in practice they fully exploited that culture. D.G. Hart observed: "People perceive evangelicalism as old-fashioned and conservative, [but] it has actually been one of the most modern and innovative forms of Christianity in using the cultural vernacular to restate . . . an ancient faith." Or, as Billy Graham disarmingly put it, "I'm selling the greatest product in the world. Why shouldn't it be promoted as well as soap?"[25]

Mass-market paperbacks, movies, radio, and television all helped evangelicals spread their message. Lindsey's *The Late Great Planet Earth* sold millions of copies in cheap paperback editions. Billy Graham's 1965 film *The Restless Ones*, addressing such edgy subjects as drug addiction and premarital sex, featured a contemporary music track and starred Robert Sampson, also seen on TV's *Gunsmoke, Ben Casey,* and *Star Trek. A Thief in the Night* (1973), by the evangelical filmmaker Donald Thompson, dramatizing the Rapture and the rise of the Antichrist, reached millions in evangelical churches worldwide.[26] As FM radio became more segmented in the 1970s, Christian stations proliferated, offering music, news, call-in shows, and special-interest programming with an evangelical slant.

Apart from some local programs and the occasional Billy Graham special, pre-1970 religious television had consisted mainly of public-service Sunday programs reflecting a liberal, ecumenical perspective, such as *Lamp unto My Feet* (CBS) and NBC's *Frontiers of Faith.* In the 1970s, by contrast, viewer-supported evangelical programming burgeoned, with Jerry Falwell and Pat Robertson in the vanguard.

Falwell was born in Lynchburg, Virginia, in 1933 to a pious mother and a hot-tempered, alcoholic businessman father who owned several service stations. After a religious conversion in 1952, young Falwell attended a Missouri Bible college and returned to Lynchburg to found the Thomas Road Baptist Church. His *Old Time Gospel Hour,* launched locally in 1956, drew at least 1.4 million viewers nationally by 1980, thanks to cable and communications satellites.[27]

Falwell's fellow Virginian Pat Robertson came from a wealthy and politically prominent family. His father, U.S. senator Willis Robertson, a conservative Democrat, opposed both the 1954 school-desegregation decision and the Civil Rights Act of 1964. Defeated for renomination after President Lyndon Johnson actively opposed him, he helped craft Richard Nixon's 1968 appeal to disgruntled white southerners. Young Pat, meanwhile, received a Yale law degree in 1955, flunked the New York State bar exam, and shortly thereafter experienced a charismatic religious conversion. He bought a defunct Portsmouth, Virginia, TV station in 1959 and made it the launching pad for his Christian Broadcasting Network (CBN). Along with Robertson's *700 Club,* a religious talk show, CBN showcased ministers, authors, and celebrities. A 1976 special, "It's Time to Pray, America!" featured President Gerald Ford. Regent University, Robertson's venture into higher education, began operations in 1978. Still greater growth and influence lay ahead. By 2000, CBN reached 180 countries with broadcasts in seventy-one languages; Robertson's *The New World Order* (1991) and other books had won a wide readership; and his Christian Coalition (1989) had emerged as a major player in the politicized evangelical movement.[28]

Pentecostals like Ohio's flamboyant Rex Humbard, the Oklahoma faith healer Oral Roberts, and Louisiana's Jimmy Swaggart (a cousin of the rock-and-roll singer Jerry Lee Lewis) further enlivened 1970s religious TV. So did Jim and Tammy Bakker with their "PTL" (Praise the Lord) program and their grandiose plans for a Christian theme park. (Sexual and financial scandals eventually did in Swaggart and the Bakkers.) Paul Crouch's California-based and charismatically oriented Trinity Broadcasting Network debuted in 1973.[29]

Media and marketing savvy, in short, fueled evangelicalism's post-1970 resurgence. Burgeoning evangelical bookstores sold religious-themed greeting cards, jewelry, baseball caps, T-shirts, placemats, planters, and home-décor items. They also promoted therapeutic and self-help books offering advice on finances, dating, marriage, depression, and addiction from an evangelical perspective. The Christian Booksellers Association's 1975 convention, featuring Johnny Cash and other performers, drew 5,000 registrants. By 1980, CBA members reported annual sales of $1 billion.[30]

Christian bookstores also marketed record albums (and soon audiotapes and CDs) by evangelical and charismatic "praise bands," soft-rock groups, and other Contemporary Christian Music (CCM) performers. Elvis Presley blazed the trail with *How Great Thou Art* (1967) and *He Touched Me* (1972). Larry Norman, whose 1972 album *Only Visiting This Planet* featured his signature song "Why Should the Devil Have All the Good Music?" proved a particular favorite.[31]

James Dobson, a conservative psychologist, won evangelical fans with his *Dare to Discipline* (1970), a child-rearing manual following biblical precepts. In 1977, Dobson launched *Focus on the Family* magazine and a daily radio program that was eventually broadcast worldwide.[32]

By the decade's end, evangelicalism's cultural presence was widely pervasive. With the financial reports, mergers, and acquisitions of the multibillion-dollar Christian music, publishing, and broadcasting industries routinely reported in *Billboard, Publishers' Weekly,* and the *Wall Street Journal,* evangelicalism's penetration of mainstream culture had reached impressive proportions. Orson Welles's narration of the film version of Lindsey's *The Late Great Planet Earth* in 1979 epitomized this melding of sacred and secular in the mass culture. These 1970s developments, in turn, laid the groundwork for further evangelical incursions in the mass culture as represented, for example, by such Hollywood movies as *The Rapture* (1991), produced by New Line Cinema, a division of the media giant Time Warner, and by the blockbuster *Left Behind* series of novels (1995–2005) by Tim LaHaye and Jerry B. Jenkins, a fictionalization of the Darby–Scofield dispensational scheme of Bible prophecy interpretation.

As in so much else, the baby-boom generation loomed large in the 1970s evangelical resurgence. As campus-based political activism and the hippie counterculture faded, a disorienting mood of cultural uncertainty ensued. While feminist, gay, and environmental causes won adherents, many young people turned to religious quests, including Zen Buddhism; Transcendental Meditation; the Reverend Sun Myung Moon's Unification Church; and the International Society of Krishna Consciousness, whose saffron-robed converts added an exotic note to airport lobbies and college campuses.

Ultimately more enduring was the boomers' discovery of evangelical Christianity. This was not their parents' evangelicalism, however. Though doctrinally strict, it was far more laid-back in style. Recruits to what was loosely called the "Jesus Movement" spurned the established denominations and staid worship services of older evangelicals. Larry Norman ridiculed traditional hymns as "funeral music." "Explo '72" a 1972 Jesus Movement rally in Dallas, had elements of a religious Woodstock. A *Life* magazine cover story featured photographs of blissful kids in colorful T-shirts. At the open-air final concert, 150,000 people turned out to hear Johnny Cash, Kris Kristofferson, and Rita Coolidge. That evening, 70,000 filled the Cotton Bowl to hear Billy Graham, football star Roger Staubach, and Florida governor Reuben Askew.[33]

Three Southern California pastors, Chuck Smith, John Wimber, and Rick Warren, devised strategies for institutionalizing this amorphous movement. Smith, a minister of the International Church of the Foursquare Gospel (founded in 1923 by Aimee Semple McPherson), came to struggling Calvary Chapel in Costa Mesa, California, in 1965. His fundamentalist sermons emphasized strict morality; biblical inerrancy; Bible prophecy; and conservative, patriarchal cultural values. But "Pastor Chuck's" casual style, humor, and conversational delivery struck a new note. His informal services interspersed charismatic praise with contemporary music featuring guitars, percussion, and trendy lyrics.

Drawing "Jesus freaks," ex-hippies, young marrieds, and surfers from nearby Huntington Beach, Calvary Chapel grew explosively in the 1970s. One early convert described the scene: "Everybody wore granny dresses and carried fur-covered Bibles and jeans and bib-overalls and tie-dyed shirts and long hair and beards. They were so wild it was scary." By 2000, Smith's empire included books, films, videos, a radio and TV ministry, a Christian music label, an academy, a college, and a retreat center in the San Gabriel Mountains. Emulating the model of proliferating fast-food franchises, some 800 Calvary Chapels had sprung up in the United States and abroad by 2000. Each, like its prototype, was theologically conservative; casual in style; and headed by a "Pastor Dave," "Pastor Ron," or "Pastor Jim."[34]

John Wimber, a self-described "beer guzzling, drug abusing pop musician," embraced evangelical Christianity in 1963. Becoming pastor of a Calvary Chapel in Yorba Linda, California, in 1977, he pursued an increasingly independent ministry featuring charismatic worship, divine healing, and the "casting out of demons." Adopting the Calvary Chapel model, Wimber's Vineyard Christian Fellowship by 2002 had 850 churches worldwide, a publishing enterprise, and a music company.[35]

Rick Warren, then a twenty-five-year-old Southern Baptist minister, founded Saddleback Church in Anaheim, California, in 1979.

He, too, wrapped his evangelical doctrine in an easygoing style, preaching in colorful Hawaiian shirts, peppering his sermons with colloquialisms, and enlivening his services with "Contemporary Christian" music. Applying the small-group strategies advocated by Peter Drucker in *An Introductory View of Management* (1977), Warren encouraged new members to join one of Saddleback's many special-interest groups. By 2005, Saddleback's mall-like complex, sprawling over 120 acres, boasted 20,000 members, and Warren's *The Purpose-Driven Life* (2002) had become a best-seller.[36]

Calvary Chapel, Vineyard Christian Fellowship, Saddleback, and other trendy evangelical and charismatic churches of the 1970s provided a model for evangelical megachurches, defined as congregations of 2,000 or more members. By 1980, some fifty megachurches, conservative theologically and characterized by easygoing informality and close-knit congregational life, were scattered across the land. By 2005, the total approached 900.[37]

Addressing the spiritual and emotional needs of Americans rattled by Vietnam, the upheavals of the 1960s, and multiplying challenges to traditional mores—exacerbated by inflation and oil shocks—evangelicalism grew exponentially in the 1970s. In the process, its leaders brilliantly appropriated the communications technologies, marketing strategies, and organizational techniques of the larger culture.

This protean movement merits attention not only as a religious and cultural phenomenon, but also for its political implications. Historically, evangelicals were no strangers to politics. Antebellum-era evangelicals had championed social causes, from antislavery to temperance, with obvious political overtones. Later evangelicals played a key role in the 1919 passage of the Eighteenth (Prohibition) Amendment.

But for much of the twentieth century, evangelicals shunned politics and even openly criticized liberal Protestants' social activism, focusing instead on denominational affairs and on monitoring members' behavior. (Southern Baptists, it was said, forbade premarital sex because it could lead to dancing.) Chastened by the ridicule heaped on the 1925 Scopes trial and by the repeal in 1933 of the Eighteenth Amendment, their activist energies flowed into missionary efforts at home and abroad, not in imposing their beliefs or remedying society's evils through political action. Indeed, as we have seen, this emphasis on personal salvation, individual ethics, and congregational life increased evangelicalism's appeal in the 1970s.

Ironically, however, many evangelicals, while targeting different issues, soon outdid their liberal counterparts in political engagement. As signs of America's growing irreligion and secularism multiplied, calls for political action intensified, and Falwell and others locked arms with politicians who professed to share their goals.[38] Though full-scale political mobilization came as the seventies ended, the groundwork was in place earlier. Lindsey's *The Late Great Planet Earth* and *There's a New World Coming* (1973) not so subtly promoted a detailed political agenda, urging Americans to support Israel's biblically rooted territorial claims; to avoid entanglement with the United Nations, a likely forerunner of the Antichrist's global rule; to build a stronger military to fight atheistic Communism; and to battle home-front secularism. Some found Lindsey's attempts to influence an already predetermined future paradoxical, but he clearly believed that individuals must not only secure their own salvation, but also strive to align America on God's side as Armageddon approached.

In 1979, having rethought his skepticism about politics, Jerry Falwell founded the Moral Majority to rally evangelicals behind candidates committed to a "pro-life, pro-family, pro-moral, and pro-America" agenda. Falwell summed up his strategy succinctly: "Get them saved, baptized, and registered."[39]

Falwell was not the only conservative leader to draw media attention. Donald Wildmon's American Family Association (1977), James Dobson's Focus on the Family and his more overtly political Family Research Council (1983), Tim LaHaye's secretive Council for National Policy (1981), Beverly LaHaye's Concerned Women for America (1979), Louis Sheldon's Traditional Values Coalition (1980), and other political lobbies used paperbacks, magazines, direct mail, radio, and TV to rouse culturally conservative evangelical voters on a broad range of emotion-laden moral issues. In Orange County, California, Chuck Smith's Calvary Chapel and other evangelical churches figured prominently in the emergence of this pivotal county as a bastion of right-wing politics.[40]

As President Ford's appearance on a Pat Robertson telecast suggests, politicians paid attention. As early as 1975, Representative John Conlan, a deeply conservative Arizona Republican associated with a shadowy religious lobby called the FaithAmerica Foundation, met with Bill Bright of Campus Crusade for Christ and other evangelicals to craft an electoral strategy that would turn worried evangelicals into voters. The conservative Republican activists Paul Weyrich, Howard Phillips, and the direct-mail expert Richard Viguerie assisted Falwell in planning the creation of the Moral Majority (Weyrich, in fact, suggested the name). Phillips's Conservative Caucus (1977), in turn, included on its staff evangelicals Robert Billings, a graduate of the fundamentalist Bob Jones University and executive director of the Moral Majority, and Ed McAteer, founder of an evangelical lobby called the Roundtable.[41]

Christian Voice (1978), a direct-mail lobby founded by conservative Baptists Richard Zone and Reverend Robert Grant, anticipated Falwell in mobilizing evangelicals politically. Declared Grant, echoing Peter Finch in the 1976 movie *Network*, "Everywhere we turn, Christian values are assaulted and are in retreat. As Christians, we are not going to take it anymore." With a membership of nearly 200,000, including 37,000 ministers, Christian Voice distributed report cards for members to rate their political representatives on "key moral issues." (Tim LaHaye's *The Battle for the Mind* [1980] included a similar checklist to help readers monitor political candidates' moral reliability.)[42]

It was Ronald Reagan, of course, who benefited most spectacularly from evangelicalism's political turn. Though not a churchgoer, Reagan sprang from evangelical soil, cultivated leading evangelicals while California's governor, often mused about the prophetic significance of world events, and endorsed the evangelical worldview on most domestic and foreign-policy issues. An August 1980 rally in Dallas, billed as a "National Affairs Briefing" for evangelical clergy and organized by Ed McAteer's Roundtable, cemented the alliance. Falwell, Robertson, and other luminaries joined 15,000 Dallas evangelicals led by the senior pastor of the city's gargantuan First Baptist Church, the Reverend W. A. Criswell (a prominent Southern Baptist some called "the Protestant Pope"), for two days of politico-religious sermonizing. The event culminated in a speech by Reagan, who, to cheers and cries of "Amen," proclaimed, "This is a nonpartisan gathering and so I know you can't endorse me, but I . . . want you to know that I endorse you and what you are doing." With the alliance thus publicly acknowledged, Reagan added the Moral Majority's executive director, Robert Billings, to his campaign as liaison to the evangelical community.[43] More than 70 percent of white evangelicals voted that November, up from around 61 percent in earlier elections, and they overwhelmingly backed Reagan. The Moral Majority alone, analysts estimate, delivered 4 million votes to the Republican candidate.[44]

As president, Reagan cultivated this vast new horde of voters. In 1983, he addressed both the National Religious Broadcasters and the National Association of Evangelicals. At the NAE's Orlando convention, he praised "intercessory prayer," denounced "modern-day secularism," and memorably described the Soviet Union as "the focus of evil in the modern world." In phrases familiar to evangelicals,

Reagan intoned: "Let us pray for the salvation of all . . . who live in . . . totalitarian darkness—pray that they will discover the joy of knowing God."[45] The evangelical alliance with the Republican Party, rooted in the 1970s, would profoundly shape the nation's political culture for decades.[46]

Though the evangelicals' embrace of Reagan received the lion's share of media attention, their political mobilization in the 1970s reverberated at all levels, from Congress to city councils and school boards. The Wheaton College alumnus Dan Coats won election to the House of Representatives in 1980. The political rise of avowed evangelicals like Dennis Hastert of Indiana, Tom DeLay of Texas, and Sam Brownback of Kansas would soon follow. Not all the beneficiaries were themselves evangelicals. Orrin Hatch, a conservative Utah Mormon, won election to the Senate in 1976. Conservative Catholics elected to the Senate in these years included Nevada's Paul Laxalt (1974), Oklahoma's Don Nickles (1980), and Alabama's Jeremiah Denton (1980). But by sheer weight of numbers, evangelical Protestant voters, constituting nearly a quarter of the electorate, played a key role in these electoral outcomes, further illustrating how pragmatic alliances in pursuit of common goals could trump sectarian differences.[47]

The Colorado Republican Bill Armstrong, elected to the House of Representatives in 1972 and to the U.S. Senate in 1978, was converted to evangelical Christianity by Bill Bright, who through the 1970s spent a week each month in Washington proselytizing in Congress, the White House, and the Pentagon. Armstrong later joined the board of Bright's Campus Crusade for Christ and, upon leaving the Senate, became president of Colorado Christian University, a fundamentalist school founded in 1914.[48]

Not all evangelicals became political conservatives. African American evangelicals, though culturally conservative, generally retained the Democratic loyalties forged during the New Deal and solidified by Lyndon Johnson's civil rights record. And some white evangelicals deplored the movement's rightward political drift. In *The Great Reversal: Evangelicalism versus Social Concern* (1972), David O. Moberg, a Marquette University sociologist, urged evangelicals to emulate their antebellum predecessors by championing social justice and the downtrodden.[49]

John Stott's social vision encompassed such issues as world hunger and environmental protection. The Lausanne Covenant (1974), issued by an International Congress on Evangelization, where Stott played a leading role, affirmed basic evangelical doctrines but in a section titled "Christian Social Responsibility" also called for "justice and reconciliation throughout human society and for the liberation of men and women from every kind of oppression." It went on: "Because men and women are made in the image of God, every person, regardless of race, religion, colour, culture, class, sex or age, has an intrinsic dignity . . . He or she should be respected and served, not exploited . . . Evangelism and socio-political involvement are both part of our Christian duty . . . The message of salvation implies also a message of judgment upon every form of alienation, oppression, and discrimination."[50]

In the same vein, the 1973 "Chicago Declaration of Evangelical Social Concerns," the manifesto of the Evangelicals for Social Action, founded by Ronald J. Sider and others, urged evangelicals living in "an unjust American society" to uphold "the social and economic rights of the poor and oppressed," to work for a "more just . . . distribution of the world's resources," to reject "a national pathology of war and violence," to protest the "prideful domination" of women by men, and to "resist the temptation to make the nation and its institutions objects of near-religious loyalty." Sider's *Rich Christians in an Age of Hunger* (1977) challenged evangelicals to address the vast disparities between the world's haves and have-nots. Jim Wallis's *Sojourners* magazine (1975) and his *Agenda for a Biblical People* (1976) struck a similar note.[51]

Clearly, a simplistic equation of evangelicalism and right-wing politics would be misleading. Nevertheless, "left-wing evangelicalism" remained a minority position. With their mass-media megaphone and potent lobbies, Falwell, LaHaye, Dobson, and their associates tended to drown out the likes of Moberg, Stott, Sider, and Wallis. The former group's stern individualistic morality and apocalyptic, black-and-white worldview, with righteousness under siege by enemies who must be annihilated, proved more appealing than the nuanced perspective of evangelicals who focused on social-justice issues and on the ambiguities and pitfalls of partisan politics.

By 1980, then, with notable exceptions, millions of American evangelicals were not only becoming politicized, but were overwhelmingly voting Republican. To be sure, the rightward political shift of the 1970s had complex sources. It included neoconservative ex-Democrats alienated by their party's lurch leftward in the later 1960s and focused on building U.S. military strength and on projecting American power abroad; whites in the once solidly Democratic South reacting against the civil rights revolution; and Midwestern and Western blue-collar and middle-class whites upset by campus activism, the counterculture, racial violence in northern cities, and what they saw as government favoritism toward minorities.[52] But intermingled with all this were religious and cultural conservatives who viewed moral issues as paramount and who saw "traditional values" as under siege in a rapidly changing society. In this category, the growing ranks of Protestant evangelicals (along with traditionalist Roman Catholics and many conservative Jews) loomed large.

The religious transformation sketched above helps one understand the political machinations entertainingly described by journalist Thomas Frank in *What's the Matter with Kansas? How*

Conservatives Won the Heart of America (2004). Using his native state as a case study, Frank shows how Republican strategists and politicians like former track star Jim Ryun and Wichita's Todd Tiahrt focus on hot-button cultural and moral issues at election time, thereby persuading working-class and middle-class voters to support a party whose economic agenda directly undercuts their own interests.[53]

Insightful as it is, Frank's dissection of early-twenty-first-century U.S. cultural politics largely ignores the religious developments that made this strategy possible. While frequently alluding to polemicists like Ann Coulter and Rush Limbaugh, he says little about Kansas's religious landscape apart from a few jeering references to the state as "a great bubbling Crock Pot of Godliness," "smug fundamentalists," "spiritual swindler[s]," and the "preternaturally pious." Broad-brush caricatures aside, Frank hardly addresses the post-1970 history or grassroots specificity of evangelical Protestantism in contemporary Kansas, including the state's 7 Christian radio stations, 22 evangelical Christian bookstores, 8 Vineyard Christian Fellowships, 10 Calvary Chapels, 148 Assembly of God churches, 297 Southern Baptist churches, and 11 megachurches where weekly attendance ranges from 2,100 to 8,500—not to mention the televangelists and prophecy-interpreting paperback writers who reach every corner of the nation.[54]

It was not Republican political operatives but a vast army of pastors, evangelists, writers, musicians, and entrepreneurs, keenly attuned to the post-1960s mood of cultural disorientation and to the media outlets, pop-culture trends, management theories, and marketing strategies of consumer capitalism, who woke the sleeping giant of American evangelicalism in the 1970s. Certainly, as Frank argues, politicians serving the interests of a privileged economic class devised strategies for tapping the movement's ballot-box potential. But the movement's genesis lay deeper than economic interests or party politics. It must be sought in the shadowy recesses of grassroots American religious life and moral concerns.

Thomas Frank is far from alone among American cultural and political observers in missing the centrality of religion, or in assuming that it can be dealt with in a few off-hand phrases. G.K. Chesterton in 1922 called the United States "a nation with the soul of a church." Eighty-seven years earlier, Alexis de Tocqueville had observed, "There is no country in the world where the Christian religion retains a greater influence over the souls of men than in America."[55] The evangelical resurgence that began in the 1970s underscores the continued timeliness of these much-quoted observations. The tectonic shifts that transformed America's religious landscape in this decade affected culture and politics in ways that resonated for decades. Indeed, their reverberations intensified in the years ahead and a generation later show few signs of diminishing.

CHAPTER 3

Make Payroll, Not War

Business Culture as Youth Culture

BETHANY E. MORETON

For many Americans, the sixties ended on May 4, 1970, with the slayings by the Ohio National Guard of four students at Kent State University, a working-class commuter campus near Akron. Captured in a photographic pietà, the young victims protesting the invasion of Cambodia graphically symbolized the gulf that separated an alienated youth culture from its national frame of reference. The dead and their mourners qualified as "our" children—the assimilated, upwardly mobile offspring of white, ethnic factory operatives, the favored heirs of the American Century. Their very presence on a college campus was the proof that the system worked.[1] If they were the enemy, then who was the ally?

Looking back on the tragic incident from the vantage point of 1978, Kent State's Goodyear Professor of Free Enterprise remembered his reaction to the news of the murders in very different terms. At the time, he had been an executive at the Griswold-Eshleman Company in Cleveland. When he read of the "violent protests" in the papers, he recognized himself as the object of the students' irrational hostility, a symbol of the establishment that provoked their self-destructive rage. As one of his students put it,

"It really wouldn't have been too healthy for a businessman here in 1970."[2]

For the bodies of the dead protesters, this retelling substituted a crucified businessman, then celebrated his resurrection on the very Golgotha of Kent State itself.[3] By 1978, the introductory business classes at Kent State were packed, and the free enterprise instructor was gratified to imagine himself as a "business missionary." His mission: "to break down the walls of Jericho and correct the many negative misconceptions about business."[4] In this task, he could rely for help upon the student activists of Kent State's Students in Free Enterprise (SIFE) chapter, one of 150 such groups around the country at the time. In 1979, the energetic club organized a "Battle of the Bands" at a bar a few blocks from Kent State's campus, awarding donated prizes to the best pro-business rock song. An entry from the local band Radio City serenaded small-scale capitalism with this tender ode:

entrepreneurship

> You know I could never be happy
> Just working some nine-to-five.
> I'd rather spend my life poor
> Than living it as a lie.
> If I could just save my money
> Or maybe get a loan,
> I could start my own business
> And make it on my own.[5]

Thus, half a decade before the Republican Party wrote free enterprise into its platform as "fundamental to the American way of life," these and hundreds of similar campus missionaries were well on their way to rehabilitating free-market capitalism and its managerial representatives on the cultural battle turf of the American campus.[6]

Learning how to speak to college students had been an explicit goal for large corporate interests from the decade's outset. Their conquest of the campus was one of the great unacknowledged victories that laid the groundwork for the Reagan revolution. Yet despite the deep pockets from which the campaigns drew support, their success cannot be reduced to a recession-driven raffle of young hearts and minds. Students embraced business values in the seventies not in a jaded materialistic hangover from the previous decade, but under the historically unique conditions of a wrenching new economic dispensation. As the dollar floated free of the gold standard and capital, unbound from the Bretton Woods controls, began its restless border-hopping, the outline of that reordered world was grasped incompletely through such ominous signs as inflation, trade deficits, the energy crisis, and stagnating household incomes. In part, student reactions expressed a realistic fear that the drawbridge was going up and that they might well be stuck on the wrong shore. At the same time, though, their sympathy depended on a narrative of the new material conditions of life that paid homage to their student predecessors—participatory, antiauthoritarian, idealistic, liberatory. They took up free enterprise as an imperiled cause, precisely because of its demonstrable woes. That an industry giant like Goodyear wanted to spread such a message seems self-evident. That the chosen messengers would include dueling guitars and an endowed Professor of Free Enterprise was not a foregone conclusion.

In 1971, Pepsico CEO and Nixon intimate Donald Kendall was lamenting the country's "economic illiteracy," which he attributed to "the Generation Gap—the chronic alienation of youth and parents, youth and religion . . . youth and free enterprise." So far, he cautioned, the hostile young had vented their spleen on draft boards and their own colleges. But could anyone doubt that the day was fast approaching when the long-hairs would come for American businessmen?[7]

Kendall's jeremiad joined a chorus from boardrooms across the country. Organized since World War II in vehicles like the Foundation for Economic Education and the American Enterprise Association, business elites had transformed themselves from "economic royalists" into the guarantors of individual liberty, the crucial stumbling block on the road to serfdom.[8] But their hard-won cultural prestige now lay in ruins. The student generation was in open revolt against the spindling and mutilation they foresaw in their white-collar futures. "Business is in poor repute these days," counseled a retail industry magazine, "and for some obvious reasons: anti-establishment social upheavals spurred by Vietnam, Watergate and its attendant corporate scandals, oil price inflation, consumerism and the ecology movement."[9] "The young take for granted the affluence which is the rule," groused *Newsweek,* and California governor Ronald Reagan wanted to know just what gave these arrogant children the right to sneer at the very men who had given them the world's highest standard of living.[10]

But help was on the way. Arizona's Republican governor Jack Williams took aggressive steps to combat the menace when in 1971 he enthusiastically signed into law a bill that created a new graduation requirement for the state's high schoolers: economics. The class would provide the young student "some foundation to stand on when he comes up against professors that are collectivists or Socialists," its sponsor explained. Governor Williams, a former radio broadcaster who had decreed an annual "John Birch Day" for Arizona, heartily concurred.[11]

Likewise, Arizona's state superintendent of public instruction had long been a strong advocate of Christianity in the schools. He distributed materials from the Austrian-inspired Foundation for Economic Education that had been funded by sponsors like GM, Dupont, and Sun Oil, but he augmented them with his own, more theologically explicit views. "Collectivism as a way of life is a manifestation of the abyss into which men sink when not motivated by the pursuit of truth and justice," the materials explained to their student audiences. To place out of the course, students could

demonstrate mastery on an exam by, for example, correctly match-
ing the phrase "Government intervention in a free enterprise system"
with its appropriate predicate, "is detrimental to the free market."[12]

By the end of the decade, twenty more states had followed Arizona's lead, mandating economics instruction that amounted to
little more than industry propaganda. In Texas, the legislature declined to appropriate money for the required class, opening the
door to sponsors like the Houston Natural Gas (HNG) Corporation. In 1977, the gas concern provided teaching materials to
twenty-three Texas school districts and trained fifty HNG employees as "business resource persons" for the schools. As the company's public relations manager put it, "Somebody had to take the
initiative."[13]

As a front in business's ongoing PR campaign, the seventies' crusade against economic illiteracy was not entirely new.[14] But the
source of hostility to business ends and means came as a shock. In
the postwar years, the main ideological competitors had been
unions, the formal political arm of the managed. Now they were
students, the future managerial class itself. With impressive and
well-funded resolve, the pro-business front of the 1970s chose to
organize, not agonize, and reached out to the students on their own
terms.

One obvious lesson to take from the new generation was how to
communicate when the whole world was watching. At the time, executives on television were providing their peers with the same rude
awakening that politicians had received from the 1960 presidential
debates: the medium was not kind to Nixonian style. Early in 1974,
representatives of the country's largest oil concerns were forced to
testify on camera to a Senate subcommittee. It was not a pretty
sight. No less of a sympathetic audience than Arizona senator Barry
Goldwater charged that industry spokesmen "seem, invariably, to
be the most poorly organized, poorly informed group of witnesses
in the whole country." Didn't they realize they were up against the

back-room whiz kids of congressional staff offices?[15] The point hit home. Heavy-handed PR tactics pioneered in the 1940s and 1950s by firms like General Electric increasingly gave way to more sophisticated, subtler messages. Professionals took over from in-house ideologues. By 1981, over 100 media consultants were renting their expertise to executives. Periodic "Communicator Workshops" taught businessmen to bond with audiences and to leave their plaid suits in the closet.[16]

The communicators' efforts to personalize multinationals like-wise included a renewed emphasis on direct contact with students, preferably by allowing smaller local businesses to stand for the whole. The U.S. Chamber of Commerce introduced its "Economics for Young Americans" kits into 12,000 schools in the mid-1970s on the condition that the local businesses who picked up the tab deploy one of their number as a "resource person" to accompany the materials into the classrooms.[17] The Knoxville Chamber of Commerce, impressed by the audio-visual materials' ability to "jazz things up" in the classroom, also instituted a program in which students and teachers would "run" a business for a day and then host a business representative as a guest teacher in exchange. The manager of a Bay Area radio station used the Chamber's materials to tutor Boy Scouts on his own time.[18] Traveling around the country to local industry gatherings and fraternal lunches, a full-time speaker for Goodyear Tire urged greater one-on-one contact: "When's the last time you talked with local educators to see what is being taught in your schools?" he demanded of his audiences, and even warned them not to neglect the home front: how about those intimate chats with your grandchildren about the role of profit? The economic recession, he pointed out, was making young audiences noticeably more receptive to these messages.[19] A bank in Chattanooga that ran ads giving "basic facts about the private enterprise system" was equally gratified by the youthful response: "The thirsty acceptance of economic truth by young people was amaz-

ing," the bank chairman explained, pointing to a wave of apprecia-
tive phone calls and letters. "Youth is brave enough to embrace
economic truth and discard myth and delusions."[20]

Students in the Watergate era, however, were not always so easily swayed by the pronouncements of authority figures. The real
challenge was to mobilize the newly self-conscious youth culture itself. As a former executive with the Dallas insurance firm Southwestern Life remembered it, the first gathering of Students in Free
Enterprise, or SIFE, convened 100 students from ten different Sunbelt campuses near the theme park Six Flags over Texas in January
1975. The students assembled there to "discuss what they might do
to counteract the stultifying criticism of American business which
was flowing from the campus, the press, and elsewhere, seeking to
tear down the very system which gave the critics their jobs and their
warm, comfortable homes . . . The kids loved it."[21]

SIFE sponsors and students came up with a new mechanism for
counteracting this corrosive anti-business sentiment. The idealistic
young free enterprisers were to return to their campuses and develop their own projects for promoting American capitalism locally, then present these public education plans in a competition to
be judged by a panel of Dallas businessmen. The winning student
collective took home a $2,500 grant to its university.[22] By 1978,
the contest had spread to 200 campuses and the prize purse had expanded to $30,000, courtesy of sponsors like Dow Chemical and
Ralston Purina.[23] "There's a virtual army of young people out there
on our side," explained the group's founder, "and we never gave
them a role to play before."[24]

SIFE tapped into a promising new resource for the wary employers of college graduates. In 1973, Oklahoma Christian College
(now University) had commissioned a Gallup poll on the political
orientation of college students. The results confirmed their worst
fears. Asked to rank ethical standards by professional fields, students placed businessmen near the bottom. Ralph Nader won the

honors in individual esteem, and the United Nations in the institutional category; the Republican Party and the CIA were last. Almost half favored nationalizing the oil industry. Moreover, while one-third of freshmen in the survey identified themselves as leftists, more than half of seniors did so. It was true: higher education in itself produced anticapitalist sentiment.[25]

But Oklahoma Christian was quick to publicize as well the poll's silver lining: its own students were significantly more conservative than their rowdy counterparts at Princeton. This datum suggested a way out for corporate donors still wary of the restive campuses. In 1971, shortly before his elevation to the Supreme Court, Lewis Powell had penned a furious memo to the U.S. Chamber of Commerce: what was business thinking, he demanded, to tolerate college radicalism when the graduates would go on to vent their hostility as the next generation of lawmakers and regulators?[26] Two years later, the chairman of Hewlett-Packard challenged the Committee for Corporate Support of American Universities to stop providing institutions of higher education with enough financial rope to hang the donors. In the future, he suggested, corporations should target support to those schools and departments that "contribute in some specific way to our individual companies or to the general welfare of our free enterprise system."[27]

Oklahoma Christian knew just the place. Following the 1973 Gallup poll, a 1976 study found that rural, male Protestants working more than thirty hours a week and studying business, math, or engineering were the most likely to be "pro–free enterprise." The most negative reactions, conversely, came from the nonreligious.[28] Thus it was among these small-town Protestant students that SIFE took hold with particular success. While the expanding access to higher education had reached the children of unionized factory workers at places like Kent State, the small Christian colleges had drawn from rural and small-town settings, often with a long tradition of on-campus enterprises at which farmers' children could work their way through a degree in Bible or a teaching certificate.

These student bodies could be impressed by the Sunbelt's evidence that economic salvation, like its spiritual counterpart, was a matter best addressed at the level of the individual conscience—it wasn't Texas that was rusting, after all. The bureaucratic corporations that dominated industrial landscapes in the North were the entrepreneurial success stories of another century. The new ones building shopping centers and fast-food outlets in the South and West were the expressions of private individuals still young—small-town boys made good. The economic vision that defined insecurity as opportunity sounded more plausible with these object lessons in sight, and business clubs and departments served their Christian campuses by preparing country kids for Dallas's gleaming new high-rises. Organizations like SIFE eased their introduction to middle-class office culture even as secretaries and accountants actually became the new American working class.

As the Young Americans for Freedom laid the groundwork for the electoral Reagan Revolution, then, organizations like SIFE prepared its economic counterpart. Especially for the newest claimants to managerial credentials, SIFE interpreted the maligned business sector as a cause, not just a job. Each fall, teams of business students and their committed instructors received "extensive motivational leadership training" and "information about current problems of the free enterprise system" at regional workshops. SIFE acquainted the trainees with promotional materials that were available for the students to take to local audiences, allowing the participants to serve as an effective grassroots distribution mechanism for corporate films and booklets. Local Rotary Clubs provided "dialogue resource persons" for the trainees, teaching students how to present their cause professionally and to garner support for their activities. SIFE groups then headed home to design creative programs for "projecting the positive side of our free enterprise system on the campus and in the community," recruiting as many as 100 additional students to log time on the projects. For their efforts, most received academic credit as well as valuable exposure to the unfamiliar world of corporate America.[29]

SIFE did not labor alone. Students in a business club at a Christian college in Arkansas learned to dress for success and made presentations in the local schools "designed to give the children a basic definition of Free Enterprise and to stress the importance of preserving the system."[30] The pupils were instructed on the virtues of consumer choice, the dangers of socialistic government control, and the importance of training from day one for their serious role as economic citizens.[31] In another innovative program, nine groups of high-school "Union Carbide Scholars" traveled each year to Washington to observe sessions of Congress, meet cabinet-level officials, and run their own mock Congress. Returning to their communities—all sites of a Union Carbide plant or office—these teen-aged ambassadors then spoke to school and civic groups. "When a young man or woman comes back into your office after attending the seminar and tells you Union Carbide has changed his or her life," explained a manager, "now that makes your week."[32]

Surveying the millions of dollars' worth of "economic education" materials pouring out of corporate PR offices in the mid-1970s, neoconservative professional intellectual Irving Kristol frankly proclaimed most of them propaganda, and ineffective propaganda at that. Even worse, he declared, honestly improving the quality of high-school economics courses would not guarantee the pro-business outcome the sponsors sought, for knowledge of economics did not necessarily mean favorable attitudes toward laissez-faire. Far more influential in shaping attitudes, Kristol contended, were experience and culture, including the culture of higher education. The repeated finding that college seniors were significantly more anti-business than freshmen did not necessarily mean that they were failing to study economics in college. Rather, their animus had "more to do with their study of literature, or anthropology, or history, or political theory—the 'value-forming' humanities."[33]

The remediation Kristol had in mind did not include reducing students' academic exposure to the liberal arts. But through changes in higher education during the 1970s, this path became a de facto solution to the business demand for college-educated yet pro-business white-collar workers. Well before the 1980s culture wars over the academic canon, the undergraduate business major became America's default core curriculum.[34]

Between 1969 and 1979, applications to undergraduate and graduate business programs both doubled nationally. The growth in business degrees conferred outstripped the growth in bachelor's and master's degrees in general. By the end of the decade, business was the single biggest major, approaching a 2:1 ratio over its closest competitor, education. A survey of college freshmen at the end of the decade showed one in four planning to major in business. Departments strained at the seams with the unexpected influx of what they conceded were usually the weakest undergraduate students. And at Berkeley, where only a decade earlier the Free Speech Movement had issued its impassioned *grito* against the commercialized "knowledge industry," business classes were so choked with students that the university had to cap enrollment.[35]

As the cold wind of recession blew across the quad, the boom in university-based vocational training for business not surprisingly came at the expense of the liberal arts, or what *U.S. News & World Report* dismissed as "personal growth." An admissions officer at George Washington University explained mid-decade that entering freshmen were looking for majors that would be "more marketable than the liberal-arts programs have been in recent years." "The sitting-under-a-tree-and-wondering-who-you-are routine has diminished," agreed a Texas business professor. "Students are looking for layers of security." A longitudinal study by the College Placement Council stressed the low salaries and long job hunts facing liberal arts graduates and recommended that the tree-sitters at least "take sufficient electives in business-related subjects to enhance their employability."[36]

The student demand for a career-oriented degree was indeed one-half of the equation, but the changes in the structure of higher education that favored a default culture of business were much more profound. The stream of federal funding that had poured into research universities after Sputnik dried up under the demands of the country's land war in Asia. Under Nixon's prodding, the National Science Foundation (NSF) instead developed research partnerships between industry and universities. During his brief presidential receivership, Gerald Ford likewise called for a greater rapprochement between business and education, and Congress responded with $10 million for career education. By 1978, the NSF required universities to find corporate sponsors for joint funding.[37]

But the lion's share of this tax-supported industrial R&D flowed to high-tech labs at the more prestigious research institutions. Less favored schools, unlikely to land a particle accelerator or a robotics program, turned instead to the self-styled science of management to attract new patrons. In 1971, a Texas business professor discovered a new market for this less capital-intensive expertise when he deployed his students to help the Small Business Administration (SBA) salvage local enterprises after a devastating tornado. Delighted with this new constituency, the SBA began paying other universities to award academic credit for free consulting by students, and christened the fledgling programs "Small Business Institutes," or SBIs. Squeezed for operating revenue, the colleges were happy to comply. By mid-decade, the number of SBIs was approaching 400, and the SBA was learning from its encounters with campuses. Its 1973 annual meeting focused on "changing concepts of education and integrating business management training into school curricula."[38]

In 1975, the dean of the University of Georgia's business school teamed up with California State Polytechnic to pitch an idea for an expanded program to the government agency. As a result of their advisory efforts, the SBA launched a system of Small Business Development Centers (SBDCs), which would at last "make available to small business not only the services of the School of Business, but the full capabilities of the universities."[39] In other words, the very basis for judging academic legitimacy could potentially shift from the pointy-headed intellectuals to their snubbed colleagues in marketing and management. The SBDCs, as a congressional hearing established, were not to be "just an appendage, a stepsister" to the academic mission. To the contrary: the question was whether the American university could prove itself "a manager of resources," rather than "just another resource."[40]

To launch this ambitious dream, the SBA turned to a series of campuses that were already actively pursuing closer ties to business, including UGA and Cal-Poly. Clients for the free consulting services of students and professors were not hard to come by. The altered economic geography of post-Fordism was throwing many older small businesses into a tailspin, while the downsized became the "newly self-employed." Congress signaled its approval by appropriating a whopping $20 million for SBDCs in 1981, with the requirement that colleges and universities find one-to-one matching funds from other sources.[41]

The political support behind this largesse had little to do with the centers' effectiveness. Reports and hearings found a spotty record and a dramatic over-reliance on undergraduates. But many constituents understood that the utility of the centers could not necessarily be measured by their economic impact alone. The end of the Bretton Woods era left bewildered small businessmen as a window dressing for the new "vast casino" of international finance specula-tion.[42] Like a failed Missouri manufacturer, many could not under-stand "why, in a country as great as ours, a small business should have so much trouble surviving."[43] The answer was not to be found in an undergraduate accounting class, but that was not really the point.

Rather, like the personalized outreach programs and the local ac-tivism on behalf of free enterprise, the college-based small business centers offered the businessman as a victim, not a bully, to impres-sionable campus audiences. As Cal-Poly's Reed Powell put it, "Young students who know of American business only through ste-reotypes are changing their attitudes in favor of the private enterprise system."[44] The program benefited students, a Chicago instructor ar-gued, by "providing an outlet for their social concern and youthful enthusiasm." It also managed to contain the danger latent in these "casualties of the free enterprise system," providing psychic support to those traumatized by the war of all against all.[45]

The march of the business major addressed anti-business senti-ment by replacing much of the "values-forming" liberal arts cur-riculum, but one subdiscipline raised free enterprise advocacy to an art form in itself. The official origin story of Wichita State Uni-versity's Center for Entrepreneurship relates the move dramati-cally:

On a Saturday morning in the summer of 1977, Professor Fran Jabara was riding his exercise bicycle while watching the television tuned to the only available entertainment—cartoons. A big limou-sine and a high-powered, manipulating, uncaring businessman ap-peared on the screen. Jabara was struck by two things: the negative portrayal of the businessman and the stereotype of business people as exclusively CEO's of large, established companies. At that mo-ment, Jabara, who had been a member of the business faculty at Wi-chita State University for 28 years, decided it was time to change society's image of business people. "We spend all of our time talking to our students about becoming president of a major corporation and we devote almost no time to thinking about the entrepreneurial process."[46]

Jabara convinced the university to back him in marketing a practical workshop on launching a small business. With the profits it generated, the professor then underwrote related academic and advocacy activities. His success turned Wichita State into an acknowledged go-to center for small colleges looking to inspire the young. Another early leader was the Church of Christ's Pepperdine University in Southern California, which attracted patronage from the author of *How I Made $1,000,000 in Mail Order* and *How to Get $50,000 Worth of Services Free, Each Year, from the U.S. Government*. During the 1970s, the number of colleges and universities offering courses in entrepreneurship and small business administration increased from eight to almost 200.[47]

Conceiving of entrepreneurship as a set of character traits rather than a function of an economic structure, the new field zeroed in on "the Entrepreneur as an Individual," in the words of a course at Georgia State.[48] The University of North Carolina treated "the psychology of the entrepreneur," while New Mexico Highlands University instructed students on "Entrepreneurs: care and feeding."[49] "The entrepreneur, through the process of innovation, becomes the principle actor in the drama of economic growth," explained the Chair of Private Enterprise at the Southern Baptists' Baylor University.[50] Southern Methodist University in Dallas elaborated breathlessly: "The life of an entrepreneur is exciting, active, challenging and rewarding . . . The entrepreneur is the captain of the ship, guiding all facets of business while maintaining speed and direction. Active entrepreneur speakers are in the midst of their careers, builders, busy in the turmoil of the organization, physically and mentally active."[51]

Here lay the answer to the postwar organization man, that other-directed drone who, in the right light, looked disturbingly like his Soviet counterpart. Texts assigned in the new classes extolled the entrepreneur as a rare and special type, not content with the ordinary round of bureaucracy in corporate life. In this guise, the entrepreneur inherited the mantle of Jeffersonian virtue from the independent farmers and the Populist rebellion—a hero for the age of the mass office, a foil to sissified bureaucrats and the distant Shylocks of Wall Street. At the same time, these young Turks embodied the countercultural values enshrined by the generation of '68: distrust of large-scale hierarchies, creative nonconformity, moral outrage on behalf of the underdog, even anti-materialism, as "their status needs [were] determined by achievements rather than clothes, office décor, or the automobiles they drive."[52]

But underneath these bold paeans ran the instructors' concern that their role models failed to live up to the virile image. Dull, uninspired visiting speakers often seemed ridiculously at odds with the entrepreneurial hero, and the risk-taking student was rarer still. The problem of "student aggressiveness," wrote a Tulane professor, had not yet been solved in his entrepreneurial classes. He had begun his courses confident that students would demonstrate "boldness and breadth of vision," but was forced to conclude that "this was an incorrect assumption." At UCLA, even five years out from the graduate course, fewer than 10 percent of the alumni had actually started a business. Most, the professor noted, realized by the end of the semester that "being an entrepreneur IS NOT for them."[53]

In fact, reported the instructors soberly, most entrepreneurship students eagerly sought work in the secure, salaried jobs of large corporations. In the face of this failure, many professors philosophically altered their mission. They would try instead to equip their students for the uncertainties that increasingly came along with the salaries and warn them away from risky ventures. As one of their favorite textbooks had it, what was needed was an action plan for "the employed, the unemployed, and the self-employed"—for who knew when and how you might change categories?[54]

Compared to the atmosphere of the previous decade, then, campuses by the late 1970s had become friendly places for business. A Harris poll of faculty at 150 colleges found that over three-quarters of them favored more contact between academe and the corporate world and that none at all urged less. "The welcome mat is out," the poll concluded with modest understatement.[55] As the neoliberal stratification of the labor market accelerated and globalized over the ensuing decades, the American university loomed as gatekeeper to the land of the saved, empowered to distribute or withhold the credentials for economic survival. Unsurprisingly, rival claimants in this deadly serious contest struggled to ensure that the yardstick for success would be marked in the units they commanded.[56] To the extent that the old heart of the university functions today as a handmaiden to vocational training or a loss leader for administration, real estate development, and biotech, the short-term outcome at least is clear.

Under the warming sun of the Reagan administration, the seeds of the seventies bloomed. In the new administration's first year, graduating business majors already outnumbered their classmates in all languages and literatures, the arts, philosophy, religion, the social sciences, and history combined.[57] The Reagan cuts in higher education further helped transform the unmarketable degree into a luxury, and programs that awarded academic credit for waged work inherited the ideal of democratic access to the life of the mind.

By the mid-1980s, too, entrepreneurial programs and free-enterprise centers had been adopted enthusiastically by many smaller campuses, where they performed virtually no research but did undertake considerable corporate fund-raising and advocacy.[58] In many cases, this pairing was originally a marriage of convenience, not a love match. Once established, however, the incubators of business values drew constituencies that could dominate the campus, from the libraries to the classrooms to a literal theme park of free-market capitalism, "the Disneyland of Economics." In the words of its own publicity, this site at Oklahoma Christian College was "the nation's only major visitor attraction designed to interpret the American Free Enterprise System. It is a 60,000-square-foot, $15-million educational attraction, designed to simplify economics and the free market system and to provide a hands-on, fun experience for people of all ages as they learn about free enterprise and the role it has played in making the United States the greatest and most profitable of all nations."[59]

SIFE likewise went on to extraordinary labor in the cultural trenches during the eighties. The young enthusiasts constructed information booths in malls and produced public service announcements for radio and talk shows for cable TV. They silk-screened T-shirts and imprinted their message on bumper stickers, milk cartons, Frisbees, billboards, and mud flaps. They popularized a grade-school rendering of Milton Friedman's "Free to Choose" series with classroom skits in Arkansas. At a busy intersection in Appalachia, they erected a tombstone inscribed "Bury the Deficit!"[60] Invigorated by enthusiastic new supporters—Dow Chemical, Coors, the Business Roundtable, and, above all, Wal-Mart—SIFE in the late Cold War linked campuses to corporate funders and trained a white-collar cadre to market economic restructuring at home and abroad. By the end of the decade, 40,000 SIFE students on 170 campuses reached an estimated 117 million people.[61] "SIFE is more than just another student group," explained the headquarters to its potential clients. "SIFE is a media network."[62]

Yet media alone, no matter how well funded, could not convince without a message that resonated for its target audience. The terms of that message recall the interpretive compromises that business made with youth culture. Two decades after SIFE's foundational gathering at Six Flags, a regional competition in Memphis's historic

Peabody Hotel played host to "SIFE-Man," a "business super-hero." Costumed in tights and a cape bearing a large dollar sign, the Christian college chemistry major had spent the preceding academic year traveling to elementary school classrooms around Jackson, Tennessee, dramatizing the need to defend free enterprise from powerful villains. This caped crusader was neither *homo economicus* nor *Übermensch*. The exuberant stunt was not a product of triumphant theories of profit maximization or creative destruction, but of the collegian's responsibility to mobilize his beloved community in defense of a democratic society, understood in market terms. "Everybody needs a hero," he explained.[63]

CHAPTER 4

Gender and America's Right Turn

MARJORIE J. SPRUILL

The 1970s are well remembered for the remarkable successes of the modern women's rights movement, which profoundly changed American society. Less well known is the role of gender issues in American politics' turn toward the Right in the second half of the decade. As the women's movement grew in strength and social conservatives mobilized in opposition, distinctly different views on women and their social roles led feminists and antifeminists into a highly visible struggle for influence during a series of state and national "International Women's Year" (IWY) conferences in 1977. The conferences, sponsored by Congress to solicit women's recommendations for federal action and attended by over 130,000 women and some men, revealed much about the two opposing groups, their fundamental assumptions, policy goals, and strategies. And despite the intentions of IWY leaders, the conferences galvanized antifeminists as well as feminists—contributing significantly to the rightward turn in American politics as social conservatives began rallying around gender issues.

Few Americans not directly involved in the 1977 IWY conferences seem to remember them, yet both feminist and conservative leaders regard the U.S. IWY conferences as watershed events in

American history—and both claim victory in the conflict. Gloria Steinem remembered the national IWY conference as a "Constitutional Convention for Women," a major achievement of the women's movement, "the sort of milestone that divides our sense of time."[1] Phyllis Schlafly regards the IWY as a major strategic blunder by feminists that played right into her hands, a "Battle of Midway" in a war between feminists and social conservatives, one that sealed the fate of the Equal Rights Amendment (ERA) and gave rise to the "Pro-Family Movement."[2]

The IWY conferences, however, produced no clear victory for either side. Rather, the IWY conflict ushered in a new era in American politics, the beginning rather than the end of a protracted struggle over women's rights, "family values," and cultural politics. Feminists felt empowered as the success of their movement was acknowledged through the establishment of what they delighted in calling "the first federally funded women's conference"; they eagerly embraced the opportunity to involve thousands of newcomers in the ongoing discussion of women's rights and to widen their base even as they developed an official answer to the question "what do American women want?" But the feminists' very success in gaining a congressional invitation to set policy guidelines was a red flag to the conservatives and impressed many of them with the need to create a sustained movement against feminism as opposed to a single-issue campaign against the ERA. The IWY-inspired debates over policy on women's and family issues contributed to the politicization of previously quiescent social conservatives and the development of the Pro-Family Movement, which grew rapidly in the late 1970s, merged with economic conservatives to empower a New Right in American politics, and helped put ERA opponent Ronald Reagan in the White House. After 1977, national politics would be increasingly polarized and gender issues would be at the heart of the dispute.

Steinem's "Constitutional Convention for Women" and Schlafly's "Battle of Midway" was formally known as the National Women's

Conference, the grand, culminating event of IWY that became so closely associated with its host city that it is often called the "Houston Conference," or simply "Houston." It received worldwide publicity. On November 18, 1977, television audiences saw scenes of Houston airports and hotels jammed with travelers, mostly female. In addition to the 2,000 elected delegates, the throngs of alternates and observers, including 100 women from 56 countries—plus 1,500 members of the press—brought the total gathered for the conference to around 20,000.[3]

Participants ranged from students and homemakers attending their first conference to celebrities, including feminist leaders Betty Friedan and Gloria Steinem; anthropologist Margaret Mead; actress Jean Stapleton (Edith Bunker on the hit sitcom *All in the Family*); and political leaders Martha Griffiths, Pat Schroeder, Barbara Jordan (the keynote speaker), and Bella Abzug, a central figure in the story. Of particular significance was the presence of three First Ladies from both national political parties: former First Ladies Lady Bird Johnson and Betty Ford, and then-First Lady, Rosalynn Carter—plus the First Lady of the civil rights movement, Coretta Scott King.[4]

The gala event was loaded with symbolism connecting the so-called Second Wave of feminism with the first. A relay team that included tennis pro Billie Jean King carried a "Torch of Freedom" to the conference from Seneca Falls, New York, the scene of the iconic 1848 conference that launched the American women's movement with its "Declaration of Sentiments." Poet Maya Angelou delivered a dramatic reading of her "Declaration of Sentiments 1977," composed for the occasion. The conference was opened with Susan B. Anthony's gavel, loaned by the Smithsonian's National Museum of American History for the occasion.[5]

The establishment of the IWY program was inspired by the U.N.-sponsored 1975 IWY conference in Mexico City, which had adopted a "World Plan of Action" to enhance women's lives.

President Gerald Ford appointed the first National Commission on the Observance of IWY, headed by feminist Republican Jill Ruckelshaus. Housed in the State Department, it was charged with developing recommendations for how the nation could become "a more perfect union" for women. Its primary recommendation was the ratification of the ERA "at the earliest possible moment." When the United Nations extended International Women's Year to a decade for women, Congress, at Bella Abzug's urging, authorized this series of state conferences and a national IWY conference to be held in 1977 and funded by $5 million.[6]

In early 1977, President Jimmy Carter appointed Abzug as chair of the IWY National Commission, which had established state IWY commissions charged with planning conferences open to all. Participants at the state level were to debate issues and vote on recommendations and delegates to send to the national conference. At Houston, the delegates were to devise a "National Plan of Action" to guide federal policy on women's issues in the years ahead.[7]

The Houston Conference was a remarkable achievement, perhaps the crest of the Second Wave of the American women's rights movement. The conference fulfilled two goals dear to the hearts of feminist leaders. First, it moved the movement beyond its white, middle-class base. In fact, the act of Congress that mandated the IWY program required that delegates elected to represent each state reflect the full diversity of the state's population. The state conferences provided transportation and child care to insure that low-income women could participate: delegates elected to the Houston Conference were fully funded. So successful were these efforts that for some minority groups, participation rates actually exceeded their percentage in the nation's population.[8]

Second, feminist leaders hoped to move beyond the internal ideological and strategic wrangling that was a hallmark of the modern feminist movement. At Houston, according to the official report, "women's rights advocates worried as much about divisions within their own ranks as they did about disagreement with the anti-change forces." Some feared jeopardizing ratification of the ERA by linking it with controversial issues, particularly government-supported child care, abortion rights, and civil rights for lesbians. Others, including National Gay Task Force leader and IWY commissioner Jean O'Leary, who urged the delegates to back her cause, urged them to be noncompromising; she invoked the example of Elizabeth Cady Stanton who persuaded cautious participants at the Seneca Falls convention to endorse the most controversial of the resolutions then being considered—woman suffrage.[9]

Amid the pageantry, films, exhibits, poetry readings, the Sweet Honey in the Rock concert, women's history lessons, and occasional spontaneous outbursts of hugging, singing, and dancing in the aisles, the delegates labored in tension-filled caucuses to resolve their differences regarding what the final "Plan" should look like. Betty Friedan was loudly cheered when she announced to the full assembly her support for the lesbian rights plank, putting aside her well-known opposition to aligning feminism with "the lavender menace."[10]

A spirit of compromise and expansiveness prevailed: the resulting National Plan of Action reflected the goals of the moderate, mainly middle-aged feminists who had launched the movement in the mid-1960s and those of the more radical and ideologically diverse group of women who entered the movement later in the decade.[11] Planks adopted covered a wide range of issues, including equal access to jobs and credit; international cooperation to advance women's rights worldwide and promote peace; aid for elderly women, disabled women, and "displaced homemakers"; and an end to sex-role stereotyping in schools and in the media. Notable was a new plank, hammered out in Houston by the Minority Caucus that, in the words of Coretta Scott King, sent a message that should "go forth from Houston," that "there is a new force, a new understanding, a new sisterhood against all injustice that has been born here. We will not be divided and defeated again." A highlight of the conference was the passage of the plank urging ratification of the ERA, which produced a long and emotional floor demonstration.[12]

Adoption of the 1977 National Plan of Action, encapsulating the goals of the diverse group of "pro-change" delegates, filled these women with a tremendous sense of accomplishment and solidarity. As one participant recalled, "Inside the cocoon of those four days of Houston, we women found sisterhood—that universal sense of being together honorably for a great cause."[13] "The Plan" was indeed a major achievement, a compendium of the goals of the American women's rights movement at its most expansive moment—one that would continue to guide feminists in future decades.[14] It did not, however, as IWY organizers proclaimed, represent a consensus among American women on what federal policy should be. Solidarity within the feminist movement was not the same as solidarity among American women.

Even within the Houston Conference, 20 percent of the delegates that had been elected by the states were social conservatives who opposed most of the planks favored by the feminists. And across town, another major gathering almost as large was taking place at the Astro Arena to protest the Houston Conference and challenge its right to speak for American women. A crowd of between 15,000 and 20,000 people from across the nation attended this rally led by Phyllis Schlafly. The rally's "star line-up" was composed of numerous conservative speakers, including attorney Nellie Gray, president of the March for Life; Dr. Mildred Jefferson, an African American physician from Boston, at-large delegate to the IWY conference, and president of the Right-to-Life Federation; Lottie Beth Hobbs, president of the WWWW (Women Who Want to be Women); and Congressman Robert K. Dornan.[15]

Obviously, feminist leaders knew from years of conflict over the ERA and abortion that they had opposition. But they had a confidence based on the strength of their convictions, public opinion polls, and a sense of momentum resulting from remarkable gains recently achieved. Thus, feminist leaders believed that other women—when exposed to new feminist perspectives—would come to accept them, that the IWY would greatly expand their base of support by serving as a "consciousness-raising session" on the grandest of scales.[16] And the IWY did indeed win many converts to the cause, but rarely from the ranks of those already opposed to feminism.[17] Again, the success of the feminist leaders in gaining this mandate from two presidents and from Congress to hold these IWY conferences served to galvanize the opposition, to politicize social conservatives, and to aid Phyllis Schlafly and her associates in expanding the single-issue movement against the ERA into a more enduring, profoundly antifeminist, and—in her words—"Pro-Family" movement.[18]

As the decade began, few would have envisioned such a turn of events. In the late 1960s and early 1970s, the conservative backlash that became visible in the campaigns of George Wallace and that Richard Nixon then manipulated to his advantage, focused on race, domestic unrest, and economics—but not gender.[19] Politicians of all stamps seemed to be jumping on the women's rights bandwagon. In the early seventies, feminists celebrated the *Roe v. Wade* decision legalizing abortion as well as congressional approval of the ERA by overwhelming margins—endorsed by Democrats and Republicans, the Left and the Right. George McGovern, Birch Bayh, Bella Abzug, and Teddy Kennedy endorsed it, but so did Richard Nixon, Spiro Agnew, George Wallace, and Strom Thurmond. Proclaiming simply that "Equality of rights under the law shall not be denied or abridged by the United States or by any State on account of sex" and giving Congress the power to enforce it, the ERA passed in the House of Representatives by 354 to 23 and by 84 to 8 in the Senate. States scrambled to ratify with little or no debate. By March 1973, only eight more states were needed. All this occurred without ERA ratification committees in most states: confident of victory, feminists had not felt it necessary to establish them.[20]

To a degree not yet visible to feminists, the major media outlets, and the general public, however, some Americans were simmering with resentment. After the publication of "A Matter of Simple Justice," the 1970 report of President Nixon's Task Force on Women's Rights and Responsibilities, a few socially conservative women began to view with alarm the apparent "capitulation" of leading politicians to the new and seemingly ascendant women's rights movement they saw as a threat to American women and to America's identity as a Christian nation, the leader of the free world—retaining its strength through the strength of its families.[21]

Interestingly, at first Phyllis Schlafly was not among them. Absorbed in writing books critical of America's defense policies, she regarded the ERA as something on the spectrum between "innocuous and mildly helpful." Brought into the fight by admirers in Florida and Connecticut, who urged her to examine the issue, Schlafly founded STOP ERA (acronym for "Stop Taking Our Privileges") in October 1972, a few months after the amendment was sent to the states.[22] Schlafly was ideal for this role because she already had a following with enormous potential for expansion. This was the supremely ironic result of efforts by Nelson Rockefeller and other liberal Republicans to limit her influence by blocking her accession to the presidency of the National Federation of Republican Women. After losing to the liberal Republicans' candidate, Schlafly and 3,000 livid supporters walked out of the Federation convention and started their own independent conservative movement complete with a monthly newsletter, the *Phyllis Schlafly Report,* and an "Eagle Trust Fund" to finance their work.[23] That Schlafly's organizing activities for the next decade took place largely outside the Republican Party put her in an excellent position to attract additional support from women of northern ethnic and white southern backgrounds who were beginning to leave the Democratic Party—early roots of the massive realignment in American politics of the late twentieth century.

By the end of 1975, Schlafly had also created the Eagle Forum, an organization that served as the nucleus for a loose coalition of social conservatives who demonstrated against the ERA and abortion and would now cooperate with one another in the battle with the feminists for control of the IWY conferences. As we understand today, far more clearly that did observers at the time, religion inspired the passion many of these women poured into their activism. Some, like Schlafly, were devoted Catholics, many being active in "right to life" groups. By the mid-1970s, religious opponents of the feminist movement also included Mormons, who played a key role in the battles over the ERA and the IWY not only in Utah but throughout the United States. And then there was the newly politicized group of evangelicals and fundamentalists—to whom denial of gender differences and separate, subordinate roles for women was not only erroneous but sacrilegious—who had previously eschewed politics as corrupting. Significantly, the IWY program inspired Christian conservatives to action just as Republican strategists began their efforts to broaden the political power of conservatives by reaching out to the religious Right.[24]

Federal support for feminist goals also angered an overlapping group of social conservatives still incensed over decisions made by Congress and the Supreme Court in the 1950s and 1960s on race and religion. In the 1970s, they were ripe to be drawn into a social movement against federal "intrusions" into the sensitive and intensely personal arena of relations between the sexes.[25] Many of these women and men were also ardent patriots and isolationists, suspicious not only of feminism but of international cooperation—certainly including the IWY with its U.N. roots and ties.[26]

Ironically, at the time that it had become politically unacceptable to be overtly racist, being overtly antifeminist became increasingly acceptable, as many women insisted publicly that there were innate differences between the sexes that should continue to guide and direct legislation. Increasingly, gender became a rallying point for a wide variety of social conservatives believing in innate, indeed divinely inspired, gender differences and hierarchies. Conservatives often spoke of feminism as a great evil rooted in secular humanism and advocating great sins, including abortion and homosexuality. It was common to link feminism with Communism and to insist that it would weaken the traditional family, the bulwark of a free America, and replace the care and influence of parents with federally run child care beyond parental control. Indeed, as the grip of the Cold War loosened, "Godless feminism" seemed to replace "Godless Communism" as a common foe around which to unite. The mobilization of socially conservative women and the fact that such a wide variety of conservative groups—many of which harbored deep suspicions of one another and were usually reluctant to work with one another—came together in opposition to feminism is one of the most remarkable developments in this story.[27]

When the act establishing and funding the IWY conferences was passed in 1975, conservatives went to battle to stop the conferences from occurring and, failing that, challenged feminists for control of them. By then, conservative opposition had succeeded in stalling the ERA bandwagon and antifeminists perceived the entire IWY program as nothing more than a lavishly funded effort to foist upon the public not only the ERA but also a whole host of other feminist goals. Schlafly, with a love of alliteration second only to Spiro Agnew, denounced IWY as "Federal Financing of a Foolish Festival for Frustrated Feminists" and condemned the national and state IWY organizing committees as dominated by "militant women's libbers."[28]

As the state conferences began in 1977, the dramatic, opposing definitions of woman's nature and social role were revealed more clearly than ever as was the conviction of each side that they were the true advocates for American womanhood. In February, conservatives were appalled when conference participants at the first IWY conference (in Vermont) adopted resolutions supporting the ERA, abortion rights, and, according to conservatives, "an additional anti-family goal—gay rights"—and elected twelve feminist delegates to represent them in Houston. When, in March, the national commission sent a list of largely feminist "core recommendations" to the state coordinating committees—which included enough conservatives for news of committee proceedings to reach antifeminist leaders—antifeminists accused the feminists of "pre-packaging" the issues to be discussed as well as the slates of delegates to be considered. Conservatives then created the "IWY Citizens' Review Committee," headed by Schlafly devotee Rosemary Thomson.[29]

Interestingly, though ERA opponents had claimed for five years that the ERA would usher in numerous undesirable feminist goals, Thomson stated that it was the IWY conferences and the resolutions the feminists were promoting that "shocked" traditional women like her and confirmed their worst fears concerning the intentions of ERA advocates. They were horrified, she said, that, if approved at the state and national conferences, these recommendations would pass as the official wish list of American women. The IWY Citizens' Review Committee quickly spread the word among church leaders and pro-life organizations, and Schlafly called her followers to action in the May 1977 *Phyllis Schlafly Report*. The results were soon evident. Congressmen were swamped with letters protesting the IWY. And conservative groups, working in loose coalitions that varied from state to state, managed what were called "takeovers" of several conferences, including Mississippi, Alabama, Missouri, Oklahoma, Ohio, Nebraska, and Utah.[30]

After the first of these, on June 16–18, 1977, in Oklahoma, state Eagle Forum leader Diane Edmonson reported that her group "relied heavily on the fundamentalist church groups here to tell their members to attend and vote against the feminist slate. The conservative participants defeated the entire list of core recommendations." Conservative columnist James Kilpatrick relished the victory, concluding that the "troops of Bella Abzug got scalped." "For the past 10 years," he boasted, "the Gloria Steinems have had things pretty much their own way. Now the Phyllis Schlaflys are venturing out of their kitchens."[31]

Conservatives were soon celebrating the fact that "the radicals [were] being challenged—and defeated . . . where concerned Americans see the dangers." In Utah, 14,000 men and women jammed into the Salt Palace in Salt Lake City, summoned by the vast Mormon women's organization, the Relief Society, to stand up for "correct principles." According to the national IWY report, they "reversed the intent of all the workshops designed by the pro-IWY State coordinating committee."[32]

In Mississippi, a coalition calling itself "Mississippians for God, Country and Family" staged a takeover notable for its stealth approach and the completeness of its victory: Although only 250 people preregistered, 1,500 attended. Many arrived in church buses and, according to the feminists, were guided in their voting by a handful of men. They adopted a set of resolutions that were completely antifeminist, pro-life, anti-daycare, and anti-homosexual as substitute resolutions and sent an antifeminist set of delegates to Houston, including the only men elected to the national conference. The delegates also included Dallas Higgins, the wife of the Grand Dragon of the Mississippi KKK, who told the press that Communists had failed to take over the country through blacks and were now trying to do it through women. IWY Citizens' Review Committee leader Rosemary Thomson denounced accusations that members of the Klan were in the Mississippi delegation, but Klan leaders bragged openly that they had "controlled" the Mississippi conference and "infiltrated" most of the state IWY meetings. The state conference organizers appointed by the federal government, a racially diverse group of moderate feminists, reported being astonished at the conservatives anger as well as their numbers.[33]

The strength of the conservatives also surprised conference organizers in states all over the nation. Indiana, Hawaii, Kansas, and Montana elected delegations that were predominantly opposed to the core resolutions proposed by the National IWY Commission. Conservatives challenged feminists in New York, Massachusetts, New Jersey, Illinois, California, and Washington—another state in which they took a "stealth approach" with 2,300 preregistering and 2,000 more than that arriving—many of whom were Mormon.[34]

In the vast majority of state conferences, however, feminists prevailed. In thirty states, participants adopted all of the "core recommendations" and in eleven states approved most of the core.[35] In New York and California, attendance soared as rumors spread that Schlafly or singer Anita Bryant—then famous for her anti-gay rights "Save the Children Campaign"—might appear in person and that social conservatives were planning to turn out in large numbers. Well-known feminist leaders, including Abzug and Steinem plus Jean Stapleton, made personal appearances in very successful attempts to rally supporters.[36]

Ellen Cohn, a feminist writing for *The Village Voice*, in an article called "Mama Said There'd Be Days Like This," recognized this as a major wake-up call for feminists. She wrote: "something totally unexpected and disturbing has happened in recent weeks. The IWY conferences, instead of providing a forum for some sort of feminism, however, diluted, have become a vehicle for anti-ERA and anti-abortion forces around the country." And she quoted a New York IWY organizer as saying, " 'Feminists can no longer make the bland assumption that their voices will dominate any women's conference.' "[37]

As the state conferences came to a close that summer, feminist leaders were pleased with the results of many of the state IWY conferences, which included substantial research on women's accomplishments and current status and the enhancement of feminist networks.[38] But they were shaken by the extent of the opposition and the ability of the conservative leaders to command the attention of the press—which had paid little attention to the IWY program until the battles for control began. More significantly, they were disturbed by the alarming progress socially conservative women were making in convincing politicians that they—rather than the feminists—were the constituency most important to please. Feminist leaders were furious when, after the last of the state conferences, Senator Jesse Helms, working with the IWY Citizens' Review Committee, held congressional hearings where conservative women from across the nation testified that they had been victims of discrimination at the state conferences. Afterward, the IWY Commission members felt considerable heat from other congressmen, and they pleaded in vain for President Carter to commit to attending the Houston Conference.[39]

Angry feminist leaders went on the offensive to "expose the disruptive tactics of the right." Schlafly, said one IWY spokeswoman, was "seeking a resurgence of the far right by exploiting the women's movement." Worse still was her apparent success. Writing in August 1977, Schlafly denounced the conferences for "rigging, ruthlessness, and railroading" and "lesbian aggressiveness" and stated: "our friends who attended the International Women's Year State Conferences have realized that, *if family-oriented Americans don't stand up and fight for their values and their legal rights now,* it may soon be too late to save the next generation from those who are trying to destroy our family structure. The libs will replace it with a society that does not respect gender differences, moral values, church, or family." And she urged her admirers, rather successfully, to join the Eagle Forum "so [that] you can be part of an effective national organization of God-fearing, highly-motivated, well-informed men and women."[40]

Led by the American Association of University Women, forty women's organizations formed a Women's Conference Network to support the IWY program. Even as feminist "Truth Squads" went about the nation holding press conferences to "rebut the false or exaggerated charges anti-change groups had been making to the press and even in Congress," conservatives again tried to prevent the Houston Conference from taking place, charging the IWY Commission with violating its congressional mandate by discriminating against conservatives and by using IWY for lobbying. Schlafly predicted that the spring and summer IWY conferences "speeded the demise of the women's movement" and that the Houston Conference would finish it off.[41]

The rising national tensions over the IWY reached Houston ahead of the delegates. The local arrangements committee had considerable support from the city, the state, and the business community, given that the local "Grass Roots Majority Pro-Family, Pro-Life Coalition" sent a mass mailing to local businesses warning that the conference was an attempt to impose sex quotas on hiring practices and to destroy both capitalism and the family. Mayor Fred Hofheinze remained supportive, but the newly elected Harris County Republican chair Jerry Smith blasted the delegates soon to come to Houston as "a gaggle of outcasts, misfits, and rejects."[42] The press swarmed the celebrities, but these included the archconservative Mississippi delegation, especially the Klan leader's wife, who expressed concern that IWY organizers were going to harass the women of their delegation by making them room with black lesbians.[43]

The National IWY Conference and the protest rally in the Astro Arena both received extensive coverage: one of the few points of agreement between feminists and conservatives was that the press seemed to relish the idea of American women engaged in a massive "cat fight."[44] Schlafly's well-dressed supporters (she generally advised that no one over twenty-five should come dressed in a T-shirt) carried signs proclaiming "We're Ladies, Not Libbers"; "Sin Is Still Sin, Even if It's Legal"; "God Is a Family Man"; and "IWY Means

Immoral Women's Year." These images were juxtaposed in the media with images of the exceptionally heterogeneous group of IWY delegates with a very different set of signs, including "Wages for Housework," "Keep Your Laws Off My Body," "Peace Is a Woman's Issue," "Lesbian Mothers Are Pro-Family," and the omnipresent "ERA YES."[45]

The two Houston gatherings demonstrated the major fault line that had developed in American society over gender issues. Participants, politicians, and the public were all confronted with the fact that there were now two clearly developed sets of ideas about what was best for American women. The Houston IWY Conference inspired the feminist participants and made them all the more determined. However, the corresponding mobilization of socially conservative women—equally fired up by their experiences during IWY—would prove to be enduring and highly influential.

In IWY Citizens' Review Committee chair Rosemary Thomson's *The Price of Liberty,* published in 1978 with a foreword by Jesse Helms, she characterized the uprising of conservative Christian women against feminism as "the story of God's women and their efforts to preserve America's traditional moral and spiritual values"—comparing it to the Great Awakening and other important religious revivals in American history that had had important political consequences.[46]

Political commentators took notice. Dick Behm observed in the *Ripon Forum,* a publication of the moderate Republican Ripon Society, that the state IWY conferences had turned into "fiercely fought conflicts between 'change' and 'anti-change' groups"—"highly significant" battles that "presage[d] a new coalition of 'social conservative' groups . . . that often hated one another before and in future [would] vote similarly." He and others noted that these groups had "demonstrated considerable skill in both coalition politics and convention plotting." These antifeminist and antigay rights campaigns, he said, could well become powerful "if teamed with the many . . . anti-gun control, anti-busing groups that have proliferated along with Richard Viguerie's mailing lists."[47] Historian Donald Critchlow, Schlafly's biographer, has argued that the 1970s mobilization of conservative women at the grassroots levels "activated a disheartened conservative movement" and laid the foundation for their rise to power late in the decade.[48]

After IWY, women's rights advocates remained hopeful about the implementation of the National Plan of Action, but they faced many disappointments. Leaders who had clashed with Carter owing to his opposition to abortion and who believed he could have done much more for the ERA were highly critical of his response to "the Plan." Though Carter's domestic policy staff went to work right away to identify areas in which progress on the Houston recommendations had already been made or was needed, many feminists believed there was too much emphasis on the former and too little action on the latter. White House insiders were well aware of the controversy surrounding the IWY conferences, and some wanted to put distance between the Carter administration and this program that, as one put it, "had gone sour." After Houston, Rosalynn Carter had opposed Abzug's appointment to the IWY "continuing committee," the National Advisory Committee for Women. The president nevertheless appointed Abzug as co-chair—with the well-respected, temperate committee member Carmen Delgado Votaw—but rarely met with committee members, who soon became indignant at having so little contact with the president they were supposed to advise. When they publicly criticized him for not fully backing the National Plan, the president—seeing them as ungrateful for his support for women's issues—allowed Hamilton Jordan to fire Abzug unceremoniously, an incident notorious among feminists as "The Friday Night Massacre." A majority of the committee resigned in protest. Carter later reconstituted the rest of the committee and new appointees as the President's Advisory Committee on Women, headed by Lynda Johnson Robb, but in Abzug's

Nat'l Plan of Action

no energy

eyes its functions were too limited. The new committee, she wrote in 1983, was "even forbidden to lobby for women's programs on Capitol Hill," which left the National Plan of Action "without an official advocacy presence there." For the rest of Carter's term, feminist leaders were divided in their attitudes toward the president. Some worked closely with him but others were openly antagonistic. NOW refused to endorse his reelection, and when he lost, aide Hamilton Jordan was quoted as saying that the feminists had got—in Ronald Reagan—exactly what they deserved.[49]

Meanwhile, feminists were uncertain about how to respond to the increasingly combative social conservatives who, emboldened by their show of strength during IWY, sought aggressively to roll back feminist gains. Betty Friedan soon sparked controversy within the movement as she called for a "Second Stage" in which feminist women and men must work together and not allow conservatives to paint the women's movement as anti-family.[50] Feminists would continue to fight for the agenda encapsulated in "the Plan" and to make significant progress toward its goals, but without the level of federal support the movement enjoyed prior to the controversial IWY conferences and without the solidarity achieved for a glorious moment at Houston.[51]

Conservative women found their champion in Ronald Reagan, who led the Republican Party to reverse its forty-year history of support for the ERA, to adopt a pro-life position—and to victory. Republican feminists protested vigorously but to no avail. In 1980, the platforms of America's two major national parties revealed how polarized the nation had become over gender issues, and "family values" had joined "women's rights" in the political discourse of the nation. Schlafly's success in politicizing, uniting, and mobilizing religious conservatives, emulated by other strategists for the Right, expanded the ranks of committed conservative activists, which enhanced their power within the Republican Party and national politics.[52]

The many victories of the modern women's rights movement, inspired and supported by profound economic and demographic changes in American society, would not be easily undone, however. The success of Schlafly and others in stopping ERA did not stop or reverse many of the other changes advocated by feminists—though without the ERA that possibility remained. Yet the hotly contested IWY conferences were instrumental in America's "right turn" even as they propelled gender issues to front and center in the nation's politics. The conferences deepened and extended feminist networks and, as Abzug noted afterward, laid the foundation for further coalition work on behalf of the ERA and other issues.[53] But these networks were soon needed to lobby against the antifeminist programs of the Reagan years and to mount feminist voter-registration drives in an effort to counter the growing activism of social conservatives who had clearly entered politics to stay. The struggle over the right to speak for American women during the IWY conferences had heightened the awareness of both feminists and social conservatives about their profoundly different worldviews and the importance of political action to advance or defend their positions. By 1980, the polarization of feminists and antifeminists had led to two enduring social movements that still compete over policy regarding women and families.

CHAPTER 5

Civil Rights and the Religious Right

JOSEPH CRESPINO

The 1970s were a boom decade for conservative evangelical Christians. *Time* magazine famously declared 1976 the year of the evangelicals. That same year, nearly 50 million people, a quarter of all Americans, identified themselves to pollsters as born-again Christians.[1] It was not their presence in the general population, however, so much as their presence in politics that attracted attention. Jimmy Carter made his evangelical faith a central part of both his personal and political identity. More important, conservative evangelical Christians played prominent roles in a variety of political efforts that sought to reclaim what conservatives saw as "family values" under threat. The litany of issues that galvanized conservative Christians is familiar: feminism, abortion, gay rights, pornography, the perceived decline in public and political morality. Absent from this list, however, is the one issue that—at least according to leading conservative activists of the day—was the most crucial in politicizing a broad range of conservative Christians.

In the late 1970s, evangelical and fundamentalist Christians rallied to the defense of independent Christian schools that they believed were under attack by federal bureaucrats in the Internal Revenue Service. Public policies that had originated in the fight

90

against white-flight private schools in the rural South were being applied to what supporters claimed were innocent Christian schools, free from racist taint. Small, independent Christian schools were forced to spend thousands of dollars in legal fees defending themselves from bureaucratic harassment by the federal government. Richard Viguerie, a pioneer in the development of direct-mail techniques and a leader in the New Christian Right, claimed that the IRS controversy "kicked the sleeping dog. It galvanized the religious right. It was the spark that ignited the religious right's involvement in real politics."[2] Paul Weyrich, the founder of Coalitions for America, a central forum for some 120 independent conservative organizations, believed that the IRS controversy more than any other issue contributed to a siege mentality among conservative evangelicals. It "shattered the Christian community's notion that Christians could isolate themselves inside their own institutions and teach what they pleased."[3]

The controversy over the IRS and religious schools deserves a central role in any account of America's turn toward the Right in the 1970s. The politicization of evangelical and fundamentalist Christians was perhaps the most salient development in the conservative political coalition that would dominate American politics for the remainder of the twentieth century. The controversy sheds light on three important intersections of race and religion in conservative politics during the decade. First, it shows the inadequacy of historical frameworks that view the 1960s as the critical decade for understanding racial politics in modern America. Conflicts in that decade set in motion legal and bureaucratic processes that redounded in unexpected and largely unexamined ways in the subsequent decade. Second, the episode underscores a key aspect of the political identity of the modern religious Right. Conservative Christians galvanized by the IRS controversy saw their fight as part of the long history of the Protestant defense of the separation of church and state; they viewed their struggle in defensive terms, as a last-ditch effort to protect Christian education from a hostile state intent on standardizing and secularizing education and citizenship in modern America. Finally, the IRS conflict highlights a strange displacement that occurred in racial politics in the 1970s. With tax lawyers creating civil rights policies, disaffected conservative groups focused their animus not against African Americans or other historically disadvantaged groups but rather against "liberal elites" and "unelected bureaucrats." Conservative Christians could nominally support the goal of racial equality—indeed, all but a small minority viewed the promotion of brotherhood across racial lines as part of their Christian duty—while vigorously opposing the remedies that federal courts and executive branch officials had devised to address historic patterns of racial discrimination.

The history of the conflict between private Christian schools and the IRS began in an unlikely place—Holmes County, Mississippi. In May 1969, a group of black parents in Holmes County filed a lawsuit, *Green v. Kennedy*, demanding that the IRS withhold tax exemptions for the three new private academies that had been founded to avoid public school desegregation. The struggle to integrate public schools in a poor rural county like Holmes was particularly difficult. By the 1960s, the mechanization of cotton production and the collapse of the plantation economy had turned Holmes County into essentially a rural ghetto. Just over 23,000 people lived in the county in 1970, down from nearly 40,000 only thirty years earlier. Holmes was more than two-thirds African American; 73 percent of black families lived below the poverty line.[4]

Since the 1950s, white elites in black-majority counties like Holmes had been the backbone of the white South's "massive resistance" to public school desegregation. By the mid-1960s, however, federal enforcement had placed southern segregationists on the defensive. In some areas, private schools became the only way for hard-line whites to avoid integrated education. The number of private schools exploded across the South in the 1960s. Their growth was often timed exactly with the desegregation of formerly all-white public schools. In Mississippi, the number of non-Catholic private schools had risen from 17 in 1964 to 155 only six years later. The Southern Regional Council estimated that in 1970 some 400,000 children were in segregation academies in eleven southern states.[5]

In rural areas with high percentages of African Americans, these new private schools often simply reconstituted the formerly all-white public school. Holmes County provides a good example. In July 1965, a federal court ordered Holmes County public schools to desegregate, at a rate of four grades per year. Within two months of the order, white residents had established three different all-white private academies. White enrollment in the public schools dropped from 771 to 28 the first year of desegregation. The next year, no white students were enrolled in the public schools.[6]

Financing for white-flight private schools became an important new battleground in the southern racial struggle. A 1964 law passed by the Mississippi legislature had provided a tuition grant of $180 to each child attending private schools; the legislature eventually bumped it up to $240 per student. Before the decade closed, however, lawsuits filed by civil rights attorneys overturned this program.[7] A similar fight took place over federal tax status for these new institutions. As early as 1967, the U.S. Commission on Civil Rights recommended that the treasury secretary confer with the attorney general to consider whether federal law "authorizes or requires" the IRS to withhold tax exemptions to racially segregated private schools.[8] New private schools in the South that depended on donations for new buildings and scholarships let potential donors know that their gifts would be tax-exempt. For example, an April 1969 fundraising letter for one of the new private schools in Holmes County urged "substantial contributions" to the school's scholarship fund. Without them, the school's directors warned, many poor white children would be forced into "the intolerable and repugnant 'other schools.' " The letter emphasized that all contributions were "deductible from your gross income for tax purposes."[9]

The very next month, black parents in Holmes County filed their lawsuit against the IRS.[10] The court granted a preliminary injunction in January 1970, barring exemptions to new private schools in Mississippi. A year and a half later, the court made the injunction permanent, establishing a series of guidelines the IRS should follow in enforcing the ruling.

In early 1970, the issue of tax policies toward white-flight southern private schools was not just of regional concern. Since Richard Nixon's inauguration in January 1969, fights over public school desegregation in the South were, as Nixon's adviser John Ehrlichman noted, "one of the burning issues of the day."[11] The Supreme Court had cracked down on recalcitrant southern school boards, and Americans of all political persuasions were eager to see how Richard Nixon would handle the issue. Nixon's campaign rhetoric combined with earlier pronouncements on school desegregation led liberals to question the president's commitment to desegregating schools. The fear was that the Nixon administration's foot-dragging on the issue was part of a Republican "southern strategy" to win white southern voters to the GOP.

When it came to the issue of tax exemptions and private schools, the Nixon administration was divided. In early January 1970, Robert Finch, Nixon's secretary of housing, education, and welfare announced that he would urge the Treasury Department to wipe out tax breaks for private schools established to avoid desegregation.[12] Southern Republicans were outraged by Finch's comment.[13] So, too, was President Nixon, who ordered an aide to tell Finch to "stay out of this." "Tell him to do the right thing for a change," Nixon barked at John Ehrlichman in an oval office meeting. "Whites in Mississippi can't send their kids to schools that are 90 per cent black; they've got to set up private schools."[14] But Nixon would eventually reverse course. In July 1970, the president ordered the IRS to institute a new policy to deny tax exemptions to racially discriminatory private schools. This decision came before the District of Columbia Court of Appeals issued its ruling to the same effect. Reporters at the time speculated that Nixon's decision was an attempt to tack back to the middle on school desegregation. Only weeks earlier, George Wallace had won a surprising come-from-behind victory in the Democratic primary race for governor in Alabama. Nixon had secretly transferred money from his own bulging reelection funds to Wallace's opponent, in hopes of getting rid of the Alabama challenger once and for all. With Wallace still alive in Alabama—and still likely to challenge Nixon in the 1972 election—Nixon decided that it was wiser politically to move to the middle on the tax exemption issue.[15]

Nixon's new policy anticipated the decision of the D.C. district court to deny tax exemptions in *Green*. It left undecided how the IRS would actually implement the policy. In *Green,* the court outlined a number of strategies the service should follow to ensure that schools were not discriminating. The IRS established its own policies based on the court's prescriptions. Civil rights groups were concerned about how the IRS would actually assess the discriminatory status of private schools. Would they simply take the schools at their word that they did not discriminate, or would the service actually require some proof of actual integration? As civil rights advocates looked on closely, a larger debate developed about the nature of the new private schools that were emerging across the country.

The desegregation of American public schools in the 1960s coincided with Supreme Court decisions that restricted the role of public prayer and other displays of religious belief. The school prayer decisions did not provoke an immediate exodus of Christians out of public schools in the same way that desegregation orders did, but by the 1970s, liberal Supreme Court decisions on public schools had created a powerful conservative drive for private education. The fight over southern school desegregation had become at least in part a fight over who got to define the nature of the new private schools that were springing up not only in the South, but across the country. Were these new private schools "segregation academies," or were they merely "church schools"?

A good example of the fight could be seen in the case of the Briarcrest Baptist School System in Memphis. The founders of Briarcrest considered their institution a Christian church school. The school enrolled 1,890 students and was supported by eleven local Baptist churches, all of them affiliated with the Southern Baptist Convention. The school claimed to have an open admissions policy as well as a recruitment program for black students, but no black students were enrolled. The chairman of Briarcrest's board believed that African American students were "pressured into staying away, feeling they'd be Uncle Toms if they came." The director of the local chapter of the National Association for the Advancement of Colored People (NAACP), however, called Briarcrest "a racist place . . . no matter what its admission policy. No black family would want its children educated in such an atmosphere." In 1973, an education task force coordinator at the Southern Regional Council summed up the belief of most civil rights supporters: "These days, Christian schools and segregation academies are almost synonymous."[16]

In the 1970s, no organization was more responsible for advancing this view than the Lamar Society, a group of liberal southerners concerned about desegregation—what was referred to as "a kind of down-home Common Cause" in one description. The organization represented a rising generation of white and black southerners committed to transforming the South's historic albatross of racial inequality into opportunity, providing a model for how a racially integrated, egalitarian society might actually function.[17] At their annual meeting in Jackson, Mississippi, in 1973, the Lamar Society saw firsthand the remarkable growth of private segregated schools in the South. The group sponsored a two-year study of southern private schools that culminated in *The Schools That Fear Built,* written by the journalist David Nevin and Robert E. Bills, an education professor at the University of Alabama. The book gave the lie to optimistic assessments that the private schools would be temporary solutions for southern segregationists. Southern private schools had caught on, Nevin and Bills argued. Operated on shoestring budgets in makeshift classrooms, these schools had inexperienced instructors using outdated pedagogy to teach a mix of Christian fundamentalism and right-wing ideology. These schools were the roadblock in the way of meaningful desegregation in many rural areas and were a drag on public school educational reform in those southern school districts in greatest need of improvement. A variety of factors helped explain the popularity of these schools: resentment against the banning of school prayer, overcrowdedness or lack of discipline in public schools, the sense that small private schools gave students and parents a real say in how the school operated. But for the authors, the central fact remained the schools' origins: "The academies were founded to perpetuate separatism. They stand as havens from integration and association with other cultures and colors."[18]

The authors admitted that blaming the southern private school movement on "racism and fear of integration" was "too simple." The earliest private schools, established in the 1960s and early 1970s, tended to be nonsectarian and were organized in rural areas on a town- or countywide basis.[19] In the 1970s, however, new private schools in the South were organized increasingly as Christian schools. Sponsored by evangelical churches and located in suburbs or metropolitan areas, these schools had a curriculum heavily influenced by conservative, evangelical theology. Some of the first wave of private schools in Mississippi fit this Christian-school model, but the vast majority did not—they were secular academies that essentially remade the all-white public schools. Over the course of the decade, however, the Christian-school model became more common in Mississippi and across the South. By 1976, the year *The Schools That Fear Built* was published, Nevin and Bills estimated that Christian schools "outnumber[ed] the older secular academies." In the end, however, Nevin and Bills found the distinction between the two "unimportant." "Despite what would seem contrary origins," Nevin wrote, "the schools in practice are so similar as to be indistinguishable."[20]

Church school defenders disagreed vehemently. They argued that although many of the schools were founded coincident with public school desegregation, church schools had their true origins in a broader set of conservative social and religious beliefs. Racism was a negligible factor, they argued, compared with the broader disenchantment with a liberal, secular culture that rejected the traditional values that had long sustained family and community life in the United States. "At least since the late 1960s, social and religious conservatism has been on the march," argued Peter Skerry, a Harvard-trained sociologist who reported on seventeen Christian schools in North Carolina for the neoconservative journal *Public Interest*. "To reduce this conservatism—and the Christian schools that have emerged from it—to racism is simply to ignore two decades of social and cultural upheaval." A study of church schools in Kentucky and Wisconsin led Virginia Davis Nordin and William Lloyd Turner to the same conclusion: "The motivation for founding and maintaining nonpublic schools appears to be more than racial prejudice."[21]

Through the mid-1970s, civil rights advocates kept pressure on the IRS to identify and deny tax exemptions to racially discriminatory private schools, including private schools founded ostensibly for religious purposes. A study by the U.S. Commission on Civil Rights that year criticized the IRS for its failure to adequately identify and deny tax exemptions to discriminatory private schools.[22]

In response, the IRS published two new revenue procedures in November 1975. The first strengthened guidelines requiring that schools maintain and make public a statement of nondiscrimination as laid down in earlier rulings.[23] The second revenue procedure went to the heart of the debate over segregation academies and private schools. It placed private church schools in the same category as secular private schools: "The First Amendment . . . does bar governmental interference with mere religious beliefs and opinions, but it does not affect the legal consequences otherwise attending a given practice or action that is not inherently religious."[24] The next year, the original plaintiffs in the *Green* case went even further than the Civil Rights Commission. They reopened their case against the IRS, convinced the service was not doing enough to identify discriminatory private schools in Mississippi. In addition, a companion case was filed that sought to apply the *Green* principle in states beyond Mississippi.[25]

By 1978, however, the reopened *Green* case had dovetailed with other information that showed that despite all the efforts of the IRS, racially discriminatory private schools were still receiving tax exemptions. In May 1978, an investigation by the U.S. Commission on Civil Rights determined that at least seven private academies in Mississippi that had been cited by the federal court as having a discriminatory admissions policy were still tax-exempt. In the face of such evidence, IRS Commissioner Jerome Kurtz admitted that the service's policies were inadequate—having schools simply declare that they did not discriminate or merely advertise the school's open-enrollment policy among minorities was not enough. In August 1978, the IRS issued new guidelines that precisely outlined the measures required in order for schools to prove nondiscriminatory status.[26] In doing so, the service initiated a political firestorm that had implications far beyond a small group of white-flight academies in Mississippi.

The new IRS guidelines started innocently enough. They created two classes of schools—"reviewable" and "nonreviewable." Schools were placed in the first category if they (1) were "formed or substantially expanded at or about the time of desegregation of the public schools," and (2) had "an insignificant number of minority students." To be in the reviewable category meant that the schools had "the burden of clearly and convincingly rebutting this prima facie case of racial discrimination showing that it has undertaken affirmative steps to secure minority students. Mere denial of a discriminatory purpose is insufficient."[27] But under the 1978 guidelines, schools not only had to have minority students enrolled; they also needed a "significant" number of minority students. In classic bureaucratese, the IRS defined an insignificant minority enrollment as less than 20 percent of the percentage of the minority school age population in the community served by the school.

The mathematical formula defining an "insignificant" minority population, more than any single factor, infuriated conservative Christians. Church school defenders fastened on the formula as evidence that federal bureaucrats were creating racial quotas that threatened church schools. Under *Green,* Mississippi schools had all along been in what the IRS was now calling the "reviewable" category (i.e., they bore the burden of proof as to their nondiscriminatory status). The rules that had been applied to Mississippi private schools could now potentially be applied throughout the country. The reaction bordered on the apoplectic. Over 120,000 letters of protest flooded the IRS in protest of the new guidelines. The response was, by one official's estimation, "more than we've ever received on any other proposal." Some 400,000 more protest letters were sent to members of Congress.[28]

The tumult over the new procedures led the service to hold four days of contentious hearings in Washington. Church school supporters from across the country were ready. Over the previous decade, conservative Christians had built new academies at the rate of two per day. One Christian organization boasted that in the 1970s a church school was founded every seven seconds. By the mid-1980s,

Christian academies were educating more than a million children. Church school supporters founded two important lobbying groups in the 1970s: the American Association of Christian Schools in 1972 and the Association of Christian Schools International, which originated in 1978 directly out of the fight over IRS policies. These organizations lobbied for favorable state and federal legislation, monitored tax and accreditation regulations, created training programs for teachers and administrators, and helped coordinate activities among member schools. Other organizations, such as Accelerated Christian Education, sold ready-made Christian curriculum materials to new schools.[29]

The IRS hearings marked a key moment in the formation of modern evangelical politics. Bob Billings, a church school organizer and former president of Hyles-Anderson College, a private Bible college in Indiana, joined with Paul Weyrich, the conservative activist, to found the National Christian Action Coalition, the chief goal of which was to defeat the IRS efforts to withdraw tax exemptions for racially imbalanced private schools. Other groups that originated from the church school controversy included the Christian School Action Committee, the Christian Legal Defense and Education Fund, and the International Association of Christian Educators.[30]

In hearings before the IRS in 1978 and before Congress in 1979, church school supporters laid out numerous objections to the IRS policy. They claimed that the policy had derived out of what Senator Jesse Helms of North Carolina characterized as "sweetheart litigation" between civil rights lawyers and federal bureaucrats. In doing so, IRS officials had usurped the right of Congress; instead of merely enforcing the laws and collecting the taxes, IRS officials were writing tax laws. They also objected to the original formulation made by civil rights advocates in the *Green* case that conceived of tax exemptions as essentially a federal subsidy. Tax exemptions were not subsidies, church schools supporters argued; if they were, then the long-standing practice of tax exemptions for churches would represent a violation of the First Amendment. By denying tax exemptions to private institutions that did not accord with the federal public policy on school desegregation, the IRS was creating a dangerous precedent in which the federal government could use the power of the purse to discourage all manners of political behavior.

Church school defenders also denounced the 1978 guidelines as a racial quota, a charge that IRS officials were quick to reject. The numerical formula was not a quota, the IRS pointed out, but merely a measure for determining which schools would fall into the "reviewable" and "nonreviewable" categories. IRS Commissioner Jerome Kurtz described it as a "safe harbor," a standard that schools could meet to ensure they were not placed in the reviewable category. Even schools deemed reviewable could meet other standards to show they did not discriminate, despite the fact that their enrollment and employment statistics cast suspicions.[31] But this explanation did little to soften the objections of conservative Christians, particularly after the service announced revisions to the original 1978 revenue procedure that allowed exemptions for Jewish day schools as well as for schools for Muslims and for the Amish. The revisions also included a provision for "a particular school which is part of a system of commonly supervised schools," language that was intended to exempt Catholic schools. Here the IRS was attempting to be as specific as it could in targeting private schools started to avoid public school desegregation. It did not want to lump in schools that had a history of religious instruction that predated public school desegregation.

Though well intentioned, these changes only further inflamed resentment among conservative Protestants, who felt that the federal government had now intentionally singled out independently run Christian schools. Many church school supporters interpreted their current struggle in light of a historic pattern of state opposition to religious freedoms, one that was at the heart of the American democratic experiment and enshrined in the First Amendment. Arno Q. Weniger Jr., the executive vice president of the American Association of Christian Schools, for example, invoked the memory of his Baptist forefathers in Virginia, who had "languished in jail until the establishment of that first amendment."[32]

Powerful Republican Party leaders were eager to champion the cause of evangelical Christians against what they alleged were secular, liberal elites with an undue concern for the rights of racial minorities. In 1979, Republicans in the House and the Senate proposed amendments to an appropriations bill that blocked the IRS from enforcing its regulations against discriminatory private schools. In the House, Robert Dornan of California and John Ashbrook of Ohio proposed three different amendments that would block the IRS from using funds to enforce its regulations. The Ashbrook amendment was the only one to survive the House–Senate conference, but it was all that was needed. Ashbrook placed a similar measure in the fiscal 1981 treasury appropriations.[33] In the Senate, leadership came from North Carolina's Jesse Helms, a long-time right-wing opponent of desegregation. In the 1960s, Helms's television editorials on WRAL-Raleigh denouncing liberal meddling were rebroadcast as radio editorials on more than 100 radio stations, most of them southern; they also commonly ended up as reprints in segregationist publications. Helms proposed legislation that went even further than the Dornan and Ashbrook amendments in stopping the IRS from enforcing its 1978 guidelines.[34]

The private school controversy also figured prominently in presidential politics. The 1980 Republican Party platform pledged to "halt the unconstitutional regulatory vendetta launched by Mr. Carter's IRS commissioner against independent schools" (this despite the fact that it was the Nixon administration's IRS, not Carter's, that first decided to deny tax exemptions). Bob Billings, cofounder along with Paul Weyrich of the National Christian Action Coalition, stepped down from his new position as executive director of the

Moral Majority to serve as religious adviser to Ronald Reagan's 1980 presidential campaign. Billings stayed on as a special assistant for nonpublic schools in Reagan's Department of Education.

In January 1980, Ronald Reagan gave a speech before a cheering crowd of over 6,000 students and faculty at Bob Jones University, a fundamentalist Christian school then involved in a suit against the IRS after having had its tax exemptions revoked because of a policy banning interracial dating. Referring to Bob Jones as "a great institution," Reagan called for a "spiritual revival" and denounced the 1978 IRS guidelines as an example of government bureaucrats establishing "racial quotas." For Reagan, this was just Jim Crow segregation operating in reverse. "You do not alter the evil character of racial quotas simply by changing the color of the beneficiary," he told the crowd. He received three standing ovations and was interrupted by applause some fourteen times. A reporter traveling with the president called the appearance "one of the warmest receptions of [Reagan's] . . . campaign."[35]

Reagan's support for Bob Jones University would become one of the fiercest controversies of his first term. In January 1982, the Reagan administration reversed the nearly twelve-year-old IRS ban on tax exemptions for racially discriminatory private schools, reinstating Bob Jones University's tax-exempt status. The move prompted a storm of protest, with critics accusing Reagan of promoting "tax-exempt hate." The administration quickly introduced a bill in Congress that would have given the IRS explicit permission to deny tax exemptions to discriminatory schools—the logic being that Reagan's opposition all along had been with bureaucrats usurping the rights of Congress. But the legislation found few supporters, and the federal court intervened to block tax exemptions for the school. The Bob Jones case reached the Supreme Court in October 1982. With Reagan's Justice Department having abandoned its case against Bob Jones, the Supreme Court took the unusual step of appointing a third party—in this case, William T. Coleman, a former secretary of transportation in the Ford administration and the chairman of the NAACP Legal Defense Fund—to submit a brief in defense of the IRS's position. In May 1983, the Supreme Court upheld the IRS's original position, ruling that the national interest in eradicating racial discrimination in education "substantially outweighs whatever burden denial of tax benefits places on petitioners' exercise of their religious beliefs." The vote was 8 to 1, with only Justice William Rehnquist dissenting.[36]

Though the Bob Jones controversy was a political embarrassment for the Reagan administration and a clear defeat for the religious Right, it exemplified a larger pattern that would characterize conservative religious politics in the closing decades of the twentieth century. Richard Nixon's decision to deny tax exemptions to discriminatory private schools was, at the time, a politically expedient solution to what seemed like the impossible task of integrating public schools in the Black Belt South. It was also an example of what John Skrentny has called the "minority right's revolution," the decade beginning roughly in 1965 that witnessed a remarkable growth in federal legislation, presidential executive orders, bureaucratic rulings, and court decisions establishing nondiscrimination rights.[37] This top-down, bureaucratically driven process was bipartisan in its orientation, yet was easily parodied by conservatives as the meddling dictates of unelected liberal elites. Republican Party operatives would continue to invoke this populist framework to position themselves as the chief defenders of conservative religious principles against a modern secularist enemy that was hostile to the interests of Christian Americans. In doing so, they dramatically shifted the debate over race, morality, and politics in modern America.

CHAPTER 6

The Decade of the Neighborhood

SULEIMAN OSMAN

In October 1973, the Brooklyn Brownstone Conference hosted New York City's first "Brownstone Fair." Made up of young white brownstone renovators, the civic group advertised the fair as a showcase for "Everything You Always Wanted to Know about Brooklyn Brownstones." Over 2,000 attendees strolled past fifty exhibits run by enthusiastic volunteers. Instructional booths offered tips on old electrical wiring, stone masonry, architectural ornamentation, and carpentry. Gardeners and horticulturists gave instructions on tree planting and care, community gardening, and negotiation strategies with the city park department. The "Community Bookstore," started by Park Slope brownstoners, displayed over a dozen "brownstone books" ranging from local histories to "how-to-renovate" guides that had been penned by Brooklyn's new middle class. Fledgling neighborhood and block associations invited potential homebuyers to visit their new enclaves. The most popular exhibit was the mortgage information table, where experienced brownstone buyers offered tips on procuring financing from reluctant banks. To cap off the event, Brooklyn Union Gas sponsored a fleet of buses to take fair attendees on tours of Brooklyn brownstone neighborhoods.[1]

As New York City's service economy flourished after World War II, small numbers of young white professionals and artists began to purchase and rehabilitate dilapidated brownstones in Brooklyn as early as the 1950s. But by the 1970s, the trickle became a flood. New York newspapers began to speak of a "back to the city" movement, a "brownstone revitalization movement," and a "brownstone revival" transforming Brooklyn and Manhattan. "Brownstoners" and "brownstoning" entered the popular lexicon to describe the hundreds of young renovators avidly renovating Victorian townhouses. "Of their own free will, in the face of considerable odds and dire predictions, a growing number of younger people have been expending great amounts of psychic energy on the purchase and remodeling of old brownstones in beat-up neighborhoods," noted the 1969 New York City Master Plan. It continued:

> The people are of all kinds—artists, writers, professionals, junior executives, civil servants, returned suburbanites . . . Their frontier is to be found in brownstone rows that have gone badly to seed as rooming houses . . . The great reservoir is in Brooklyn. Brooklyn Heights has been almost completely renovated, splendidly so, but to the south and east lie large areas with potentials to be tapped: Cobble Hill, Boerum Hill, Carroll Gardens, Fort Greene . . . They are proud of being culturally in tune with the City, proud that their neighborhood has so many different kinds of people. They are proud most of all of the difficulties they face. They are, they like to believe, the new pioneers.[2]

Brooklyn brownstone renovators were not alone. In Atlanta's Inman Park, Boston's South End, Toronto's Yorkville, the District of Columbia's Capitol Hill, and other inner-city districts around the country, a new urban middle class hungrily purchased and rehabilitated aging Victorian homes. By 1976, an Urban Land Institute study found versions of brownstoning in a majority of the nation's 260 cities with populations exceeding 50,000. In cities with populations of 500,000 or more, three-quarters were experiencing significant private rehabilitation. Surveys showed that renovators in all cases were overwhelmingly young, white, highly educated, and white collar.[3]

Brownstoning represented more than a simple renovation fad. As they created enclaves with names like "Park Slope" and "Boerum Hill," rehabilitators sought to reestablish a sense of local place and community in an alienating urban environment. Pioneers started block associations, organized street festivals, and opened food co-operatives. They penned local histories of Victorian townhouse en-claves and fought for historic district status. Others spearheaded tree-planting drives and cleared abandoned lots to found commu-nity gardens. As they dug through concrete sidewalks, brownston-ers symbolically and literally hoped to "sink their roots" into the earth, reconnecting rehabilitated neighborhoods to a pastoral past. "It's exciting. Something really happens to your soul when you re-alize you've had a part in planting a tree," explained a Brooklyn block association member in 1971.[4]

The white-collar brownstone neighborhoods of Brooklyn and Manhattan were the most powerful front of a national "neighbor-hood movement," "neighborhood power," or "community revolu-tion." "A decade ago, no survey of urban America focused on 'neighborhood power,'" wrote the *Los Angeles Times* in 1979. "Today, neighborhoods are a focus of city action. The 1970's have seen a remarkable flowering of grass-roots groups revolting against the heavy hand of bureaucracies, reasserting their own turf." "Their names are a jungle of abbreviations and acronyms," wrote the *New York Times* that same year. "AID (Against Invest-ment Discrimination) in Brooklyn; N.W.B.C.C.C. (North West Bronx Community and Clergy Coalition); C.B.B.B. (Citizens to Bring Broadway Back) in Cleveland; ROBBED (Residents Orga-nized for Better and Beautiful Environmental Development) in San Antonio; PAR (Playland Area Residence) in Council Bluffs, Iowa;

UWE-COACT (United West End-Citizens Organization Acting Together) in Duluth, Minn., and so on."[5]

As part of a decade considered the nadir of American cities, the neighborhood movement is largely absent from urban history. Written in the wake of the postwar urban crisis in Rustbelt cities and forged in the fires of the 1960s urban riots, most descriptions of the 1970s cityscape read much like the conclusion of a coroner's report. Much like a police forensics team, urban historians recount a series of lethal blows—suburbanization, deindustrialization, white flight, urban renewal—to explain how and why 1970s cities lay dead. More than just a tale of economic collapse, the 1970s mark a political death, a decade in which the nation shifted rightward. As in-migrating African Americans clashed with an increasingly conservative and racially hostile white-ethnic working class, the fragile coalition that made up the New Deal urban liberal coalition ruptured. The "dead" city of the 1970s—with its boarded-up homes, empty stores, impoverished schools, and shattered glass surrounded by lifeless and sterile sprawling suburbs–appears briefly in an epilogue to this autopsy of urban America.[6]

There is much reason for the bleak description of cities in the 1970s. By all measurable economic standards, American industrial cities in the Northeast and Midwest were in deep crisis. Decimated by decades of white flight and the loss of industry, the American industrial cityscape seemed to be decomposing. Downtown retail sales dropped 48 percent in Baltimore, 38 percent in Boston, and at a similar clip in other declining central business districts around the country. Boston, Pittsburgh, Philadelphia, and Chicago lost over a third of their manufacturing during the years 1967–1977. Cities like Saint Louis, Baltimore, and Cleveland appeared to hemorrhage people as white residents and increasing numbers of middle-class African Americans fled to the suburbs. Segregated, depopulated, and with high concentrations of poverty, large sections of New York City, Chicago, and Detroit were a tragic patchwork of abandoned buildings, empty stores, and rubble-strewn empty lots. Adding to the woes of local residents, cities in the 1970s were unsafe. After a surge in the late 1960s and early 1970s, urban crime rates stabilized at distressingly high levels. In Detroit, homicides rose 345 percent from 1965 to 1974 and plateaued thereafter. By 1978, seven out of ten New Yorkers expressed fear of walking a block away from their homes. The reason for the nationwide rise in crime and subsequent drop in the early 1990s remains unknown. But as even the most conservative "law and order" mayors struggled unsuccessfully to put a dent in robbery and murder rates, politicians and residents by the mid-1970s resignedly accepted crime as a permanent feature of the urban landscape.[7]

But while the image of burnt-out tenements and shuttered stores looms large in public memory, American cities were not dead. In fact, they were the epicenter for a dynamic wave of political activism. In San Francisco, New York, and Chicago, the neighborhood movement was the hidden drama in a decade remembered as dead air between the tumult of the 1960s and the economic revival of the 1980s. "An army of journalists, policymakers, social scientists has begun to discover that a 'neighborhood movement' forms a kind of invisible saga of the decade," wrote neighborhood activist Harry Boyte in 1979, "below the antics of Presidents, rock stars and football heroes."[8]

The neighborhood movement forms a crucial missing piece to a fuller, more nuanced understanding of the oft-misunderstood 1970s. Rather than the hangover of sixties radicalism or the triumph of conservatism, the neighborhood instead reflected a new spirit of localism that was neither exclusively Left nor Right. Where New Deal liberalism celebrated large institutions, comprehensive planning, social science, and cooperation between big government and big business, 1970s "neighborhoodism" valorized smallness, intimacy, voluntarism, subjectivity, and privacy. The 1970s introduced a postindustrial reimagining of the declining industrial city.

Rather than a dead landscape, the empty factories and dilapidated Victorian homes of older cities were repositories of symbols and memories for returning suburbanites, African American activists, white ethnic revivalists, historic preservationists, and new urban white-collar professionals. Rather than an intermission between two dynamic periods of urban history, the 1970s extended and transformed the participatory community movements of the 1960s and set the groundwork for economic revival and gentrification in the 1980s.

Whether referred to as the "neighborhood revival," the "community revolution," or "neighborhood power," the neighborhood movement consisted of an eclectic collection of seemingly unrelated urban revolts. In African American areas, neighborhood power was an outgrowth of the black power insurgency that in the late 1960s had challenged both black machine bosses and national civil rights organizations. Young pastors of Baptist and Presbyterian churches made up one wing of the insurgency. With strong links to southern churches and the civil rights movement, urban pastors brought a faith in issue-driven protest politics and spearheaded well-publicized picketing campaigns in cities around the country. A second wing of "insurgents" was made up of young anti-poverty workers introduced to politics through Great Society community action programs (CAPs) without ties to the local Democratic machine. Where the civil rights pastors brought a passionate faith in direct action and protest politics, CAP leaders brought a strong belief in decentralization and community control. Regarded by mainstream civil rights organizations and machine politicians as "militants," this new generation forged a new style of "black power" politics that was hostile to centralized control, ambivalent about government intervention, based in protest politics rather than backroom dealing, preoccupied with cultural authenticity, and rooted in a belief in neighborhood self-determination rather than in integration. Once filled with 1960s revolutionary fervor, by the 1970s, the black power insurgency matured into an organized political movement seeking electoral gains and seats in government.[9]

The white backlash of the 1960s also produced new white ethnic leaders who were independent of the Democratic machine and preoccupied with the concept of "neighborhood." As crime rates soared in the late 1960s and early 1970s, new law-and-order "populist conservatives" like Philadelphia's Frank Rizzo and New York's John Marchi ran angry, racially charged, anti-establishment campaigns against incumbent mayors. The anti-busing movement also established a cadre of female grassroots political leaders like Boston's Louise Day Hicks and Buffalo's Alfreda Slominski who in the 1970s ran for political office. Attacking downtown interests and powerbrokers, eulogizing safe, white ethnic enclaves, demanding community control over schools, and calling for neighborhood preservation, white backlash politicians echoed the black power celebration of the urban neighborhood.[10]

But brownstoners and other white college-educated residents of gentrifying enclaves remained the most powerful wing of the neighborhood movement. "In recent years neighborhoodism has been growing in New York, particularly in neighborhoods dominated by brownstones rather than high-rises—the Village, Chelsea, a half-dozen partly renovated areas in Brooklyn," noted Calvin Trillin in 1975. "The new version of neighborhoodism, often led by middle-class house renovators, is geographical rather than ethnic; it is organized around residence on block rather than membership in, say, an Italian Catholic Church." "What started as a thousand or so families seeking a 'buy' in a home became . . . a true community of interacting neighbors," wrote a hopeful Vance Packard of brownstone Brooklyn in his 1972 bestseller *A Nation of Strangers*. "The block organizations or other groups now have gala cookouts with each neighbor contributing a native dish. There are champagne breakfasts in the park in the spring and block festivals for young and old . . . Park Slope is not unique in New York. The 'brownstoners' have recently been creating authentic communities out of rundown areas on the Upper West Side, in Chelsea, on the Lower East Side in Manhattan, and at Cobble Hill, Boerum Hill, and Fort Greene in Brooklyn."[11]

Throughout the 1970s, these disparate groups came together in an assortment of seemingly paradoxical coalitions. "In the public media, such activism generally seemed a crazy-quilt array of protests, without apparent themes in common," explained activist Harry Boyte of the "backyard revolution." "While one community fought redlining by the banks, another planted urban gardens. The same group might simultaneously oppose school busing, make alliances with black homeowners, and patrol against criminals." "The three groups here have damn little in common," explained a Park Slope resident in 1971 of blacks, blue-collars, and brownstoners in the politically active Brooklyn enclave.[12]

When city activists spoke of "neighborhood power," it was primarily a call for political reform. Like generations of urban reformers before them, neighborhood groups attacked the crony network of Democratic machine politicians that still dominated politics in most older American cities. Whether they were black power activists fighting for control of local wards, anti-busing leaders lambasting city hall, or white-collar brownstoners attacking "bossism," neighborhood activists fought acrimonious battles against older ethnic clubhouse politicians. Hostile to the informal system of bribes, backroom deals, patronage, and favors that undergirded urban machine politics, neighborhood groups championed direct democracy, town hall meetings, and a revival of Jeffersonian democracy. Rather than professional political parties, neighborhood groups were pointedly volunteer organizations. "Community organizing is the mass participation side of democracy," argued Joe McNeely of Baltimore's Southeast Community Organization. "It goes back as far as Tocqueville observing a New England town meeting." "The ideal of neighborhood government rests upon the belief that people can and should govern themselves democratically and justly," stated the National Association of Neighborhoods in its 1976 "Neighborhood Bill of Responsibilities and Rights." "The neighborhood is a political unit which makes this possible, since the smallness of their neighborhood enables all residents to deliberate, decide and act together for the common good."[13]

But aging politicos playing dominos in local Democratic clubs were not the primary targets of the neighborhood activists. Instead, they described a far more ominous new "machine" spreading outward from downtown. The neighborhood movement was a crusade against "planners" and "big developers"—all epithets for the New Deal coalition of realtors, planners, business leaders, politicians, civic groups, and nonprofit institutional directors who since World War II had spearheaded a program of urban redevelopment in cities around the country. Urban renewal projects, city expressways, school integration plans, public housing, and other centralized government development schemes had sparked widespread and scattered protests throughout the 1960s. But by the 1970s, thousands of antidevelopment neighborhood organizations formed a decade earlier coalesced into a powerful, nonpartisan political wing with influence on the local and national level. With a visceral hostility to bureaucracy and centralized power, this new cadre of political activists lobbied Congress, funded campaigns, and ran for office on platforms challenging "downtown interests," "power brokers," "city hall," or, simply, "The Man."[14]

Neighborhood politics of the 1970s marked a dramatic departure from earlier drives for municipal reform. Where Progressives and New Dealers had once put their faith in strong executives and rationalist city managers, 1970s activists called for the decentralization of political control and municipal services to neighborhoods. They were deeply suspicious of regional planning and emphasized the unique needs of local communities. Whether African Americans protesting "negro removal," white ethnics resisting busing, middle-class whites fighting the demolition of townhouses, or mixed-race coalitions fighting urban expressways, all expressed a deep distrust of mega-institutions, expertise, universal social programs, and private–public consensus. They shared their dislike equally for big business, big labor, and big government, championing instead grassroots institutions. They lionized voluntary service, self-determination, and "do-it-yourself" bootstrap neighborhood rehabilitation. "The theme is unequivocally anti-big, pro-participatory and pro-accountability," explained the editors of *Social Policy* in 1979 about the "new politics via the neighborhood. "People want to be unencumbered by what they perceive to be government sloth and to be protected from corporate excess. In that dualism there is a bridge between popular anti-statism and leftist anti-corporate strategy which perhaps can be built."[15]

Rather than a shift rightward, the 1970s marked a shift inward. Neither exclusively Left nor Right, the politics of the 1970s was militantly local. "A new 'localism' [is] sweeping neighborhoods across the United States," wrote the *Christian Science Monitor* in its 1977 series "A Nation of Neighborhoods." "Largely in response to neglect by big government and failure of such 'top down' solutions as model cities, urban renewal, and the war on poverty . . . the 'new localism' is simultaneously conservative and radical, willing to preserve traditions of 'turf' and home ownership with confrontation tactics . . . Neighborhoods have become 'the politics of the 1970's.' "[16]

Neighborhood organizations, Harry Boyte pointed out, were part of a larger shift toward voluntarism in 1970s urban America. In 1979, the National Commission on Neighborhoods listed more than 8,000 major community organizations in cities around the country. A 1978 Gallup poll found that 64 percent of Americans hoped to volunteer on committees concerned with neighborhood issues. A 1977 *Christian Science Monitor* poll found that one-third of residents in communities of 50,000 or more had participated in either a neighborhood protest or sweat-equity rehabilitation campaign. A majority polled were willing to participate in direct action to "defend their neighborhoods" in the future. A 1979 *Harvard Business Review* study of 175,000 blue-collar workers found a broad acceptance of "sixties-style movement values." Other polls found a similar widespread faith in grassroots action, public participation, and participatory democracy.[17]

But more than a political revolt against central planning and undemocratic urban redevelopment schemes, the neighborhood movement marked the ascension of a new type of urbanism. The 1950s and 1960s union leaders, corporate CEOs, housing reformers, luxury apartment developers, racial idealists, and racial conservatives who spearheaded urban renewal and highway development were an eclectic lot representing a myriad of political views. But they all shared a belief in modernity as a solution to the city's ills. With new highways and public housing developments, planners hoped to create an open and dynamic cityscape. They turned to modern architecture that favored functional design, geometric form, smooth surfaces, open space, light, and bigness. By improving transportation systems and centralizing power in city hall, leaders hoped to "integrate" a chaotic city. Originally a corporate management term that described the efficient communication between disparate parts of a large bureaucracy, civil rights leaders borrowed the phrase to make "racial integration" part of the postwar liberal agenda. Last, modernists had a faith in renewal, a liberatory process that allowed man to break free from the limits of place and time, where the new constantly replaced the old, where difference was integrated into a universal whole, and where human ingenuity facilitated the inevitable march of progress.[18]

The 1970s "neighborhood," in contrast, represented a dramatically different romantic urban ideal. A Victorian industrial cityscape that Progressive reformers once deemed frighteningly modern and

New Dealers dismissed as obsolete was turned to by 1970s community activists as a source of authenticity. Instead of rejecting old and decaying factories, trolleys, and townhouses, 1970s activists relished their historic character. Rather than turning to new transportation technology to break free from the constraints of the city, neighborhood activists lambasted the effects of the car and airplane on urban community life. They instead celebrated an older Victorian street grid that encouraged walking, face-to-face contact, and intimacy. Where modernists once spoke of integration, activists now championed "mixed uses" and "diversity." Rather than renewal, neighborhood groups talked of preservation: preserving old buildings, preserving ethnic identity, preserving authentic communities. Originally written as polemical tracts against urban renewal in the early 1960s, Jane Jacobs's *Life and Death of American Cities* and Herbert Gans's *Urban Villagers* in the 1970s became canonical texts for young urban enthusiasts. Jane Jacobs's sentimental industrial "urban village," home to mustachioed white ethnic grocers, friendly policemen, colorful pushcart vendors, and elderly grandmothers cooking tomato sauce, inspired a burst of neighborhood activism. Angry white ethnics, urban hipster pioneers, and excited white-collar townhouse renovators all turned nostalgically to the deindustrialized landscape as a refuge from suburbia, modern highways, and bureaucratic alienation. African American activists similarly evoked images of a black community with spontaneous street folk culture, mom-and-pop stores shielded from mass consumer culture, and townhouses home to a historic black aristocracy.[19]

If urban redevelopers once spoke of "renewal," the 1970s neighborhood movement marked a symbolic "return" to the past. In Brooklyn, new block associations cultivated urban gardens and started food cooperatives with talk of reviving the borough's preindustrial agrarian landscape. Other white middle-class brownstoners described themselves as coming back from the suburbs to reinhabit townhouses once home to a Victorian bourgeoisie. As they scraped paint off marble fireplaces, emptied trash from nonfunctioning dumbwaiters, and at times evicted the poor, they hoped to restore decaying mansions to their former aristocratic grandeur. "Brooklyn could be to Victoriana what Williamsburg [Virginia] is to Early Americana," exclaimed a Park Slope newsletter in 1975. "There is a developing market for all types of Victorian reproductions . . . Such an industry—on a small scale—has already sprouted in San Francisco. But the 19th Century *belongs* to Brooklyn."[20]

With the ascension of the black power and ethnic revival movements, newly assertive ethnic activists looked to the declining industrial landscape as a site of imagined ethnogenesis. For African American activists, the industrial city replaced the rural South as a symbolic site of unassimilated ethnic origins. Where a New Deal generation of black civil rights leaders once hoped to obliterate the ghetto and allow free access to the suburbs, 1970s black neighborhood groups encouraged the middle class to return to their roots or find their ancestry in the center city. Preservation of local community and urban cultural heritage uneasily coexisted on the civil rights agenda with calls for downtown reinvestment and economic development programs.[21]

White ethnics also produced versions of what might be called *Brooklyniana:* a nostalgic collage of memories of Dodgers pennants, pushcarts, stickball, mama's cooking, cries of *fuggedaboutit,* and other ethnic kitsch commemorating the city *ante-Negro.* In fights against scattered-site housing projects, expressways, and busing programs, ethnic revivalists transposed pastoral imagery of Old World peasant life to the urban landscape. "We are very folksy, plain spoken, plain living, Harry Truman types," explained Gloria Aull, founder of a southeast Baltimore anti-expressway neighborhood group. "Really our communities are like European villages, whether you go to Greek town, Little Italy, Highlandtown, or Fells Point. And what are we characterized by? First of all, we view the neighborhood as our home, and our relationship with our restaurants, our businesses, our candy stores at the corner . . . We lived through the think-tank, master-plan programming, where we were all going by rescued by VISTA."[22]

In the era of the "Me Generation," the city of the 1970s was a "Me City." Planners, artists, and residents rejected the metanarratives of master plans, transportation systems, mass consumer culture, and universal government programs. Instead, they viewed the cityscape as subjective, private, and intimate. The city could not be generalized, but instead each individual or community contributed to a multiplicity of viewpoints. Rather than an integrated system, the city of the 1970s was a diverse mosaic, a "delirious" collection of independent enclaves. When some aging New Dealers complained that the city had become ungovernable, they missed the point. The neighborhood movement believed not only that the city couldn't be governed, but that it shouldn't be. "We were criticized for not recommending some big national program," explained Gail Cincotta in 1979, as chairperson of the National People's Action. "We don't want any more big government programs. It was big government programs that destroyed our cities."[23]

Much of the language of the neighborhood movement—bureaucracy, alienation, and the search for authentic community—emerged during the countercultural and New Left movements of the 1960s. But the sixties were more a decade of transition in which an older New Deal generation tried to incorporate community demands into bureaucratic programs. The Great Society marked not the golden age of postwar liberalism, but an awkward attempt to reconcile a New Deal faith in scientific government programs with neighborhood activist demands for local distinctiveness and community control. As a typical reform mayor of the late 1960s, New York's John Lindsay was a "local modernist" hybrid, uneasily straddling two paradigms of urban reform. As a Cold War liberal, Lindsay was entranced with new computer technology and cybernetics, hiring McKinsey consultants to use "Program, Planning, and Budgeting Systems" technology to centralize and rationalize city bureaucracy. At the same time, he spoke in spiritual terms about alienation and the need for community. Lindsay created a housing superagency centered in city hall, while experimenting with "little city halls," precinct community councils, and school decentralization programs. While he maintained a faith in highway building, his plan for a Cross-Brooklyn Expressway called for community involvement, minimal dislocation, pedestrian walkways, and residential space. His first urban housing task force in 1966 was led, paradoxically, by archenemies Jane Jacobs and urban renewal power broker Edward Logue.[24]

But by the 1970s, the neighborhood revolt against city hall had become a rout. In cities around the country, powerful community groups brought city development projects to a grinding halt. In 1972, protests by interracial anti-highway groups stopped expressways in Chicago, Philadelphia, and Boston. Faced with rising debts and widespread political resistance from local neighborhood groups, New York City in 1970 announced that it would not commence new urban renewal projects. In 1965, the city and state assisted with or built over 21,000 units of housing. By 1970, the number had dropped to about 10,000, half of which were in the massive Co-op City development project built on empty land on the outskirts of the city. In 1974, Saint Louis made headlines by dynamiting its massive Pruitt-Igoe housing complex. But cities everywhere quietly abandoned low-income public housing development. From 1963 to 1971, northeastern and midwestern cities built over 40,000 public housing units. From 1971 to 1977, that number dropped to a paltry 4,000. Faced with mass protest around the country, most of the major candidates of both parties in the 1972 presidential campaign turned against busing. The 1974 *Milliken v. Bradley* ruling, protecting suburbs from inclusion in busing programs, confirmed the nation's turn against both regional planning and top-down racial integration schemes.[25]

Neighborhood groups also scored a series of victories against large corporations. In the late 1970s, interracial coalitions of middle-class renovators and working-class residents around the country won battles against banks over the issue of redlining. In Brooklyn, anti-redlining activists picketed banks, lobbied politicians, gathered signatures, and contacted local papers. In 1977, Against Investment Discrimination, a local activist group, organized a "withdrawal week," during which residents withdrew $875,000 from the Greater New York Savings Bank. The bank immediately agreed to their terms. Citibank in 1977 also announced a pilot program to commit $10 million in mortgages for one or two-family homes (most of them brownstones) in Prospect Heights, Park Slope, and Flatbush.[26] In 1975, the National People's Action, a national organization of neighborhood groups, successfully pressured Congress to pass the Home Mortgage Disclosure Act, despite resistance from the banking lobby. The act required financial institutions to disclose to the public the areas in which they granted loans. While homeowners battled redlining banks, networks of tenant groups in the 1970s also coalesced to form powerful national lobby groups. By 1979, tenants organized coalitions in twenty states to block changes to rent control laws and legal protection for tenants.[27]

In the early 1970s, neighborhood coalitions of white ethnics, white-collar professionals, and African Americans began to win their first local elections. In 1972, after a series of acrimonious and increasingly narrow defeats, reform Democrats in Brooklyn won their first campaign against the regular Democratic club. Cobbling together a coalition of brownstoners, Blacks and Latinos, and working-class ethnics, Michael Pesce and Carol Bellamy eked out primary wins against two incumbents for the state assembly and state senate. Politicians with roots in the neighborhood movement won mayoral races around the country: among them were Jane Byrne in Chicago, Dennis Kucinich in Cleveland, and Nicholas Carbone in Hartford. Some of the nation's new black reform mayors similarly beat local machine candidates by forming coalitions among white-collar professionals, anti-development groups, and black activists.[28]

By the mid-1970s, "neighborhoodism" was no longer a movement of dissent, but the foundation of state and federal policy. In the 1960s, community activists knocked heads with a downtown establishment who believed strongly in state-sponsored redevelopment plans. But in a country struggling with high oil prices, inflation, and urban debt, the 1970s neighborhood movement dovetailed seamlessly with a new corporate skepticism about government bureaucracy and fiscal waste. Volunteerism, rehabilitation, sweat equity, neighborhood power, cultural heritage, and historic preservation replaced modernization and renewal on the urban agenda. In New York City, with federal funds cut off for construction, rising debts, and rows of abandoned brownstones and tenements sitting empty in a city with a crushing housing shortage, a new generation of "Jane Jacobsian" officials turned to sweat equity and private rehabilitation as potential solutions to the urban crisis. In 1973, the city started the Neighborhood Preservation Program to provide tax incentives and low-interest loans to neighborhood groups involved in rehabilitation. In 1975, the city amended its J-51 law to provide tax incentives for property owners who converted industrial space into residential units. Hoping to turn black and Puerto Rican renters into brownstone pioneers, the city considered adopting an "urban homesteading" bill modeled after experimental programs in Wilmington and Baltimore. The programs allowed low-income "homesteaders" to buy city-owned abandoned property for one dollar provided they rehabilitate them up to set guidelines. In 1973, new city planning commissioner and self-described "neo-Jacobsian" John Zuccotti announced a shift from master plans to "mini-planning," with a particular emphasis on "diversity, community preservation, humanistic 'streetscapes' and a view of the city as a composite of neighborhoods."[29]

"Thinking small" was also the new mantra in Washington as federal policy shifted toward volunteerism, choice, local control, and market-driven reform. The Housing and Community Development Act of 1974 replaced the centrally administered Model Cities with the Community Development Block Grant Program, in which grants were given directly to cities to spend on small projects with minimal guidelines. Rather than fund new public housing construction, the Community Development Act of 1974 initiated both the Section 8 rent voucher program and an Urban Homesteading Demonstration project. The 1976 Tax Reform Act gave tax breaks for private rehabilitation of buildings. While singing the praises of small traditional enclaves, new fiscally conservative officials shrank expenditures for increasingly cash-strapped cities. Shortly after he threatened to veto a federal bailout of New York's impending bankruptcy ("Ford to City: Drop Dead," read the famous *Daily News* headline), President Gerald Ford appropriately declared 1976 "The Year of the Neighborhood."[30]

Although their achievements remained modest after a decade of widespread urban industrial decline, neighborhood activists in 1980 could still point to signs of remarkable success. While cities like Saint Louis and Detroit remained depopulated and economically depressed, powerful neighborhood movements in cities such as San Francisco and New York were the catalyst for dramatic revivals in the 1980s. Fragile enclaves founded in the previous decade became the templates for a new burst of neighborhood organizing. Rather than modernist urban renewal projects or massive public expenditures, young renovators relied on sweat equity and private initiative to rehabilitate hundreds of abandoned homes. Veteran neighborhood activists were fully entrenched in positions of power. A new generation of urban planners, city politicians, and architects in the 1980s no longer spoke of slum clearance or new highways, but instead of "festival marketplaces." Political mechanisms were in place to ensure community input into city development projects.

The powerful Landmarks Preservation Commission in New York City spearheaded a comprehensive historic preservation program with full cooperation of the city government.

Yet the spoils of the 1970s neighborhood revolution were not evenly distributed. While blue-collar and poor nonwhite areas continued their steady decline, white-collar professional enclaves prospered. Rather than reviving the industrial base of older cities, the neighborhood movement both benefited from and facilitated the growth of postindustrial economies in cities like New York and Boston. Downtown developers and anti-development neighborhood activists had an oddly symbiotic relationship. Cities with healthy financial and media sectors attracted to the city thousands of lawyers, architects, reporters, academics, bohemian artists, and white-collar workers eager to start neighborhood groups. But more ironically, the 1970s neighborhood movement created fertile soil for the flowering of the 1980s corporate landscape. In their search for anti-bureaucratic authenticity in the inner city, brownstoners acted as pioneers for the bureaucratic institutions they reviled. New corporations moved to the center city to tap a growing pool of educated workers. Risk-averse developers found safe, improving areas in which to build new condominiums. Universities looked to expand in peripheral student neighborhoods. It is no coincidence that New York and San Francisco were coastal centers for both financial services and the counterculture.[31]

By the 1980s, few residents in New York or San Francisco spoke anymore of a neighborhood revolt or brownstone revitalization movement. Instead, newspapers, academics, and housing advocates spoke ominously of the gentrification of Brooklyn.[32] Where brownstoning once embodied the countercultural ethos of the 1970s, gentrification evoked for the public the new ruthless capitalist spirit of the 1980s. Where Vance Packard once talked of young idealists restoring authentic community in an alienating world, political activists now spoke of developers and home renovators destroying fragile ethnic enclaves. Brownstoners once lionized by the press in the 1970s for fighting city hall were now cast as villains.

In many ways, the neighborhood movement had changed from its plucky roots in the 1970s. Starting in the 1980s and continuing for two decades (with a short recession in the late 1980s and early 1990s), real estate prices in downtown New York, Boston, and San Francisco skyrocketed. Where once brownstone pioneers struggled to convince banks and realtors to consider investing in their enclaves, Park Slope and other Brooklyn areas were awash in speculation. Brownstoners saw the prices of their townhouses soar. Renters complained of rent gouging. During the abandonment crisis of the 1970s, housing activists pressured the city to launch programs to support private rehabilitation. In the speculative market of the 1980s, however, activists attacked the same city programs for subsidizing the displacement of the poor. In place of artists or low-income squatters, wealthy speculators used city tax breaks and legal support to convert tenements and industrial lofts into luxury apartments. Real estate brokers cynically invented historic neighborhood place names to draw clients into poor neighborhoods.[33]

As its romantic urban aesthetic became mainstream, neighbor-hoodism was targeted by a new cynical school of postmodern critics. The neighborhood was once the embodiment of the 1970s revolt against bureaucracy, corporate skyscrapers, mass consumer culture, and modernity. By the 1980s, however, large corporations included historic symbolism and eclectic styles into their designs of skyscrapers, supermarkets sold organic food displayed in rustic wooden pushcarts, and speculators built nostalgic Victorian-themed suburban enclaves. Rather than celebrating a triumph of the 1970s counterculture, urban intellectuals saw irony in a city that resembled a "theme park." Neighborhood reformers were dismayed to see that former activists-turned-mayors, when dealing with the hard-nosed realities of public office, could quickly become as corrupt as their machine predecessors or partners with the "downtown establishment." In New York, Edward Koch, once a Greenwich Village reformer, emerged as the first conservative brownstoner mayor to recentralize power in city hall while culturally reveling in white ethnic kitsch.[34]

As inner-city New York and San Francisco became increasingly expensive, many activists lamented that their "hip" neighborhoods were becoming increasingly white. "Diversity" referred less and less to racial integration and more to the cosmopolitan tastes of a new urban bourgeoisie. A "what-are-you-in-the-mood-for" diversity allowed white-collar residents to select from a selection of ethnic restaurants, Ashtanga yoga studios, independent foreign film theaters, and quirky cafes. Although people of color bustled around Brooklyn's brownstone enclaves, few actually lived there. With a "diverse mosaic" of Korean grocery stores, El Salvadorian busboys, Pakistani newsstands, Dominican livery drivers, and West Indian nannies, brownstone Brooklyn after 1980 was highly dependent on a poorly paid immigrant service economy. In the 1970s, New York-based television shows like *Welcome Back, Kotter* and *All in the Family* wrestled with race and class in a changing city. By the 1990s, a new generation of popular shows like *Friends* and *Sex in the City* presented an astonishingly racially homogeneous view of white-collar city life.[35]

But rather than a story of corporations co-opting a grassroots neighborhood movement, the transition from brownstoning to gentrification was more natural. The neighborhood revolt was an anti-institutional movement with both conservative and liberal strains. As a celebration of local place, 1970s neighborhoodism was an important corrective to the excesses of postwar modernism. In a Cold War society entranced by bureaucracy and technology, activists reestablished the importance of local community, history, and ethnicity. In a decade when cities were being abandoned by fleeing residents and indifferent government officials, passionate volunteers rebuilt and restored written-off communities with their sweat and guts. But in their populist battle against bureaucracy, neighborhood activists attacked municipal programs, public housing, integration initiatives, and affordable chain stores that poorer residents depended on. And by rejecting all forms of government planning and by lionizing voluntarism and private space, the "decade of the neighborhood" unleashed the unfettered real estate market that 1980s activists complained about. Ironically, the most strident critics of gentrification in the 1980s were brownstoners themselves.

CHAPTER 7

Cultural Politics and the Singer/Songwriters of the 1970s

BRADFORD MARTIN

Writing in 1971, legendary rock critic Lester Bangs dubbed budding superstar singer/songwriter James Taylor one of the "glory boys of I-Rock," music that was "so relentlessly, involutedly egocentric that you finally stop hating the punk and just want to take the poor bastard out and get him a drink, and then kick his ass, preferably off a high cliff into the nearest ocean." Though this level of violence might seem excessive, Bangs proceeded to fantasize about murdering Taylor with a broken-off bottle of Ripple.[1]

Bangs's antipathy for Taylor's musical sensibility—its solipsism, its self-absorption, and the privileged nature of the emotional life it expressed—typified the objections of rock critics weaned on 1960s music that focused outward, engaged with pressing social and political issues, and adopted a noisier, more anti-authoritarian rock 'n' roll aesthetic. In some ways, this critique aptly characterized the singer/songwriters of the 1970s. On one level, the path from 1960s rock to the 1970s singer/songwriter movement reflected a larger narrative of transformation from the search for the beloved community to the search for self, from concern with social justice and global peace to the quest for inner peace, from fighting to liberate the oppressed to the triumph of personal liberation. Many of the singer/songwriters' memorable lyrics suggested a longing for therapeutic self-communion, from Taylor's "rock-a-bye sweet baby James," to Jackson Browne's revelation that "it seems to me / that there may never be / A better chance / to see who I am."[2] For the singer/songwriters, self-discovery, often accompanied by retreat from the outside world, loomed at a premium.

These musings were not restricted to the movement's male troubadours. On the contrary, women songwriters, led by Joni Mitchell, Carly Simon, and Carole King, also proved capable of intensely personal introspection. One observer remarked that Mitchell "devoted much of her considerable talent—a near three-octave range . . . to exploring the exquisite pain of her amorous ups and downs."[3] Mitchell, in particular, pointed the way for female singer/songwriters to achieve a subjective voice as artists with an integral personal vision, escaping the confines of their traditional roles within the music industry as one-dimensional chanteuses or sex objects. Conversely, male singer/songwriters explored the more sensitive, "feminine" regions of their emotional range more often than had the 1960s rockers who preceded them. This prompted critics who championed what amounted to a prohibitively male and even macho ideal of rock to condemn 1970s rock's "softness" and emasculation. Debates about the singer/songwriters resounded with gender politics, a cultural reflection of the broader transformations wrought by the contemporaneous women's movement.

Although the singer/songwriters were the embodiment of the "Me Decade," as the 1970s came to be known, there was more to this group than meets the eye. Tellingly, many of these musicians banded together as Musicians United for Safe Energy (MUSE) to stage the week-long No Nukes concerts, which protested nuclear power and served as a forerunner to 1980s "mega-events," benefiting causes from African famine to American farmers. Seen in this light, the singer/songwriters' odyssey did not necessarily mark a retreat from political commitment and cultural rebellion. Instead, it signaled the emergence of a new kind of cultural politics that simultaneously accommodated and voiced suspicion of the decade's emergent conservatism. In this movement, the singer/songwriters benefited from Americans' growing distrust in government and weakening identification with traditional political institutions in the 1970s, a development that left the cultural realm more important and with greater legitimacy as a shaper of politics. By decade's end, the singer/songwriters' status as authentic artists who could speak in a personal voice came to enhance their political influence.

Underlying this phenomenon was a shift in the American cultural marketplace toward more specialized niches in the early 1970s. As the counterculture waned and the New Left's visibility ebbed, rock music increasingly explored its newfound status as art. Beginning with the Beatles' *Sgt. Pepper's Lonely Hearts Club Band,* and running through a bevy of primarily British bands, ranging from Emerson, Lake & Palmer and Yes, to the Moody Blues and Pink Floyd, art rockers nourished and fed off of a critical establishment that had elevated rock's status to the mantle of art. Capitalizing on radio's emphasis on album-oriented rock and on the music industry's eagerness to exploit it, this mind-oriented form luxuriated in protracted aural explorations that often evoked, or were enhanced by, the psychedelic drug experience. Despite this link to mind-expanding inner experience, and live stage shows that featured elaborate technological spectacles of lighting and sound to facilitate the journey, art rock seemed curiously disconnected from the vein of personal emotional life that the singer/songwriters mined. Additionally, art rock bled African American influences out of rock 'n' roll in favor of a "high seriousness" that sought to imbue rock music with the prestige of an elite cultural form.[4]

In doing so, art rock resembled another specialized form that cohered, at least initially, for a discernibly white working-class male market—heavy metal. The early 1970s emergence of bands like Led Zeppelin, Black Sabbath, and Deep Purple represented a musical aesthetic that rejected countercultural ideals of peace and love in favor of frank sexuality; a flirtation with the occult; and hard macho, often misogynist posturing. With the exception of the occasional electrified appropriation of an early black bluesman, heavy metal shared art rock's seeming absence of African American musical influence, its lack of humor, and its pretensions to classical instrumental virtuosity. A subset of hard rockers, led by Kiss and Alice Cooper, donned gaudy makeup and elaborate costumes and embellished arena shows with effects ranging from rockets, smoke bombs, police lights, and fake executions to live animal antics with chickens and snakes. While these acts still projected the aggressive masculinity that pervaded heavy metal at large, their visual image, featuring spandex and gold lamé pants and heavy mascara, revealed an androgynous strain whose gender ambiguity was more overtly explored in the glam or glitter rock phenomenon epitomized by David Bowie and the New York Dolls.[5] As distinguishable genres spawned by the music industry's fragmentation in the 1970s, art rock, heavy metal, and glam shared much with the singer/songwriters. For one thing, the fan base of these genres was almost exclusively white, as fragmentation tended increasingly to segregate music with distinct appeal to black audiences, most notably soul and rhythm and blues.

This division of music audiences along racial lines was encouraged by a simultaneous political shift at the beginning of the decade. Although soul and R&B had enjoyed growing popularity among white audiences in the 1960s, the wave of integrationist civil rights goodwill that had facilitated this crossover had crested by the new decade, a phenomenon that then became visible in the music's declining sales. In 1972, black artists began to rebound onto the pop charts, thanks to the emergence of a depoliticized soft soul sound that resonated with a broad audience that the more militant, cultural nationalist expressions of Otis Redding, Wilson Pickett, and James Brown could not reach after the 1960s. The resurgence of African American pop also benefited from the new inroads black performers like Stevie Wonder and Marvin Gaye made in the album-oriented format—a development that paralleled the singer/songwriter's use of albums as a forum for authentic creative expression.[6]

Shared among all of these strands of early 1970s popular music was a retreat from politics, a tendency to avoid referencing the most pressing issues of the day in favor of fanciful artistic visions, personal longings, and a growing embrace of commercialism. Where in the 1960s the Grateful Dead's Bob Weir had said, "If the Industry is gonna want us, they're gonna take us the way we are . . . Then if the money comes in, it'll be a stone gas," by the 1970s, Alice Cooper's comment, "I am the most American rock act. I have American ideals. I love money," came to epitomize the sentiments of growing ranks of musicians toward their industry and commercial ambitions.[7]

The singer/songwriters straddled a fine line between commercial ambition and creative personal expression in a way that few other 1970s popular musicians could manage. One way of gauging the parameters of the singer/songwriter genre is to examine figures who can help define its limits. For example, one rock historian contends that Elton John served as a "transitional figure from the early 1970s sensitive singer to the mid-1970s excessive rock star," yet the fact that he did not write his own lyrics combined with his flamboyant costumes and stage antics placed him clearly outside of the genre.[8] Likewise, Billy Joel's early music evoked some of the singer/songwriter style, but his rock overtones and unabashedly pop ambitions quashed any serious attempt to include him in this group. Bruce Springsteen and Neil Young presented more complicated, ambiguous cases. Before his landmark commercial breakthrough *Born to Run* (1975), Springsteen's first two albums, *Greetings from Asbury Park, NJ,* and *The Wild, The Innocent, and the E Street Shuffle,* which appeared at the height of the singer/songwriter movement, shared much of its sensibility. The solo acoustic accompaniment on his early ballads reflected the influence of Bob Dylan and the 1960s folk revival, while the sincere emotionality of his singing mirrored the singer/songwriters' emphasis on authentic personal experience. And yet the swirling casts of characters and multiple perspectives in his songs, their window into working-class rather than middle-class lives, and the E Street Band's clearly rock 'n' roll backing pressed the genre's boundaries and ultimately shattered them with Springsteen's post–*Born to Run* rock superstardom. Neil Young traversed a similar journey, sharing much with the singer/songwriters in his early solo years, but adopting a proto-grunge sensibility in his Crazy Horse years that had existed in muted tones all along.

The same forces that channeled popular music into specialized markets in the early 1970s steered the singer/songwriters toward largely white middle-class, often educated audiences that came of age in the 1960s and valued the same kind of personal authenticity that imbued these troubadors' work with artistic integrity. This led to the ironic development that ever larger, more impersonal musical conglomerates scurried to seek out the singer/songwriters' most authentic, personal expressions because they commanded an exalted status in the cultural marketplace. Though never completely eschewing the politics—of egalitarianism, nonviolence, and ecology—of their 1960s predecessors, the singer/songwriters, along with like-minded counterparts in 1970s art and popular culture, forged a new kind of political message that was more informal, gradualist, and outside the scope of institutional change than the previous decade's expansive utopian strivings had been. In doing so, these artists came around to engage, or reengage, in politics and social issues as they journeyed into middle age, in ways that sought to reconcile authentic self-expression, creative autonomy, and commercial ambition with larger communitarian and global concerns.

Despite this emphasis on authenticity, the singer/songwriters' creative expressions did not evolve unfettered by marketplace concerns. The boom years of the singer/songwriter phenomenon, 1970–1976, coincided with a growing recognition of the industry's power within commercialized entertainment as a whole. By 1973, the music industry was reaping $2 billion annually, a figure that eclipsed the combined total of Hollywood and professional sports.[9] In the late 1960s, corporations gained a growing sense of rock music's profitability, and of the commercial potential of its baby boomer audience, whose tastes embraced diverse musical styles. A selective sampling of the performers at Woodstock, which included Richie Havens, Sly and the Family Stone, Santana, Janis Joplin, and Jimi Hendrix, reveals an interracial lineup of performers, with eclectic, syncretic musical styles playing to a predominantly white countercultural audience. This reflected the multicultural nature of music circa the late 1960s and signified a brief moment when such eclecticism enjoyed commercial viability.

In the mid-1960s, however, Gulf and Western's takeover of Paramount Pictures signaled the beginning of an era of large-scale consolidation in the media and communications industries that contained the seeds of a new order for American popular music. This trend intensified in the 1970s, as many large corporations previously uninvolved in the music business realized rock's commercial potential and started to gobble up labels. In the most notorious example, the Kinney Corporation, best known for its ownership of parking lots, acquired Warner Brothers, forging the Warner Communications empire. By 1974, music industry consolidation had reached a point where the top four record companies accounted for half of all sales, with CBS and Warner alone representing 40 percent of total sales. With ownership by large conglomerates came a push to rationalize the market to guarantee, as much as possible, a steady stream of sales and profits. One consequence of this trend was the gradual erosion of the autonomy of smaller entrepreneurs who were music lovers and advocates, as they became embedded in a system that required fealty to quarterly earnings statements.

David Crosby described an experience that became increasingly common for musicians from the 1980s onward: "You'd go to a meeting with a record company and there wouldn't be a guy there who knew that you had written a new song and thought that was cool, there would be a guy that knew that he had moved 40,000 pieces out of Dallas that month, and he had no idea pieces of what."[10] In the 1970s, this process was just under way, and the music industry's primary economic strategy involved catering to discrete markets and specific demographics. One noticeable outcome was the breakdown, or fragmentation, of 1960s rock's more unitary and multiculturally oriented audience and the emergence of a number of identifiable genres, including the music of the singer/songwriters.[11]

Fragmentation within the music industry, combined with the premium on "authentic" self-expression and personal liberation that was a legacy of the 1960s counterculture, created the cultural space for singer/songwriters to address the longings, aspirations, and dissatisfactions of white middle-class audiences in their words and music, and record labels consciously marketed with this demographic in mind. Advertisements emphasized the singer/songwriters' artistic integrity and unalloyed authenticity. One series of Warner-Reprise ads for Joni Mitchell mobilized the genre's supposedly noncommercial purity as the basis for commercial promotion, claiming "Joni Mitchell Is 90 Percent Virgin." This ad referenced the fact that Mitchell's sales amounted to barely 10 percent of Judy Collins's, but also (to Mitchell's chagrin as it turned out) sought to exploit her sex appeal. Other ads in the series— "Joni Mitchell Takes Forever" and "Joni Mitchell Finally Comes Across"—touted the sincerity and hard work that went into the artist's creative efforts, as reflected in the length of time it took her to produce each new album.

Record industry management also bought into the notion that bottom line concerns coincided with the notion of maximizing the singer/songwriters' freedom to pursue their unique creative paths. The management team of Eliot Roberts and David Geffen, who ultimately achieved fame as an entertainment industry entrepreneur par excellence, oversaw Mitchell, Jackson Browne, and Crosby, Stills, Nash, and Young, among others, and formed Asylum Records, at least in part, to "minimize the contractual pressures on singer-songwriters who wanted to work at their own speed."[12] The presumed confluence of the singer/songwriters' open-ended creative process and profitability reflected a rare moment in the annals of American popular culture when art and commerce appeared to mesh seamlessly. As Roberts summed up his approach to creative talent, "Be sensitive, you'll make more money."

Music critics proved just as essential as record companies to the singer/songwriters' ascendancy, for not all of them were as hostile as Lester Bangs. In *Rolling Stone*, Stephen Holden diligently promoted emerging singer/songwriters, and Jon Landau's review of Carole King's *Tapestry* gave that album much of the momentum that resulted in its staggering number of millions of sales. Moreover, 1970s critics did not always remain impartial arbiters of artistic merit; rather, they occupied an ambiguous position often intertwined with the music business. In addition to Holden and Landau, such notable critics as Dave Marsh, Robert Palmer, Bud Scoppa, and Paul Nelson served the music industry in various capacities, from writing liner notes, to performing publicity work, to scouting new talent in Artist and Repertoire departments. The small handful of important critics who were positioned to "break" important new performers during the early 1970s routinely reaped the benefits of record company largesse.

To some extent, this collusion among critics, artists, and record companies simply amounted to the latest iteration of a recording industry phenomenon harkening back to the payola scandals of the 1950s. But this 1970s version cohered in its own unique social circumstances, including the ascendancy of the rock critic as cultural gatekeeper and chief publicist of the rock lifestyle, which fused elements of hippie culture, notably hedonistic drug use, to a consumption-oriented ethos of personal liberation.

Widely applied in the 1970s, the term *singer/songwriter* gradually expanded to describe a broader diversity of musical expression. The term's proliferation signified its power to evoke certain distinctive musical and stylistic elements. Initially, the label referred to performers who composed their own music, wrote their own lyrics, and sung them themselves, typically providing their own musical accompaniment along with sparse instrumentation. That this kind of music warranted a unique name indicated its break with popular music conventions of the past, namely, the use of professional composers who toiled in New York City's Brill Building to create catchy tunes for others of presumably greater star quality to front—from Frank Sinatra and Connie Francis to Johnny Mathis and Aretha Franklin. But the singer/songwriter movement also harked back to other musical traditions from the previous decade, most notably to the folk-music revival's use of solo acoustic guitar accompaniment, and especially to its preeminent figure, Bob Dylan. Jackson Browne cited Dylan's influence—especially his social conscience songs such as "Talking World War III Blues," "The Lonesome Death of Hattie Carroll," and "Blowin' in the Wind"—on his earliest musical stirrings. While these songs came right out of the pro–civil rights, pacifist politics of the 1960s folk revival, Stephen Holden noted the special influence of *Another Side of Bob Dylan,* on which Dylan's solo acoustic compositions favored interpersonal relationships and avoided social issues. As Holden remarked, "after Dylan, songwriters felt free to forgo the conventional niceties of note-to-syllable word setting and exact rhyme."[13]

Dylan's liberation and transformation of the length and structure of songs echoes through the singer/songwriters' descriptions of their own approaches to songwriting: "It was my literary period," Browne remarked of his early career. "Long-form rambling songs in iambic pentameter with the run-on philosophical attitude. I was searching bleary-eyed for God in the crowds."[14] James Taylor similarly suggested that his songwriting sprang from the intersection of his own emotions with unconscious musical experimentation.[15] For Joni Mitchell, songwriting functioned as an investigation of the self, "self-analysis of sorts," though "not just for the sake of spilling my guts or taking off my clothes, so to speak in public."[16] While denying exhibitionism, Mitchell nevertheless emphasized the centrality of her own experiences as a starting point for her songs. Although the singer/songwriters shared Dylan as a common source of liberation from more restrictive pop songwriting forms, they did not share his tendency to write from the perspective of other characters and individuals, as epitomized by his celebration of Rimbaud's idea that "I is another." With the singer/songwriters, "I" was unmistakable.

The musical expression of the singer/songwriters' inner lives became the genre's defining feature. A *Time* magazine cover story on James Taylor hailed the singer/songwriters as "the major pop innovators of 1971," noting their abandonment of "electrified guitar and wall to wall loudspeaker banks" in favor of acoustic guitar and sparse instrumentation. The story ultimately identified the hallmark of the singer/songwriter movement as the unmediated personal expression of a singular artistic voice, the "exquisitely melodic reflections of a private 'I.' "[17] The singer/songwriters were not alone in embracing this aesthetic. On the contrary, their ease in claiming the mantle of solo creative visionary paralleled other 1970s arts and cultural developments, most notably the New Hollywood movement in American cinema, whereby the notion of filmmaking as a collective enterprise was supplanted by an idea that films were supposed to express the uniquely personal and individual artistic visions of their directors, who were now elevated to the status of auteurs. Similarly, the 1970s witnessed the collision of the theater and art worlds, resulting in the ascendancy of new hybrid theater auteurs who sought to maximize directorial control over productions as well as in the growth of performance art, a form that often relied on the intensely personal autobiographical insights of an author–performer, as epitomized in the work of Spalding Gray.

For the singer/songwriters, as for many auteurs in other media, this movement coalesced amid an atmosphere of privilege, shared emotional concerns, and homogeneous audiences. Taylor grew up the son of a doctor of independent means who eventually became dean of the University of North Carolina Medical School. Rock writers frequently noted the rarified lineage of Taylor's wife for most of the 1970s, Carly Simon. Daughter of Richard Simon, cofounder of the publishing giant Simon and Schuster, observers referred to the "patrician generosity" of Simon's singing and remarked that the suggestive cover photo of her *Playing Possum* album revealed "an upper-class coquette."[18] Browne benefited from access to living and rehearsal space at Abbey San Encino, the Southern California mansion that his grandfather had built, and which was immortalized by the cover art of Browne's *For Everyman* album. While Mitchell hailed from a more middle-middle-class childhood (her parents were a grocer and a schoolteacher), piano lessons and art school were nevertheless part of the background she brought to her songwriting.

The singer/songwriters' relatively privileged circumstances and shared concerns were reinforced by a web of social and romantic connections. Taylor was married to Simon for over a decade; Mitchell shared romances with both Taylor and Browne (not to mention David Crosby and Graham Nash); Simon dated Cat Stevens.[19] These romantic entanglements existed alongside a set of overlapping musical relationships. The singer/songwriters relied on a stock group of accomplished Hollywood studio regulars for backing instrumentation. Although this group contained a multitude of talented musicians, it centered on drummer Russ Kunkel, bassist Lee Sklar, guitarist Danny "Kooch" Kortchmar, and keyboardist Craig

Doerge, a quartet that became known as "The Section" and recorded several albums in its own right. Kunkel's work ran the gamut of 1970s and 1980s popular music, yet his reputation dated from the praise he earned for his work on the early Taylor albums, with "his subdued but funky bass drum work and artful . . . fills adding a surprising but welcome hipness to the soft acoustic Taylor sounds."[20] Kunkel also played on recordings by Browne, Mitchell, and Simon. Browne explained that he hired Kunkel and The Section as his live backup band as soon as he could afford it, calling them "the best guys I could find," and credited Kunkel with the idea of recording his 1977 *Running on Empty* as a single live album of all new material rather than as a double album of predominantly older songs.[21]

Kortchmar's acquaintance with Taylor began as a friend and bandmate during their teenage years and continued through many of Taylor's most successful recordings. He also worked extensively with Browne, earning co-songwriting credits on a handful of tunes, and was featured on King's landmark *Tapestry* LP. Doerge played on some early 1970s David Crosby/Graham Nash collaborations and became a standard fixture on Browne's tours and live recordings, also appearing on Taylor's *One Man Dog*. The Section, and the singer/songwriters' shared pool of backing musicians as a whole, shared a kind of soft rock competence that contributed to a musical aesthetic designed to underscore the confessional nature of the singer/songwriters. Their style provided subtle but poignant commentary and refrained from upstaging the lyrics with ostentatious displays of solo virtuosity or cathartic hard rock dissonance. To many rock critics, this was anathema.

Both sympathetic and hostile commentators focused on the "softness" of the rock. In his *Creem* review of Taylor's *One Man Dog,* Bangs ironically touted the singer/songwriter's "nice, lulling melodies and inoffensive lyrics," as preferable to some "hotshot Rock and Roll albums like the new Black Sabbath."[22] Bangs's sardonic commentary encapsulates 1970s rock critics' main objection to the singer/songwriter movement: it wasn't rock 'n' roll. The idea that rock could be soft represented a new concept in the early 1970s, one that the singer/songwriter movement helped forge. This proved a bitter pill for many veteran rock critics like Robert Christgau, who confessed that his disdain for Taylor stemmed from his own bias as a "fanatical rock and roller."[23] This sentiment also extended to the singer/songwriters' live performance styles. A *Rolling Stone* review of a Browne concert in the Arizona desert observed that the singer chafed at the crowd noise, as the concertgoers turned into "a howling horde—a definite mismatch for Browne's basically gentle, reflective music."[24] No less a refined publication than *The New Yorker* reviewed a Taylor concert at Carnegie Hall, approvingly commenting on the "polite applause" and noting that the audience approached "the event as entertainment rather than as the gathering of any tribe."[25] For more culturally conservative music critics, then, the singer/songwriters marked a welcome development in a rock 'n' roll landscape that increasingly abandoned countercultural festivals, in which a "Do your own thing" credo prevailed, for a new era that privileged quieter introspection, even if it increasingly took place in indoor, paid-admission, reserved-seating venues.

But for veteran rock critics, the singer/songwriters signaled a selling-out of rock 'n' roll's promise. Whether they were looking to early rock 'n' roll as a rare cultural space in 1950s America, where class and racial mixing were permissible, or to the 1960s dream of cultural radicalism and collective spiritual transcendence, such veterans disdained the singer/songwriters' softness and seeming lack of social outlook. One review of a Cat Stevens concert mocked the British singer/songwriter's habit of performing sitting down and opting to generate excitement by shaking his "head and locks." At Taylor's Radio City concert, he announced that he had married Simon earlier in the day. Responding to his fans' contention that Taylor looked elated, Christgau retorted, "I wonder what he looks like when he's asleep."[26]

Criticism of the singer/songwriters' mellow side often intersected with class antagonism. Bangs simultaneously criticized Taylor's privilege, noting that he "holes up in a Martha's Vineyard bungalow far more than is healthy for any growing boy," as well as his softness, speculating that his fans empathized with him so much "they'd like to curl up into foetal balls and contract till they disappear."[27] Christgau wrote off Simon's own image of liberated independence, which inspired many young female fans to identify with her, as "a function of economic privilege."[28] He also criticized Taylor's "spoiled collegiate drawl," overlooking the fact that the singer had dropped out of high school at Milton Academy, earned his degree at the renowned Boston-area mental health facility McLean Hospital, and never attended college. Still, even that résumé bore enough residue of privilege for Christgau to confess that he had taken a poster from one of Taylor's albums and scrawled upon it: "Eat felt-tipped death, capitalist pig!"

The veteran rock critics attacked the singer/songwriters' softer, less abrasive, more widely accessible tones as a crass ploy for commercial appeal to bourgeois fans. "Taylor is leading a retreat," Christgau asserted," and the reason us rock and rollers are so mad at him is simply that the retreat has been so successful. We assume that there is something anarchic in all of us, something dangerous and wonderful that demands response, not retreat."[29] The most damning accusations against the singer/songwriters charged that they had domesticated rock, depoliticized popular music, and commercialized personal experience, while maintaining a perspective that reflected class privilege and detachment from the masses.

But the critics missed the subtler political message of the singer/songwriters—the way they carved out a new form of antiestablishment politics for an increasingly conservative age. Even at their confessional height, these musicians grappled with broader social and cultural changes, including women's liberation, the liberalization of sexuality, new definitions of masculinity and femininity, and rising environmental awareness.

In the early 1970s, the sheer novelty of a woman singing her own compositions about her own experiences often sufficed to generate cultural resonance. The lyrics of Mitchell's early work demonstrated the freshness of a subjective female voice. Critics noted that such intense self-concern may have come off as egotism in a male artist, but for a woman, it constituted an "act of defiance."[30] And Mitchell's lyrics demonstrated engagement with the era's most pressing issues that amounted to more than the autobiographical introspections on which her reputation rested. In "The Fiddle and the Drum," "Big Yellow Taxi," and "Ladies of the Canyon," she offered glimpses of antiwar lament, ecological critique, and communitarian creative sisterhood. "Help Me," Mitchell's only Top 10 single, released in 1974, portrayed the sexual revolution as a one-way street of male prerogative that exploited women. Yet the song also served notice that women's pleasure was now on the agenda.

Browne mined much the same terrain on his first four albums, those that most epitomized the singer/songwriter genre. "Looking into You," "I Thought I Was a Child," "The Times You've Come," "Late for the Sky," and "Here Come Those Tears Again," among others, try to balance the need for love, the pleasure of sexuality, the desire for freedom, and the impulse to do right by one's lover, even as the definition of what's "right" is in flux. In "The Pretender," Browne memorably examined the dilemma of being "caught between the longing for love and the struggle for the legal tender."[31] Though often misinterpreted as a wholesale capitulation to materialism and inauthenticity, the song's pulsating bass line and lilting piano melody combined with vocals that shun irony throughout also make it a song of resolve. The narrator manages to soldier on even after he has come to an intellectual and emotional realization of the material crassness of the workaday world.

Browne also revealed the rising ecological sensibility in "Before the Deluge." This song exposed the abuse of nature for power and depicted the earth exacting its revenge through natural catastrophe, prefiguring Browne's later turn to antinuclear activism with Musicians United for Safe Energy. But even before that, the singer/songwriters began to think political, even if the personal still predominated in their music. In April 1972, Taylor and King, along with Barbra Streisand and Quincy Jones, performed at the Los Angeles Forum in "Four for McGovern," a benefit event for the Democratic presidential candidate that charged audience members, including Joni Mitchell and David Geffen, up to $100 per ticket and raised more than $300,000. Taylor's performance occurred during a two-year hiatus from performing live, suggesting that his commitment, or at least his depth of feeling, was more than casual. In 1976, Browne helped organize a benefit that included Linda Ronstadt, The Eagles, and Jimmy Buffet and raised over $100,000 for California Proposition 15, a referendum to limit the use of nuclear power that ultimately failed. Later that year, many of the same performers teamed up for a benefit for Jerry Brown's presidential campaign, though there were intimations that their performances may have taken place under pressure generated by prominent radio programming executive Paul Drew's involvement.[32] By 1976, the singer/songwriters had grown wary of mainstream politics and increasingly pursued their activism independently. It was only in the 1990s, after almost two decades of conservative dominance, that they joined the Hollywood Left to renew a cultural alliance with mainstream Democrats against the Republican Right.

Browne lent his music to this independent activism, performing in some twenty benefits for Left or liberal causes between 1974 and 1976, from antinuclear initiatives to Tom Hayden's senatorial bid. One noteworthy benefit aided the Arcosanti Project, architect Paolo Soleri's ecologically minded city of the future in the Arizona desert, and netted $10,000. The *Rolling Stone* review of this event noted that the morning-after debris, a mess of cans, bottles, and food scraps, demonstrated that at least a critical mass of Browne's fan base was out of sync with Arcosanti's ecological message.[33]

This was less true at the September 1979 Musicians United for Safe Energy Concerts in New York City's Madison Square Garden. As a principal organizer of this event, Browne drew together many luminaries, not only singer/songwriters, such as himself, Taylor, and Carly Simon, but also Crosby, Stills, and Nash, Springsteen, the Doobie Brothers, and Tom Petty & the Heartbreakers. The concert series used the music event to raise awareness of the perils of nuclear power and to tout the virtues of alternative energy sources in a country still reeling from the shock of Three Mile Island earlier that year. MUSE produced and distributed a triple album and concert film, further spreading the message, and establishing the concerts as a model for socially engaged musical mega-events like Live-Aid and Band-Aid in the 1980s and beyond. A sixteen-page booklet accompanying the album featured reflections on the legacy of Three Mile Island, an article on radiation's effects on the human body, a profile of nuclear power whistle-blower Karen Silkwood, and statements from the musicians, explaining what drew them to participate in the concerts. Simon's statement was particularly telling, as it cast her concern with the hazards of nuclear energy in terms of her role as a parent and her responsibility to future generations.[34] This reflected an obvious truth about the singer/songwriters circa the late 1970s— they were growing up.

By the mid-1970s, the singer/songwriters had exhausted themselves and the emotional twists and turns of their own lives as the wellspring of songwriting inspiration. These musicians, who had gravitated to their own emotional lives and loves as a creative fountain, were discovering a more planetary and politicized set of adult concerns. Taylor recorded songs, such as "Millworker" and "Brother Trucker," that departed from his own privileged background and dared to explore, at least lyrically, the trials and tribulations of the blue-collar work world. Taylor also overcame reservations about his audience's "awareness of the political nature" of benefit concerts and played to raise money for the independent presidential candidate John Anderson in the run-up to the 1980 election.[35] Carole King has consistently married her post-1970s music to politics and public issues, from testifying before a congressional subcommittee on forests and forest health, to performing at fundraisers and appearing at speaking events on behalf of 2004 Democratic presidential candidate John Kerry, and joining with Taylor and others "in a non-political effort" to raise awareness of global warming.

Of all the singer/songwriters, Jackson Browne embedded himself most deeply in political and social causes from the 1970s onward. He made two highly politicized albums in the 1980s, *Lives in the Balance* and *World in Motion,* and in 2002 he was awarded the John Steinbeck Award, honoring artists whose work exemplifies commitment to environmental and social values. Though the singer/songwriters' activism has sometimes coincided with sound commercial impulses, and occasionally highlighted a desire to protect the privilege that wealth and fame afford—such as Taylor's opposition to a gravel mine abutting his northwestern Connecticut property and Mitchell's similar stance against a proposed fishery in British Columbia—in general, their activities have demonstrated a consistent concern for the public interest.[36]

In the early 1970s, the singer/songwriters adjusted to the new national mood. Amid a widespread disappointment with the possibilities of liberal reform, even among erstwhile leftist radicals, they developed a new, softer, more personal style. Their emphasis on authentic expression reflected a wider distrust of the establishment that revealed itself in 1970s film, theater, art, and politics, as well as in music. But this inward focus proved temporary. The reemergence of the singer/songwriters' political sensibility illustrated that their movement had been no simple capitulation to more conservative times.

Like so many Americans in the seventies, the singer/songwriters sought refuge in the cultural realm from the disappointments they found in national politics. Eventually, their personal expressions became the foundations for a new activist political sensibility, often countering the new era's prevailing politics. As in so many other areas, rising conservative political strength could not entirely overwhelm an ever more liberated popular culture. "With everyone from the president on down" suppressing the truth, Jackson Browne sang in "For America," he and his fellow artists would have to wait "until the land of the free is awake" and "her conscience has been found."

CHAPTER 8

Financing the Counterrevolution

ALICE O'CONNOR

In late 1969, executives at the Ford Motor Company (FMC) began
to grow wary as news of yet another in a series of periodically
threatened boycott campaigns trickled in. Like earlier such campaigns, this one, organized by the newly formed Committee of
Families Opposing Revolutionary Donations (F.O.R.D.), urged
"loyal American citizens" to boycott and form pickets around
FMC dealerships in protest against the activities of the "largest of
all leftist organizations, the Ford Foundation."[1] Technically, both
the automaker and the foundation could claim independence of
one another—and they did. Separately incorporated and run by an
independent professional staff, the Ford Foundation had gradually
reduced its FMC stock holdings in the years since the company
went public in the 1950s, and with the acquiescence of the family.[2]
Accurate or not, such claims did little to placate agitated dealers or
FMC executives, who for years had been complaining that even the
foundation's hypercautious support for civil rights was hurting
sales throughout the South. The foundation, for its part, had reason to be more skittish than usual. Under fire for a series of controversial grants for black voter registration, New York City school
reform, and bereaved members of Senator Robert F. Kennedy's

148

staff, it had been the clear target of provisions in the recently passed Tax Reform Act of 1969, which tightened the rules for tax-exempt foundations.

There were two other things, though, that made the Southern California–based F.O.R.D. action appear more threatening in comparison to the earlier southern campaigns—and that point to the changing dynamics that would make the 1970s an important decade of organizing on the Right. First, it was better organized, better funded, and national in reach, with reported incidents in each of the company's thirty-five dealer districts nationwide and rumors of a total of $150,000 in pledges from "five West Coast conservative businessmen."[3] Clearly, this organization was tapping into new sources of regional resentment and opposition aimed at the Ford Foundation's liberal stance. Subsequent investigation found the F.O.R.D. group to be linked to a number of "far-right" organizations, including the Washington, D.C.–based Liberty Lobby; the Christian Crusade, headed by Tulsa evangelist Billy James Hargis; and the Association of American Voters; as well as to the California remnant of George Wallace's 1968 third-party bid for the presidency. Acting as director and official spokesman for the group was Hurst B. Amyx, operating in Los Angeles out of his American Center for Education, a well-endowed conservative media outfit that counted among its backers Phillips Petroleum, Pepperdine University, and businessman Henry Salvatori, a major funder of conservative causes and a Republican Party activist.[4]

Second, while echoing earlier critics on the subject of the Ford Foundation's racial "militancy," F.O.R.D.'s list of grievances was broader in scope. Among those included in its lengthy broadside of "un-American" Ford Foundation grantees were the "pro-Soviet" Council on Foreign Relations, the "ultra liberal" John F. Kennedy School of Government at Harvard University, the "Negro militant" A. Philip Randolph Fund, and the "cybernetic liberal-left oriented RAND Corporation"—all part of a larger pattern of subversion

only recently manifest in the rise of black power and campus unrest. The Ford Foundation was, in the phrase of a pamphlet issued
by the American Conservative Union in 1969, among the handful
of powerful liberal "Financiers of Revolution" that were undermining the nation with grants to subversive causes. Directing its demands to FMC chairman and foundation trustee Henry Ford II,
F.O.R.D. called on the business executives on the board to retake
control of the fruits of capitalist enterprise by diverting foundation
funds to "groups that are striving to strengthen and preserve this
nation's concepts and principles."[5]

Much to the relief of foundation and FMC executives, the incipient nationwide boycott never got much beyond the occasional action and short-lived picket lines. Henry Ford II, grandson of the
company's founder and longtime foundation trustee, was publicly
forthright in his defense of what was then the country's largest philanthropic enterprise, telling one Southern California plaintiff that
"the officers and staff of the Foundation are loyal, high-minded citizens dedicated to trying to find new ways to make life more worth-
while for all of us—and especially for the poor, the underprivileged
and the undereducated."[6] F.O.R.D. itself dissolved amid internal
factionalism. After a few months of foundation staff meetings and
exchanges to placate worried car dealers, the threat seemed to have
died down for good, according to an outside consultant, who in
September 1970 predicted that any damage to the company would
soon "be dissipated by the success of the new 'Pinto' car—which
currently seems assured."[7]

Taken on its own, this episode offers an especially ripe portent
of the currents that, in taking firmer hold, would make the coming
decade so significant in the right-wing transformation of American
political culture. To start with the most obvious, there was the fact
that before decade's end the predictions of Ford's consultant had
been precisely reversed. The promise of the Ford Pinto had literally backfired—hastily produced to outmaneuver the German and

Japanese in the expanding subcompact market, the car exploded upon rear impact because of a design flaw—to become yet another icon of American economic and cultural decline. Right-wing critics of the Ford and other foundation "financiers of revolution," on the other hand, were on the verge of realizing, with the election of President Ronald Reagan, a monumental victory in the emerging conservative counterrevolution. We can also find broader symbolic meaning in the dynamics of the F.O.R.D. protest: the shift from deep South to Sunbelt; the implied threat to the Fordist industrial economy; the joining of evangelical and right-wing business forces. There is also the anti-establishment populism that, at the very same moment, had presidential speechwriter Pat Buchanan urging his boss to score one with the "forgotten Americans" by snubbing the "high-bouncing fairies from Lincoln Center" in the annual Freedom Medal awards, and instead to "lay one on Roy Acuff, founding father of country and western music, a Nixon supporter with a special niche in the hall of heroes at the Grand Old Opry in Nashville, TN."[8]

But the real significance of the episode is that within a few years these groups did not need to be threatening boycotts against the FMC. They had a different way to channel their opposition to the liberal establishment: foundations, and a policy establishment, of their own. Not long after the grassroots efforts of F.O.R.D., the Liberty Lobby, and the American Conservative Union had fizzled out, a smaller, more elite group of conservative activists tapped into much the same sentiments and suspicions to mount an alternative, decidedly top-down effort to redirect philanthropic wealth to more "pro-American"—and pro-capitalist—causes. Acknowledging the futility of recapturing the fortunes of the Ford, Carnegie, Rockefeller, and other major foundations for the conservative cause, they instead turned to an alternative network of foundations and individual philanthropists to bankroll the conservative movement in a way it had never been bankrolled before: not merely, as in the past, with funds for scattered, uncoordinated movements, obscure free market seminars, or promising political candidates, but with funding for the deeper infrastructure of ideas, institutions, and talent incubators through which, especially in an era of declining party influence, the parameters of both policy and political possibility were being discussed, debated, and reconstituted in Washington, D.C. A new generation of conservative funders would build—in the terminology significantly adapted from the Trotskyist Left—a wide-ranging conservative "counterintelligentsia" to break what they saw as a Left-liberal stranglehold on American politics and culture while establishing limited government, free enterprise, hard-line anti-Communism, "traditional" family values, and individualism as prevailing political norms.

Thus, in a tightly focused strategy that emphasized funding for conservative individuals, institutions, and, above all, ideas, a handful of leading conservative foundations, with comparatively limited assets and admittedly conservative ideological aims, provided what one praiseful publication later called the "venture capital" for the proliferating array of conservative think tanks, advocacy organizations, professional associations, university-based research institutes, publications, and policy advocacy organizations that, since the 1970s, have played a major role in the sweeping reorientation of policy and political culture to the Right. Prominent among these foundations were several that have only recently come to attention as major funders on the Right: the Lynde and Harry Bradley, Adolph Coors, Earhart, JM, Koch Family, Sarah Scaife, Smith Richardson, and, the one I focus on most closely in this chapter, the John M. Olin Foundation. While varying, sometimes even conflicting, in emphasis, from the hard-line libertarian, to the Christian fundamentalist, to the neoconservative Right, the core funding they collectively provided for organizations started or significantly reinvigorated during the 1970s—now-prominent organizations such as the Heritage Foundation, the Cato Institute, the Manhattan Institute, and the American Enterprise Institute (founded in 1943)—and for a whole host of conservative publications and "public interest" law firms helped to make that decade a "seedtime" of conservative reform and counter-revolution. Though hardly alone in financing the rise of the right-wing policy establishment—which over the years has garnered billions from wealthy individual donors, direct mail solicitations, and membership dues—their activism constitutes a significant new presence in recent American politics and has brought new meaning to the terms "movement" and "social change" philanthropy, terms generally reserved for funders on the Left.

To be sure, this was not the first time that conservatives, feeling besieged by a liberal conspiracy to insinuate values variously labeled "collectivist," "internationalist," culturally "relativist," and downright "un-American" into every corner of American life, had sought to channel philanthropic dollars toward the defense of free enterprise. Funds from the free-market Volker Foundation, for example, were earlier critical in helping economist Milton Friedman and others to make the University of Chicago an outpost of anti-Keynesian thought in the postwar United States. Nor, as critics on the Left as well as foundation officers themselves have been quick to point out, were even the more liberal of "liberal establishment" foundations meant to do other than to make "the world safe for capitalism"—albeit by softening its blows.[9]

But three things came together to make the 1970s a turning point in the long-standing conservative battle against the liberal policy establishment and to transform what in the past had been scattered, isolated efforts into a full-throttled philanthropic movement with long-lasting effects. One was the central role played by the small but influential group of formerly Left and liberal intellectuals known as neoconservatives, both in reformulating—and at times straying from—traditional conservative ideas and in using foundation funds to translate them into political action. Second was the coalition-building work of a number of heterogeneous but similarly Right-thinking political operatives and policy entrepreneurs—people like

neoconservative "godfather" Irving Kristol; Republican congressional staffers Edwin Feulner and Paul Weyrich, who founded the
Heritage Foundation; direct mail pioneer Richard Viguerie; the corporate lobbyist and Business Roundtable impresario Charls E.
Walker; "pro-family" activist and Eagle Forum founder Phyllis
Schlafly; and treasury secretary, energy "czar," and Wall Street ty-
coon William E. Simon. These were people who, like those identified
in a series of political ads produced by the National Conservative
Union, believed in the sanctity of private property, free enterprise,
low taxes, the traditional family, and law and order—and who were
willing, despite ideological differences, to find common cause with
one another in ferocious animosity toward liberalism. The coalition-
building behind the conservative foundations, however, reflected a
class-conscious strategy that had little to do with the people in those
ads, the white ethnic working class, or country music fans in
Nashville. Instead, as we shall see, it focused on the creation of an alliance between business and conservative intellectuals—a counterrevolution from above.

The third feature anchoring the newly resurgent conservative
foundations to the experience of the 1970s was their emergence—
amid the dwindling economic prosperity, confusing "social revolutions," ongoing racial divisions, deepening alienation from
government, and shifting political alliances that shook up the New
Deal political coalition—as part of a broader political movement
built on the values of individual freedom, property rights, hard-line
anti-Communism, moral-cultural traditionalism, and limited government. It is in this sense that right-wing foundations were most fully a
part of the realignments that started in the 1970s and that have come
to fruition not only with the growing influence of conservative ideas
and ideology but with such important shifts in late-twentieth-century
political economy as the subordination of the state and civil society
to the private market; the political erosion of the idea that there is a
difference between private wealth and the public interest; and the

shift in the direction of redistributive policy to favor wealth, capital, and property over labor and an increasingly concentrated group of "haves" over an expanding segment of "have-nots."

In mobilizing philanthropy for the conservative cause, movement activists were tapping into decades of built-up frustration and resentment against the power of what, in the conservative imagination, was an ever-expanding establishment—an interlocking directorate of politicians, lawyers, academics, policy intellectuals, media executives, union officials, public interest activists, and even some corporate executives who were predominantly liberal in orientation and located in the Ivy-League northeast. While hardly the only or even the most ubiquitous of its institutional avatars—the Brookings Institution made it to the top of Richard Nixon's enemies list—the big foundations like Carnegie, Rockefeller, and Ford stood out to critics from across the ideological spectrum as especially potent symbols of the liberal establishment's wide and interlocking reach over the nation's political, economic, and cultural life. Indeed, liberal foundations could be found behind just about every cause, organization, and major study the postwar Right found objectionable—from Keynesian economic planning and U.N.-style internationalism to the American Civil Liberties Union and the NAACP; from Gunnar Myrdal's *An American Dilemma* and Alfred Kinsey's "sex studies" in the 1940s and 1950s to public television's Children's Television Workshop in the late 1960s. Equally significant, big philanthropy had long been to the Right an especially egregious symbol of what they considered to be liberalism's hostility to capitalism and other core American values. Foundation executives were, in the eyes of their right-wing critics, using the fruits of great capitalist fortunes to "destroy or discredit the free-enterprise system which gave them birth."[10] Charges of foundation un-Americanism were behind a set of kangaroo-court-like congressional hearings at the height of the McCarthy era in the 1950s. For all the conspiratorial paranoia they tapped into, those hearings captured the central elements of an oppositional critique that would be rehearsed and reprised in such influential right-wing venues as William F. Buckley's *National Review* for decades to come.

It was within the much-changed environment of the 1960s and into the 1970s, however, that conservative activists would turn the compendium of conspiratorial charges into a counteroffensive. Amid the ongoing turmoil and divisiveness of war, racial violence, social protest, counterculture, and the emerging "law and order" response, the country's biggest foundations and all that they stood for had become an especially volatile target for critics of the liberal establishment, from the Left as well as the Right. The reign of Mc-George Bundy—the ultra establishment, Ivy League–bred, former national security adviser for both Kennedy and Johnson—as president of the Ford Foundation (from 1966 to 1979) was especially telling in this regard: having come under fire for backing the foundation's move into unprecedented (albeit, by some lights, limited) degrees of activism in civil rights, environmentalism, and public interest law, Bundy was still presiding when Henry Ford II dropped a bombshell by resigning from the board in 1977, citing the staff's disengagement from the foundation's capitalist roots. In the meantime, a rising generation of right-wing political activists—many of them veterans of the 1960s conservative student movement or of the devastating 1964 Barry Goldwater campaign—were beginning to organize through Washington-based as well as grassroots channels to build an infrastructure of organizations dedicated to conservative policy and advocacy. Galvanized by what they saw as the virtually unstoppable juggernaut of the counterculture, the rights revolution, and the regulatory/welfare state, they felt equally alienated by the moderate mainstream of the Republican Party. Such alienation was only heightened, for conservative congressional staffers such as Edwin Feulner, by the absence of readily available conservative policy analysis in key legislative debates. Along with this came an awareness, honed from years on the political margins, that the proverbial "battle of ideas" was above all about political power: the power to set, dominate, and ultimately win the terms of policy debate.

This awareness of the literal power of ideas, when funded, publicized, and mobilized for movement purposes, was a crucial factor behind a related development in the political culture of the 1970s, and the one most immediately consequential for the project of financing a counterrevolution from above. That development was the burgeoning activism among conservative intellectuals and business elites, in a mirror image of the very executive suites, think tanks, university classrooms, and foundation boardrooms that grassroots activists had long viewed with skepticism. Similarly catalyzed by the "social revolution" of the 1960s, they cultivated a critique of the foundation-funded liberal establishment that—minus the overt anti-intellectualism of earlier right-wing critics—brought intellectual respectability and sophistication to largely familiar charges of creeping collectivism, cultural relativism, internationalism, and liberal elitism. To these charges conservative ideologues added a broader analysis linking the pillars of liberal thought and policy—Keynesianism, welfare statism, regulation, and, especially, racial and gender egalitarianism—to economic and cultural decline. But even more than a common analysis of the country's economic woes, two core ideas animated business executives and intellectuals behind a new brand of philanthropic activism. With them, conservatives would embark on a strategy of counterorganizing and institution building that was designed at once to learn from, rival, and, ultimately, defeat the liberal foundation establishment at its own game.[11]

One was the conservative counterpart to an idea earlier popularized by economist John Kenneth Galbraith in his best-selling *The Affluent Society* (1959): that a hallmark of the postindustrial polity was the emergence of an elite "new class," heavily dominated by intellectuals, artists, and various knowledge professionals who were poised to displace the old capitalist ruling class as the arbiters of culture and the common good. But while Galbraith saw the new class as the potential vanguard of a less pecuniary, more enlightened, and leisure-oriented society, for conservative intellectuals the "new class" concept came to refer to the intellectuals and professionals—largely innocent of the nuts and bolts of capitalist enterprise—who promulgated an antibusiness bias not simply as a matter of predisposition or ideology but to justify their own existence. The new class, as Austrian émigré economist and conservative icon Joseph Schumpeter had forecast in the early 1940s, was sowing the seeds of capitalist destruction with its undying allegiance to redistributive welfare statism and its hostility to the virtues of capitalist wealth—but most of all in its insatiable quest for the power, as neoconservative columnist Irving Kristol told his *Wall Street Journal* readers, "to shape our civilization—a power which, in a capitalist system, is supposed to reside in the free market."[12]

Second, and closely related, was an idea that built off of the "new class" analysis and that, though not entirely new in conservative political circles, was beginning to gain wider currency among conservative business executives in their efforts to establish a more effective presence in Washington. Wholeheartedly embraced by William E. Simon in his best-selling 1978 memoir *A Time for Truth* and in numerous speeches before business groups, this was the idea that conservatives needed to build a "counterintelligentsia" to combat what Simon called the "dominant socialist-statist-collectivist orthodoxy" reigning in universities, government agencies, and policy institutes, and in the philanthropies that funded them.[13] Simon was here echoing what Justice Lewis Powell had earlier written in a memorandum to the National Chamber of Commerce just months before his 1971 appointment to the Supreme Court.[14] Warning of an "assault on the enterprise system" stemming from the likes of Ralph Nader, Charles Reich, Herbert Marcuse, and what he depicted as an overwhelmingly Left-liberal bias on campuses and in the media, he called on the chamber to end its practice of "appeasement" by cultivating its own "faculty of scholars" to produce and disseminate pro-business scholarship; by creating a network of business interest law firms to combat the public interest law movement; and by convincing universities to do more to represent the virtues of capitalism.[15] It was Simon, though, who took the lead in popularizing the idea (his book was excerpted in *Reader's Digest* and published by Reader's Digest Press) and in promoting an aggressive strategy of foundation funding. Simon urged corporate leaders and conservative intellectuals to join together at the forefront of a movement to reestablish capitalism and limited government as the reigning orthodoxy in Washington, above all by giving "grants, grants and more grants in exchange for books, books and more books." Such a project, Simon recognized, would require a new kind of foundation and a deliberately orchestrated countermobilization. It would also require a fundamental shift in the very philosophy of philanthropy that, in Simon's view, had animated the liberal establishment's appropriation of wealth. No longer could business afford to subsidize the critics of capitalism lurking within the halls of academic and public policy institutions. No longer should business apologize for what it was best at—the accumulation of wealth. No longer should the captains of capitalism tolerate the philanthropic "appeasement" of the enemy by allowing the fruits of their enterprises to be channeled to soft-hearted liberal projects and dissent.[16]

So where, if the so-called socialist-statist-collectivist orthodoxy really was so pervasive, were the "freedom-loving" intellectuals to be found? In this, as in so many other aspects of their rise to political power, the strategists of the conservative Right would literally turn to the Left—specifically, to the group of scholars and writers once identified to varying degrees with the Communist, social democratic, and/or liberal Left who, as Simon saw it, had "grasped the importance of capitalism" first in their growing recognition of the dangers of Communism, and subsequently in their growing disillusionment with liberalism. The intellectuals most readily identifiable as "neoconservatives"—Kristol, sociologist Nathan Glazer, political scientist James Q. Wilson, theologian Michael Novak, philosopher Sidney Hook, and, for a time, Daniel Patrick Moynihan—had academic credentials. But it was on the pages of Kristol's *The Public Interest* (cofounded with Glazer and Bell), in Norman Podhoretz's *Commentary,* and more and more in such bastions of free enterprise as *Fortune* and the *Wall Street Journal* that they would make common cause with the free market and corporate capitalist Right. As veterans of New York's Depression-era Trotskyist and subsequently the postwar non-Communist Left, they were practiced in the ways of public intellectuals and elite opinion making, as well as in Cold War cultural battles against Soviet Communism (Kristol had been editor of the CIA-backed magazine *Encounter* in the 1950s). They also differed from more traditionally laissez-faire conservative thinkers in their willingness to use the apparatus of policy-making, including the state, to realize their ideological objectives. Especially important, amid heated debates over issues such as welfare, affirmative action, and the enduring "urban crisis," neoconservatives proved adept at constructing an increasingly incendiary and distorted narrative of liberal excess and moral decadence—a narrative that cast business elites, along with the white working class, as mutual victims of forces bent on denying their rights. By the late 1970s, it was becoming clear that the neoconservatives were to be the entrepreneurs of conservative policy, as they began to join their more traditional counterparts in newly invigorated conservative institutions such as the American Enterprise Institute, to appear with greater frequency in the pages of traditionally liberal journals like *The New Republic* and the *Atlantic,* and on occasion to hobnob with politicians in the corridors of government power.

No single figure captured the combination of intellect and entrepreneurship Simon was looking for better than Kristol, who, as a virtual one-man brains trust, provided the basic analysis and even recommended the ghostwriter (the libertarian writer and author of *The News Twisters* Edith Efron) for Simon's *A Time for Truth.* By then, Kristol had emerged as the iconic neoconservative, the "godfather" of the group of former liberals for whom the term was coined in the early 1970s. Through wide-ranging connections in publishing, conservative politics, and think tanks such as the Heritage Foundation, Hoover Institute, and the American Enterprise Institute (where he was a resident fellow), Kristol would subsequently be credited with brokering the connections that brought the Laffer Curve and supply-side economics to the attention of *Wall Street Journal* editorialist Jude Wanniski, thence to the offices of Congressman Jack Kemp, and ultimately to the Reagan White House.[17] Kristol was also, as one of the major promulgators of the "new class" polemic in his *Wall Street Journal* columns, ideally situated to broker the relationship between neoconservative intellectuals and the business elite.[18] Indeed, like his alliance with Simon, Kristol's positioning put him in the middle of a business-political elite that was as thoroughly ensconced in the traditional northeast corridor and in "old economy" sources of wealth as it was in the Sunbelt. It also points to the 1970s as the beginning of a major ideological repositioning in key segments of the old-line establishment business press—the *Wall Street Journal* editorial page chief among them—that would later be found in newer media outlets as well.

But the aim of the intellectual-business alliance urged by Simon, Kristol, and Lewis Powell was not just about reviving and recognizing their mutual interest in conservative, free-enterprise ideology and ideas. It was about getting business to recognize its political power as an interest group—by urging it to exercise its economic power with more consciousness of its interests as a class. First and most immediate, this would mean ending business support for all the liberal causes, and Left-leaning faculty, it aided and abetted through "mindless subsidizing of colleges and universities whose departments of economics, government, politics, and history are hostile to capitalism and whose faculties will not hire scholars whose views are otherwise," wrote Simon.[19] It also meant learning the lesson, as Lewis Powell put it in his memo to the Chamber of Commerce, "long ago learned by labor and other self-interest groups. This is the lesson that political power is necessary; that such power must be assidously [sic] cultivated; and that when necessary, it must be used aggressively and with determination—without the reluctance which has been so characteristic of American business."[20] Ultimately, Simon acknowledged, the battle of ideas would have to be won in party politics as well as in the academy and boardrooms—beginning with a transformation in the Republican Party from the vaguely business-oriented, ideologically moderate "Stupid Party" of a Nelson Rockefeller to the party of principled free enterprise.[21] Perhaps most important for both Powell and Simon was for business to recognize that free enterprise, and liberty itself, was truly under siege from the reigning orthodoxy. In mounting the counteroffensive, the "new foundations" Simon envisioned would not be above the political fray. Irving Kristol put it bluntly in his own *Wall Street Journal* missive to corporate philanthropists: "when you give away your stockholders' money" he wrote, "your philanthropy must serve the longer-term interests of the corporation. Corporate philanthropy should not be, cannot be, disinterested."[22] Kristol's column, notably, was occasioned by the front-page news of Henry Ford's resignation from the Ford Foundation board.

Henry Ford's departure did not spark a slew of sympathy resignations. But the resignation did make a deep impression on conservative businessman John M. Olin, whose newly expanded and invigorated foundation would soon emerge as a leading force in the aggressive counterestablishment philanthropy envisioned in *A Time for Truth*.[23] For Olin, as for others in what was then just beginning to come together as a conservative movement philanthropy, Ford's resignation became the ultimate vindication for (re)turning philanthropic dollars to the defense of embattled free market capitalism—and, by limiting the lifespan of his foundation, for keeping those dollars out of the hands of professionals who might use them to subvert "donor intent." For Simon, who in previously recorded transcribed interviews with ghostwriter Edith Efron had referred to the Ford Foundation staff as "liberal freaks," the timing was also fortuitous: about to leave the Department of Treasury to return to Wall Street, he had agreed to join the John M. Olin Foundation as board president.

The son of a prominent midwestern munitions manufacturer, John M. Olin (1892–1982) had succeeded his father as president of the family-owned Olin Industries in 1944, subsequently overseeing the 1954 merger that made the Olin Mathieson Chemical Corporation one of the largest manufacturers of agricultural chemicals and recreational weapons in the United States and that moved the company headquarters to New York City. He had also made a name for himself as a thoroughbred racehorse and dog breeder and avid hunter—Olin and his wife were pictured in their hunting gear on the cover of *Sports Illustrated* in 1958, and he was later initiated into the Hunting Hall of Fame. The John M. Olin Foundation, established in 1953, was chiefly devoted to a combination of mainline charitable causes, anti-labor groups, and small conservative colleges for much of its first two decades, while Olin personally donated a good deal to his alma mater, Cornell University, where he sat on the board of trustees. By the early 1970s, retired and reportedly disgusted by what he saw as the Cornell administration's capitulation to "militant black radicals" in the student unrest of 1969, he began to think seriously about shifting the foundation's focus to a more aggressive defense of the free enterprise system he saw being challenged on campus. Turning to his one-time chief labor negotiator Frank O'Connell, in 1973 Olin started laying the groundwork for what would become the core emphases of the foundation for the next forty years: the foundation's overriding purpose would be to strengthen the cultural as well as the economic and political underpinnings of the "American system of democratic capitalism." O'Connell, in the meantime, had consulted widely with staff members at the Volker, Earhart, Koch Family, Smith Richardson, and other leading conservative foundations, while immersing himself in the free market literature that had become their common currency. By 1977, the Olin Foundation was giving away nearly $1 million annually based on a $12 million endowment—minuscule in comparison to the Ford Foundation's $2.35 billion endowment and $160 million in expenditures, but also more strategically focused on "supporting scholars and think tanks that favor limited government, individual responsibility, and a free society." It was also drawing attention for its grants to the likes of the Hoover Institution, the American Enterprise Institute, the Heritage Foundation, and Milton Friedman's hugely successful public television series based on his book *Free to Choose*, a free-market answer to a popular series hosted by John Kenneth Galbraith two years earlier. A subset of the major Right-minded foundations meanwhile had begun to meet informally in a group known as the Grantmakers Roundtable, convened by Leslie Lenkowsky of the Smith Richardson Foundation, and later formalized as the Philanthropy Roundtable, an organization that is now located in Washington, D.C., in offices adjacent to the American Enterprise Institute. Interviewed in the *New York Times* at the time, Olin stated his ambition "to see free enterprise re-established in this country. Business and the public must be awakened to the creeping stranglehold that socialism has gained here since World War II."[24]

Even more than his public profile, it was Olin's recruitment of Simon that put the foundation on the conservative movement map. As neighbors in summer homes in Easthampton, Long Island, the two men had recognized in each other a shared zeal for saving free enterprise—a zeal that would lead one columnist to label Simon the "Billy Graham of capitalism" and that Simon would exude in stumping the message of the best-selling *A Time for Truth* in the months after its release.[25] As board president, Simon brought more structure to what remained a small organization, despite a massive increase that would bring the endowment to $125 million and annual expenditures to a peak of some $20 million in the decades following Olin's 1982 death. He also brought Irving Kristol in as a consultant and hired a protégé of Kristol's, Michael Joyce, as executive director. Joyce, an Irish Catholic who dated his own turn away from Democratic Party loyalties to the Party's nomination of Left-liberal George McGovern in the 1972 presidential race, was then directing a joint Simon–Kristol venture called the Institute for Educational Affairs (IEA).[26]

Created in 1978 with start-up funds from such leading conservative philanthropies as the Olin, Scaife, JM, and Smith Richardson Foundations, the IEA offers an early example of what, with gathering momentum in the 1970s and early 1980s, would distinguish this newly energized brand of conservative philanthropy from its mainstream counterpart. First and foremost, of course, was its explicitly ideological commitment: the IEA was set up to launch the conservative counterintelligentsia by steering corporate philanthropic dollars to conservative intellectuals. The idea was to combine Kristol's talent for spotting promising scholars with Simon's connections in the world of business and finance. Second was conservative philanthropy's equally self-conscious cultivation of a "revolutionary" or "counterrevolutionary" sensibility, a sensibility reflected not only in the proverbial "war of ideas" but in the way conservative foundations carried it out. Thus, after failing to draw substantial corporate support (corporate foundations, for the most part, were too much invested in burnishing the company image for diverse constituencies), the IEA shifted its focus to funding the network of conservative student newspapers that had begun to crop up on elite campuses. That network would soon become a stepping stone for budding gadflies such as Dinesh D'Souza, who with Olin funding and a perch at the American Enterprise Institute would later go on to write truly incendiary attacks on the academy (*Illiberal Education,* published in 1991) and on racial egalitarianism (*The End of Racism*, published in 1996). More significant than such particulars was the broader shift that IEA's redirection indicates: toward creating institutional "beachheads" on influential elite campuses, where, conservatives believed, their ideas were most embattled. The legacy of this approach can be seen in a whole host of generously endowed university centers that bear the foundation's name and that would nurture a great deal of the scholarship underlying the right-wing policy agenda. Under the direction of philosophy professor and best-selling author Allan Bloom (*The Closing of the American Mind: How Higher Education Has Failed Democracy and Impoverished the Souls of Today's Students*, 1987), the University of Chicago's John M. Olin Center for Inquiry into the Theory and Practice of Democracy helped to spark a revival of the deeply antiliberal political philosophy of Leo Strauss, with its emphasis on the importance of moral virtue as the basis of the polity. The John M. Olin Institute for Strategic Studies at Harvard, founded by political scientist Samuel Huntington as a counterpoint to what conservatives alleged was an antiwar bias in academe, became a training ground for a foreign policy and national security establishment that, from a variety of ideological perspectives, was more open to the use of American force. The Olin-funded "beachheads" that would prove most far-reaching, however, were associated with what is known as the Law and Economics movement. Itself inspired by the largely successful postwar movement to preserve, then to revive free-market and rational choice thinking in economics, the Law and Economics movement aimed to extend these methods and principles to legal analysis and to jurisprudence as well. Economic analysis, in the works of such leading proponents as Richard Posner and Richard Epstein (both affiliated with the University of Chicago Law School), would be used to maximize the values of market efficiency and individual choice in the law. With more than $50 million in funding since 1977, the Olin Foundation subsidized the movement's more widespread institutionalization, from its original outposts at the University of Miami, George Mason University, and the University of Chicago, to Harvard, Yale, Stanford, the University of Michigan, and Georgetown. Significant for more than its immediate business applications—for which it drew corporate as well as foundation support—this movement would subsequently provide the basic legal doctrine for deregulatory shifts in antitrust, environmental, and other areas of law and policy.

Still other distinctive features of the conservative philanthropic movement would be seen in the patterning of Olin Foundation grants, with their emphasis on long-term institutional investments in conservative think tanks and in public conversation-changing books aimed at undermining liberal assumptions on issues ranging from welfare, affirmative action, public education, and crime policy, to "tort reform." In its support for such associational, movement-building vehicles as the Federalist Society, a host of legal and legislative training institutes, and publications including Irving Kristol's Cold War revivalist foreign policy journal *The National Interest,* Olin was ensuring that the ideas the foundation was funding would be widely circulated to the people who would put them into practice. In these and other ways, the foundations keyed themselves to the needs and the momentum of the conservative movement—and never more so than in its transition from opposition to establishment mainstream. There was a sense, as Michael Joyce put it in 1981, that Ronald Reagan's election was a "kind of fruition" for the "ideals [they had] been supporting." Key to this sense of triumph, according to neoconservative scholar and philanthropoid Leslie Lenkowsky, was the devotion that united all the new breed of foundations—to the "future well-being of the system that gave rise to the foundations in the first place, namely capitalism."[27]

But of all the practices that distinguished Olin and the other conservative foundations, none says more about the significance of the 1970s than that highlighted by Olin Foundation Executive Director

James Piereson in a 2004 speech before one of the movement's sig-nature creations: the State Policy Network (SPN), a web of state-level research and funding organizations devoted to conservative policy advocacy. Established in 1992 as a kind of trade and profes-sional organization for such free-market think tanks as the Heart-land Institute (Illinois), the Goldwater Institute (Arizona), the Texas Public Policy Foundation, and the Pacific Research Institute, SPN currently boasts membership in all but a handful of states. Piereson took the opportunity to confirm what for many in attendance was hardly cause for celebration. Honoring the wishes of its founder, the John M. Olin Foundation would soon be closing its doors. It was in something of a backhanded compliment to the movement's old nemesis, however, that Piereson underscored the significance of the changes set in motion during the 1970s. The strategy that had helped conservatives "turn the tables" on the liberal establishment was bor-rowed from none other than McGeorge Bundy's Ford Foundation, which, in Piereson's eyes, as in the eyes of those original car dealer-ship boycotters, had been using its links to a network of elite institu-tions and intellectuals to make the demands of the civil rights, feminist, environmentalist, welfare rights, and associated movements a permanent part of American political culture and governance. Here, ultimately, was how the financiers of counterrevolution had most fully contributed to conservatism's success. In a strategy adapted from the liberal opposition, they brought their own move-ment from protest to politics.[28]

PART TWO

THE BATTLE OVER
POLICIES AND POLITICS

CHAPTER 9

The White Ethnic Strategy

THOMAS J. SUGRUE

JOHN D. SKRENTNY

In July 1970, Richard Nixon summoned Rocco Siciliano to the White House. A deputy secretary in the Commerce Department and veteran of the Eisenhower administration, Siciliano had extensive experience in personnel management issues. But his professional expertise had nothing to do with this visit. What made the Utah Republican a compelling visitor to the Oval Office was his Italian heritage. "When I arrived," he recalled, "[Secretary of Transportation and Italian American] John Volpe was there . . . The president talked about minorities—about Italian-Americans and other ethnic groups. He wanted to know what we could do to get them more involved, to get them to understand what his administration was all about." Nixon had discovered "white ethnics"— and believed that their support was essential to his political future. Desperate for advice, he sought the counsel of ethnics in his own administration. "It was a strange, strange meeting; he was quite agitated," Siciliano told interviewers years later.[1]

Nixon was not alone in the discovery of white ethnicity. "PIGS— Poles, Italians, Greeks, and Slavs"; "unmeltable ethnics"; and "white ethnics" burst onto the American scene in the early 1970s, grabbing

171

the attention of politicians, policymakers, pundits, and activists. These second- and third-generation descendants of European immigrants became the embodiment of Nixon's "Silent Majority," a group alienated by the civil rights movement, betrayed by liberals, and simmering with "middle-class rage." Of course, ethnic political activity was hardly new. Ethnicity-based organizations flourished at the turn of the century, mostly as mutual benefit associations.[2] Ethnic lobbying on foreign policy issues had a long tradition as well.[3] Both the Democratic and the Republican parties had long-standing "nationalities" divisions that focused primarily on international issues of interest to "hyphenated" Americans. By the late 1960s and 1970s, however, politicians were refashioning their political strategies to capture northern urban Catholics disaffected with liberalism. New York created an affirmative action program for Italian Americans. Presidential candidate Jimmy Carter awkwardly pledged to preserve the "ethnic purity" of white urban neighborhoods. Cities sponsored ethnic festivals, drawing white suburbanites to downtown parks where they could sample kielbasas or corned beef and cabbage, listen to traditional music, and buy "Kiss Me I'm Lithuanian" (or Irish or Croatian or Polish) lapel pins. Ethnicity also pervaded popular culture, from the remarkable success of Mario Puzo's *The Godfather* to commercials that featured "Anthony," an Italian boy rushing to his immigrant mother on Wednesday, "Prince Spaghetti Day." What observers called the "ethnic revival" also attracted public intellectuals, journalists, and community leaders who worked to "conserve" ethnic neighborhoods, resurrect long-forgotten ethnic cultures and customs, and create ethnic studies programs.[4]

How was it that ethnic identities took on new importance in 1970s-era America? In the years following World War II, most social scientists concurred that ethnicity was disappearing in the United States, through the inexorable process of "assimilation." Schoolchildren learned that America's "melting pot" had amalgamated European immigrants of all varieties, although ethnic affiliations remained salient in urban politics and especially in structuring some sectors of the labor market.[5] "Foreign" Americans were absorbed into mainstream political institutions, as the flow of newcomers from southern and eastern Europe was stanched by restrictive immigration policies, and as linguistic ties to the "old country" weakened. Formerly tight-knit ethnic communities dissolved under the pressure of suburbanization. The number of foreign-language newspapers plummeted as their readers aged and the younger generation lacked the language skills and interest to sustain them. National parishes— nonterritorial congregations established by the Catholic Church to cater to immigrants—struggled for survival, their pews empty and their communicants graying. Rates of intermarriage across ethnic— and increasingly religious—lines skyrocketed. And in metropolitan areas, where black–white racial differences were inscribed on the landscape, interethnic differences paled in contrast to the still-bright color line. By the early 1970s, observable ethnic differences—if not ethnic identities—appeared to have broken down.[6]

The thinning of ethnic affiliations came at a moment when a wide range of Americans challenged what they saw as the blandness, conformity, and homogeneity of postwar mass culture. The ethnic revival became a sort of counterculture—an attempt to restore "authenticity" into a soulless modernity. "Many Americans who try to live in the modern, American suburban lifestyle," wrote Michael Novak, an influential commentator on ethnicity, "are restless and unsatisfied. All sorts of materials in their psyche are suppressed." Novak gave voice to a quest for authenticity, tradition, and family among second- and third-generation immigrants who had attenuated connections to the communal world of their parents and grandparents. Some cultural entrepreneurs, mostly entertainers and restaurateurs, capitalized on a new interest in "authentic" ethnic music, dance, or food. But in a society where shopping malls were rapidly supplanting neighborhood shopping districts, where chain stores drove out "mom-and-pop" establishments, and where

Top 10 radio and three-network television drew audiences away from foreign-language broadcasting, immigrant culture remained on the margins. Ethnicity was but one option in a menu of cultural choices available to Americans in the cultural marketplace of the 1970s.[7]

Ethnicity in the 1970s was, to a great extent, performative. People asserted their ties to their Old World ancestors by eating pierogies, dancing *céilí,* or serving seven fishes on Christmas Eve. But the revival of ethnicity was much more than a search for authenticity through cultural expression. It was also the expression of political aspirations and grievances. It reflected the economic, political, and social insecurity of Americans, especially those whose parents were working-class European immigrants, whose hold on middle-class status was precarious. It was the product of the rapidly shifting terrain of race relations in the United States, particularly of challenges to the very legitimacy of the racial hierarchy, of blackness and whiteness, that had formed the politics of European immigrants, their children, and grandchildren in the critical years between the New Deal and the 1960s. The ethnic revival provided Americans of European descent a new vehicle for asserting citizenship rights at a moment when it grew increasingly illegitimate to make claims on the state on the basis of whiteness. Elected officials and policymakers responded to ethnic insecurities and claims—but in ways that were largely symbolic. White ethnics achieved token, discursive political attention but ultimately not policy recognition.[8]

The ethnic revival took the form that it did in response to black militancy and the government policies that were developing in its wake. Although whites, including ethnics, supported (at least by the measure of public opinion surveys) laws that forbade racial discrimination, they resented remedial and race-conscious public policies as "special treatment" for blacks. Whites reacted to affirmative action, calls for educational desegregation, and demands for open housing with a newfound assertion of their own group identities.

Political elites sometimes reinforced the new ethnicity. Political consultants, attuned to the fragmentation of the traditional Democratic coalition, looked for creative ways to win the allegiance of disaffected voters. Ethnicity became politically salient at a moment when both parties were struggling to appeal to white working-class voters. New polling and surveying techniques made it possible to identify sub-niches of the population and to target them specifically, through symbolic gestures of inclusion and affiliation.

That the ethnic revival occurred on the Nixon administration's watch played a crucial role in the reconfiguration of Republican politics in the 1970s and beyond. Nixon and his fellow Republicans took advantage of resurgent ethnicity but directed it toward conservative ends. In doing so, they fashioned an atavistic cultural populism that stoked ethnic and middle- and lower-class white insecurities regarding race, morality, and patriotism. In the hands of Republican operatives, white ethnicity was a system of values that hearkened back to "tradition"—a romanticized past of hard work, discipline, well-defined gender roles, and tight-knit families. The GOP appealed to ethnic anxieties about blacks by supporting rollbacks of new civil rights policies, or by pushing "law and order" instead of helping ethnics or all groups improve their class positions. By appointing Poles and Italians to visible offices and talking often of white ethnic pride, the Nixon administration sought to shake the GOP's image as the party of country club WASPs; likewise, by campaigning in ethnic neighborhoods, Nixon hoped to woo those voters who saw the Democrats as the party of acid, amnesty, and abortion. Moreover, activists and intellectuals joined the government leaders in stoking ethnic identity as they sought to understand, steer, or augment the politically potent and potentially destructive consciousness. Even if the ethnic revival proved to be ephemeral in many respects, it was both cause and symptom of the political, cultural, and economic fragmentation of the United States that was full-blown by 1980.

Nothing was more formative to the revival of ethnicity than the legacy of the black freedom struggle in the 1960s. The civil rights movement destabilized the racial categories that had, to a great extent, subsumed ethnic identities in the period since the Great Depression. One of the most salient features of the New Deal and World War II was that political and economic institutions had incorporated European ethnics into an ostensibly universalistic but deeply racialized political order. New Deal housing programs allowed working-class ethnics—many of whom had aspired to single-family homeownership—the resources to purchase their own houses. In the process, however, federal policies divided cities into racial territories, places where white identities were reinforced by mortgage programs that deemed blacks to be actuarially unsound. Military service during World War II brought together Americans of a wide range of ethnic backgrounds (with the exception of blacks, who were segregated into their own units). Suspicions about the loyalty of Slavs, Italians, and Jews to the American state withered on the battlefield. On the home front, progress was slower, and discrimination against ethnics was strong enough that Roosevelt urged the nation's employers to give them equal opportunities. At war's end, the GI Bill—and its educational, housing, and medical benefits that were distributed unevenly by race—brought the sons of immigrants into the ranks of fully entitled citizens. Through the 1920s, southern and eastern European immigrants struggled to various degrees with the burden of racial inferiority. By the 1940s, except in restrictive immigration laws still on the books, the American state identified them as white. Ethnics also identified themselves as white Americans, and interethnic differences were muted by the fact that they were not part of the most significant, visible, and subordinated "race"—African Americans.[9]

The inscription of race onto the institutions of the New Deal and World War II state did not, however, go uncontested. Throughout the country—and especially in the northern cities that were home to most European immigrants and their children—increasingly assertive civil rights organizations challenged segregation in housing, employment, and education. By the 1960s, those struggles had borne some fruit: African Americans, in small numbers, peppered northern urban institutions, gained prominence in urban politics, and became increasingly assertive in the workplace. One of the most important contributions of the black freedom struggle—still terribly incomplete by the 1970s—was its delegitimation of overt racist language. By the early 1960s, the vast majority of northern whites professed color-blindness, at least when questioned by pollsters and survey researchers. They supported, at least nominally, the goals of racial integration in housing, employment, and education. The rhetoric of colorblindness—which would survive, even as racial inequalities persisted in nearly every arena of American life—was a crucial legacy. To be sure, racist language persisted, especially in everyday conversations in white working-class communities. But it lost much of its political force. Media portrayals of angry, irrational whites—of overt race hatred—rendered race-based claims on citizenship, challenges to the state, and critiques of civil rights much less potent than they had been even twenty years earlier. Northern whites would have to find another political language to assert their interests.[10]

The rise of black nationalism further shifted the terms of the debate. Northern urban whites—the group that would soon be redefined as "white ethnics"—responded to African Americans who asserted their group identity by using their common "blackness" as a vehicle for creating political solidarity and for making claims on local, state, and federal governments. In the most important early treatise on black power, Stokely Carmichael and Charles V. Hamilton described black political identity as a version of ethnic pluralism. *"Before a group can enter the open society, it must close ranks. By this we mean group solidarity is necessary before a group can operate effectively from a bargaining position of strength in a pluralistic society."*[11]

By the end of the 1960s, the decline in the political efficacy of the language of whiteness combined with a growing awareness of the power of group-specific identity as a tool of political mobilization and claim making. If whites—no longer able to make claims on the state in terms of their race—were to be recognized politically, they would have to fashion a new group identity, or identities. The rise of white ethnics—the assertion of (especially) Italian, Polish, and other southern or eastern European identities—was at heart the politics of recognition. "We spend millions and the Negroes get everything," stated Paul Deac, head of the National Confederation of American Ethnic Groups, "and we get nothing."[12] John Pankuch of the National Slovak Society believed that "if the ethnics begin to speak as one voice maybe somebody will pay attention to us as well as them."[13] But in the political climate of the civil rights and black power eras, ethnicity was necessary but not sufficient. For the category of "white ethnic" to sustain political claims, its members needed to draw analogies between their condition and that of officially recognized minorities, most notably African Americans. They would need to recover two histories—one of the group's past triumphs, a filiopietistic ethnic past to forge a common ethnic identity to supplant the broad category of whiteness, and the other a history of group oppression, of shared suffering, that would allow them to gain political recognition on the same terms then enjoyed by blacks—as well as a widening circle of other aggrieved minorities, including Latinos, American Indians, and Asian Americans. As a young Barbara Mikulski wrote in a *New York Times* op-ed, "We called ourselves Americans. We were called 'wop,' 'polack' and 'hunky.'"[14]

But a white ethnic politics driven by economic, social, and cultural insecurities could move in different directions. One path started with an ethnic past but foresaw a less-ethnic future, and was committed to conserving present positions and fending off encroachments and threats from a variety of sources. White ethnics, even those who were economically successful, narrated family histories of discrimination and poverty overcome through individual initiative. Their upward mobility was recent, hard-won, but still precarious. In this context, they resented government efforts to help blacks. "If I hear the four hundred years of slavery bit one more time," complained a blue-collar white to journalist Pete Hamill, "I'll go outta my mind." Just as ethnics established themselves in American society as a result of perseverance, hard work, and discipline, so too should blacks lift themselves up, without the aid of special pleading or special preferences. Ethnic difference became salient in a politics that sought to erase black militant or government recognition of difference. This politics used appeals to simple fairness and equality: we are not that different from them, so why should they receive government help when we did not, and why should we have to pay in the form of "reverse discrimination" for them to succeed—or worse, leapfrog—over us?[15]

The issue of crime also contributed to a defensiveness among urban ethnics. Media images of black criminality along with rising murder and theft rates stoked fears that the social order was unraveling. Urban elected officials, especially mayors like Sam Yorty (Los Angeles), Richard Daley (Chicago), Roman Gribbs (Detroit), and Frank Rizzo (Philadelphia) denounced urban disorder and called for expanded police power. Fearful of an unraveling social order, many ethnics enthusiastically joined the call for law and order—or took matters into their own hands. Popular Newark vigilante Tony Imperiale bragged to *Newsweek* magazine: "We came down here one night with eight guys and kicked the crap outa [*sic*] 22 junkies."[16]

The other path, taken by many white ethnic leaders, began with similar assumptions but ended in a different place. With an emphasis on the poorer urban ethnics, these progressive leaders sought common cause with other minority groups and deployed an assertive political language of difference. They responded to new political incentives for Americans to assert nonwhite identities by invoking a narrative of ongoing victimization. Rather than fight special efforts to help racial minorities, these ethnics wanted to join them. Why should blacks be singled out as beneficiaries of affirmative action and targeted policies when Poles, Italians, and Greeks were themselves economically marginalized by ongoing discrimination in favor of Anglo-Saxon Protestants? An Irish American made a similar argument. "In Boston, they had signs like 'No Irish Need Apply' on the jobs. So why don't the American government compensate me?"[17] In this politics, ethnicity was front and center, along with class and status. Both versions of ethnic politics appealed more to urban than to suburban ethnics; they gave voice to the insecurities of those who were "left behind" and living in the closest proximity to blacks.

The politics of ethnic resentment found its most forceful interlocutor in the Slovak American theologian and philosopher Michael Novak, then on a political odyssey that would lead him from the Catholic Left to the American Enterprise Institute. In his 1972 best seller, *The Rise of the Unmeltable Ethnics,* Novak offered a populist defense of white ethnics against charges of racism. The white Chicagoans who threw rocks at the Reverend Martin Luther King Jr. and the open-housing advocates were not, at heart, racists. Their anger grew from their insecurity and, above all, their abhorrence of the Protestant perfectionism of the marchers. The "tactic of demonstration is inherently WASP and inherently offensive to ethnic peoples," he argued. "A protest march is a moralizing finger jabbing into a neighborhood sick to death of being moralized." In a theme that a whole generation of academics would repeat in their explanations of white "backlash," Novak argued that ethnics did not despise blacks so much as the elitist, suburban liberals who were supposedly the architects of busing, affirmative action, and the War on Poverty. At the core of Novak's argument was an assertion of the primal racial innocence of "whites" from southern and eastern Europe. "Racists? Our ancestors owned no slaves. Most of us ceased being serfs only in the last two hundred years."[18]

Some advocates of an assertive ethnic politics rejected Novak's defensive posture toward race. They argued for a "positive" notion of ethnic identity as a counterweight to racial defensiveness. A prominent exponent of this approach was Irving M. Levine, the urban affairs director of the American Jewish Committee. In late 1967, Levine launched the National Project on Ethnic America (NPEA). His goal was to wean white ethnics from "a strictly negative anti-black agenda" and to instead push them to be "conscious of their own realities." This required "a new breed of ethnic leaders . . . who are as visible as the demagogues trying to exploit ethnic fears."[19] In the late 1960s, NPEA sponsored a series of conferences on "the problems of white ethnic America" and "consultations on ethnicity" that attracted ethnic community organizers, academics, unionists, and religious activists. While encouraging black–white cooperation, Levine also supported programs to enhance ethnic consciousness and pride, including ethnic studies in the schools and political activism to improve ethnic neighborhoods. The Ford Foundation, a major benefactor of nonwhite political and legal mobilization (see Chapter 8 in this volume), recognized Levine's efforts with a $260,000 grant in 1971.[20]

Taking yet another tack was prominent Catholic cleric and activist Monsignor Geno Baroni. An Italian American from a blue-collar town in central Pennsylvania, Baroni shared Novak's sympathy with what he called the "economically, culturally, socially, and politically alienated and disillusioned" white ethnics.[21] But Baroni did not agree with Novak's critique of civil rights activism. He had cut his teeth as a supporter of the black freedom struggle and, in 1963, had helped organize Catholic support for the March on Washington. By the end of the 1960s, Baroni sympathized with the black power insurgency and made a case that white ethnics should—like black nationalists—organize among themselves.

In his view, the creation of strong urban communities—both black and white, respectful of their differences but aware of their common economic plight—was the only possible antidote to rising racial tensions.[22] Public recognition of white ethnic groups would bring harmony and not division. The Ford Foundation helped Baroni establish the National Center for Urban Ethnic Affairs at the Catholic University of America. The Ethnic Affairs Center, like the NPEA, held conferences with academics, union heads, and religious officials and local ethnic leaders. Baroni would go onto work for the Carter administration, where as a domestic policy staff member he pushed for urban policies to "conserve" ethnic neighborhoods that were under siege by urban renewal, disinvestment, and depopulation.[23]

While Novak defended ethnics against charges of racism and Levine and Baroni tried to diffuse racial conflict, other ethnic leaders analogized the economic plight of working-class whites with that of African Americans and demanded inclusion in federal, state, and local civil rights programs. Activists for Italians and Poles led tightly focused lobbying efforts to gain inclusion in federal affirmative action regulations. An early provocation was a reporting form, developed in the final months of 1965, that the new Equal Employment Opportunity Commission (EEOC) required of employers. The EEOC's list of America's minorities (using language common at the time) included only "Negroes," "Spanish Americans," "Orientals," and "American Indians." White ethnic leaders challenged the legitimacy of the categories. For example, Vincent Trapani, state president of the New York Federation of Italian-American Democratic Organizations, complained that EEOC statistics "will disclose discrimination *but not for all minority groups*" (emphasis in original) and that "It is obvious that minority groups such as Italian-Americans, Polish-Americans, German-Americans, Irish-Americans, Jewish-Americans and others, will not be revealed." Avoiding racial claims but responding to the new incentives being created by civil rights policy, Trapani argued that white ethnics had suffered discrimination and that it was illegal for the EEOC to exclude national origin, which was, after all, a protected category under Title VII of the Civil Rights Act of 1964.[24]

The Polish American Congress (PAC) collected employment data by ethnicity in an attempt to force the government to recognize Poles as an official minority. Most active in Chicago, PAC-sponsored studies in 1969, 1972, and 1977 showed that Polish Americans were statistically underrepresented in state and federal government jobs.[25] PAC's Illinois Division and the Joint Civic Committee of Italian-Americans commissioned a study on the executive representation of Poles, Italians, Latinos, and blacks in Chicago's 106 largest corporations. The data supported their claim that Italians and Poles were underrepresented on corporate boards and executive positions—even if their numbers were still better than those of Latinos and blacks. Poles made up 6.9 percent of the area population, but only 0.3 percent of the corporate directors and 0.7 percent of the officers. "Latins" were 4.4 percent of the population, but 0.1 percent of the directors and officers. Fifty-five of the 106 corporations did not have any Poles, Italians, blacks, or Latinos as directors or officers. Ninety-seven had no Polish officers, while 104 had no Latinos. Italians fared only somewhat better.[26]

Through the 1970s and early 1980s, white ethnic groups continued to complain of underrepresentation in the professions, the upper ranks of corporate America, and institutions of higher education. When the Supreme Court considered the legality of affirmative action in higher education in the *Bakke* case, PAC lawyer Leonard Walentynowicz wrote an amicus brief arguing that the UC-Davis Medical School plan should be struck down until justified with a study that documented ethnic groups' experiences of discrimination and underrepresentation. Walentynowicz voiced a common ethnic grievance: "Why are 'Whites' who never practiced discrimination, but fought for and championed equality, and who themselves suffered discrimination obliged to continue to suffer simply because other whites practiced racial discrimination?"[27] Walentynowicz argued that the category "white" should be broken down, to emphasize the distinct, unequal experiences of different ethnic groups. Italian and Polish leaders also pressured Weldon J. Rougeau, the head of the Office of Federal Contract Compliance, to include their groups in federal affirmative action regulations for government contractors, so that they could burst through glass ceilings limiting their employment.[28] Other organizations representing Catholics, Poles, and Italian Americans pressed their claims for full minority status in hearings before the U.S. Commission on Civil Rights.[29]

The failures of white ethnic activists to persuade the federal government to include eastern and southern European ethnics in affirmative action regulations did not indicate a lack of interest in these groups inside the Beltway. Polish American Democrat Roman Pucinski, who represented a mostly blue-collar Chicago district, complained of the EEOC's failure to count white ethnics and argued that the policy should be scrapped or revised to include them.[30] Other Democrats and also Republicans saw political gains in siding with white ethnics. For example, in 1974 House hearings on civil rights in higher education, Jack Kemp (R-NY) joined New York Democrat Mario Biaggi in demanding that EEOC chair John Powell Jr. explain the exclusion of Italian and Polish Americans from federal civil rights efforts.[31] Even Conservative Party senator James Buckley of New York argued that the federal government should include white ethnics in affirmative action programs or eliminate affirmative action altogether.[32]

Most congressional efforts to win ethnic support were, however, less controversial than affirmative action. They emphasized programs to enhance group pride and to build self-esteem, especially among youth. Chicago's Pucinski spearheaded a drive to create "ethnic heritage centers" where all Americans, white and nonwhite,

could learn about and celebrate ethnic ancestry. Pucinski pulled together a multiethnic group of cosponsors for his bill, including
African American John Conyers (D-MI), Mexican American Edward Roybal (D-NM), and Japanese American Spark Matsunaga
(D-HI).[33] "This Nation thrives on a deep sense of ethnic community," argued Pucinski. "We have oversold the value of homoge-
nization, sacrificing the diversity of our pluralistic society for the
sake of uniformity." Echoing arguments made on behalf of Latinos
and bilingual education (which he also supported), Pucinski contended that "many of our ethnic groups have developed a profound
sense of cultural inferiority" while others "have even totally for-
saken their ethnic bonds." "The most serious casualties of this
quasi-cultural obliteration have been the young," Pucinski explained, who were the " 'Forgotten Young Americans,' with no
feeling of belonging in our heterogeneous society." Ethnic Heritage
Studies Centers would develop curriculum materials on a particular
group's "history, geography, society, literature, art, music, language, drama, economy and general culture" and "contributions to
American heritage." In this way, "Every one of the 51.5 million
students in the primary grades and high school could study, in
depth, about the ethnic culture of his own family and forefathers,
and about their contributions to the American way of life." Senator
Richard Schweiker (R-PA) introduced a similar bill in the Senate in
January 1971.[34]

   After proponents dropped the idea of creating costly centers,
Congress moved quickly to pass a more symbolic law. The 1972
Ethnic Heritage Studies Act authorized grants to create ethnic heritage programs for elementary and secondary schools under the
guidance of a National Advisory Council on Ethnic Heritage Studies.[35] The program was small: Congress gave it an $8.3 million ap-
propriation for four years—despite strong demand for funds (the
Office of Education received more than 1,000 proposals, at least
one from every state, from more than fifty different ethnic groups

for only forty-two available grants).[36] In May 1976, Andrew Greeley grumbled that the program was "tokenism with a vengeance, a sop thrown at the ethnics to keep them quiet."[37]

The claims of the ethnic intellectuals and activists found a hearing in a most unexpected place—among the largely Protestant circle of advisers around President Richard M. Nixon, himself a Quaker from Southern California. Nixon and his aides were keenly attuned to the increasingly fractured political world of the late 1960s and early 1970s. Nixon and his closest aides had no deep sympathy for ethnic revival: its cultural forms were foreign to them. (Michael Novak snidely remarked that "the Nixon White House could be a cabinet for Kaiser Wilhelm: Kissinger, Haldeman, Erlichmann, Ziegler, Schultz [sic]."[38] But Nixon officials saw the possibility of real political gain by exploiting divisions in the Democratic Party. Nearly every group of voters was available for the plucking. The GOP would woo southern whites, who were opposed to civil rights, through an embrace of states' rights and anti-busing rhetoric. A combination of family-values conservatism and support for bilingual education would win Hispanics' allegiance. Even black power advocates might be seduced by Nixon's embrace of "black capitalism" and his support for race-targeted government contracts and small business loans.[39]

Of all the groups that the Nixon administration hoped to capture, the most important were northern blue-collar whites, especially those who lived in states like New York, Illinois, Ohio, Indiana, and Michigan, whose swing votes could be decisive in close elections. In January 1970, Nixon directed chief of staff H. R. Haldeman to build "our own new coalition based on [the] Silent Majority [of supporters of Nixon's Vietnam policy], blue collar, Catholic, Poles, Italians, and Irish."[40] Speechwriter and adviser Patrick Buchanan argued that "Our future is the Democratic working man, Southern Protestant, and Northern Catholic—and ethnic" and that the White House personnel office needs "an 'ethnic' man" to be "on the lookout for Italians and Poles and Irish Democrats who stood with the President, and who are the backbone of this new majority."[41] In a review of several articles on the white backlash, aide Harry S. Dent wrote that "we must realize that old political loyalties have been dissolved by the racial situation and that we have an unprecedented opportunity to garner votes in large blocks. To capitalize on this opportunity we need a carefully conceived 'master plan' for the Administration to implement."[42] Exactly which groups, beyond the ubiquitous Italians and Poles, were to be included in the category of ethnics was anybody's guess. Nixon himself sometimes included Mexican Americans in his list.[43] Moreover, Nixon's political team used other pseudo-demographic categories in which ethnics were prominent constituents. Ethnics held a welter of interchangeable, if not wholly equivalent identities: they were at once "Middle Americans," Catholics, union members, and working class. Which of those identities would gain the most political traction? The question generated intense discussion in Nixon's inner circle.

Labor secretary George Shultz was a prominent advocate of the class component to ethnic appeals. In this view, ethnics were mostly lower-middle class to working class and often struggling to make ends meet. In response to an article by Pete Hamill in *New York* magazine on "The Revolt of the Lower-White Middle Class" and a *New York Times* article on how Roman Catholic voters tended to vote against the candidates who were identified as sympathetic to minority groups, Shultz told Nixon, "They are immigrants, or sons of immigrants, and feel insecure about their own place in the mainstream of American society. They tend to live in neighborhoods that the blacks are most likely to move into, and whose schools blacks' children might attend. They sometimes have jobs that they feel blacks aspire to attain, and they get wages that are only slightly above liberal states' welfare payments. They suffer a real sense of 'compression' on both the economic and social scales."[44]

Shultz may have emphasized working-class issues, but he was not about to embrace pro-union liberalism. There were limits to the Nixon administration's political opportunism. The Republican Party was in flux during the Nixon years, cleaved by tensions between the moderate Rockefeller wing, whose most articulate members came from the "Northeast establishment," and the insurgent Goldwater/Reagan wing, which built a constituency in the Sunbelt among small entrepreneurs, suburban workers in the military-industrial complex, and libertarian ranchers and farmers. For all of their differences, both groups shared skepticism toward organized labor. The Nixon administration—which famously suspended the Davis-Bacon Act for a period in 1971—was not about to practice a politics of social class that emphasized sharing of economic power.[45]

To target white ethnics—but without reinvigorating unionism—Shultz pushed two policies. The first, though lacking an explicit ethnic component, was implementation of the so-called Rosow Report. Shultz had directed assistant secretary Jerome Rosow to study the problems of low-income workers. Rosow's report and recommendations received the backing of several high-ranking officials, including chief of staff Bob Haldeman, domestic policy adviser John Ehrlichman, resident liberal Daniel Patrick Moynihan, and chief architect of the "southern strategy" Harry Dent. Nixon chose not to act on the report, however, and the reasons seemed clear enough: Rosow offered a blueprint for an expanded welfare state. He recommended improved access to education, funds for childcare, tax reform, new workplace regulations, and having government act as the "model employer." More generally, Rosow called for more status to blue-collar work and sounded a note of empathy with white ethnic insecurity: "our system of values signals that something is very wrong when conscientious, able, and hardworking people cannot make it."[46]

The other major policy backed by Shultz similarly had a class component but also emphasized the progressive or assertive strand of ethnic politics. This was the Labor Department's December 1971 proposed regulation that would extend affirmative action to "members of various religious groups, primarily Jews and Catholics, and members of certain ethnic groups, primarily of Eastern, Middle, and Southern European ancestry, such as Italians, Greeks, and Slavic groups." This proposal would complete the expansion of the Labor Department's affirmative action policy, which began in 1969 with the "Philadelphia Plan," requiring hiring goals and timetables for blacks, Latinos, Asians, and American Indians in the Philadelphia construction industry. In 1970, "Order #4" made affirmative action mandatory for all government contracts that were over $50,000 and employed fifty or more people, and "Revised Order #4" added women to the list of minorities.[47] The white ethnic version was weaker than the Labor Department's affirmative action regulations for other minorities—it lacked the hiring goals and timetables, was limited to management jobs, and depended on complaints from white ethnics or community groups to be enforced. Still, the proposed regulations were similarly directed at government contractors and called for a remedy to the "underutilization" of these ethnic groups if contractors were found to be discriminating against them.[48] However feeble the regulations, business leaders and some White House staffers complained that white ethnics did not deserve government help and, in any case, would be difficult to count. The final version of the regulations was watered down to the extent that they became meaningless.[49]

Political advisers like Dent, Haldeman, and especially Charles Colson were far more influential than Rosow and Shultz in shaping Nixon's ethnic strategy. Joining Colson was a team of aides, including Michael P. Balzano, an Italian American and former sanitation worker, whose blue-collar ethnic pedigree lent some authenticity to the efforts.[50] Their plans for attracting ethnic voters gestured to the assertive and progressive strand of ethnic politics, but took a conservative path that emphasized ethnics' social and cultural insecurities. They emphasized strategies to meet what Colson called "our immediate objective," namely, "to keep Labor split away from the Democrats" in service of the "long range target . . . to make them part of our 'New Majority.'" To that end, Nixon asked Haldeman and Colson to devise a plan for "developing our strength with the labor unions and union leadership" by "picking them off one by one." Nixon officials reached out to conservative unionists like Teddy Gleason of the Longshoremen ("on a patriotism kick second to none") and forged ties with unions that represented culturally conservative workers, including "all of the construction trades . . . clearly our most fertile ground." The administration even saw the United Auto Workers (UAW)—longtime Republican foes—as ripe for the picking. Colson wrote off UAW president Leonard Woodcock as "a socialist who will never support us." But he was hopeful in making inroads among the UAW rank and file, who were "among the most conservative in the union movement," and among local UAW leaders, "who are strongly patriotic, anti-student, and keenly aware of the race question."[51]

Ethnic voters, stated a white ethnic political strategy report from Colson's shop, represented a "tremendous resource." One key to winning their support, the report argued, was challenging the Department of Housing and Urban Development's "dispersal" housing policy—that is, efforts to use scattered-site subsidized housing to integrate white neighborhoods. The romantic depiction of tight-knit ethnic neighborhoods under siege provided a compelling—and politically palatable—justification for opposing residential integration. Another strategy sought to tap into ethnic fears of crime and general social disorder. The report argued that "the President's strong 'law-and-order' position, and the actions that have followed it, should be particularly popular among ethnics," adding that "Of special note are the President's stands against racial strife, student unrest, busing, pornography, and drug abuse and the achievements he has made in each of these areas."[52] Colson and his aides also

called for sustained high-profile efforts to win the ethnic vote—
for example, through support of the inexpensive ethnic heritage
programs.[53]

But Nixon avoided policies that affirmed white ethnicity. The
ethnic heritage programs and the Labor Department's affirmative
action for white ethnics withered from lack of White House support. Nixon's appeal to white ethnics ultimately resulted in a series
of cost-free symbols of ethnic appreciation and gross appeals to
ethnic insecurities and resentments.[54] Instead of ethnic affirmative
action and ethnic heritage centers, Nixon issued a National Heritage Day Proclamation and made speeches celebrating the contributions of immigrants and their children to America. Nixon, his
aides, and the First Lady made appearances at white ethnic events
and parades. At one Italian American picnic, Nixon told the approving crowd that he felt like he had Italian blood. During the
1972 campaign, Nixon shored up ethnic support by appearing at
the newly opened Museum of Immigration on Liberty Island. And
with great fanfare and after intense lobbying from ethnic leaders
as well as from Laszlo Pasztor, head of the Republican National
Committee's Nationalities Division, the White House appointed
ethnic Americans (like Rocco Siciliano and Michael Balzano) to
mostly minor positions and dispatched them to various ethnic
gatherings and celebrations.[55] Instead of implementing the Rosow
Report, the Nixon team continued to appeal to the cultural conservatism of parts of the urban working class by building personal
relationships with union leaders, all the while cutting spending on
federal contracts, implementing anti-union policies in the Department of Labor, and presiding over trade policies that accelerated
the long process of capital flight from the cities that were home to
most working-class ethnics.[56] Nixon officials appeased white
working-class discontent by embracing law-and-order rhetoric,
rolling back many Great Society programs, and nationalizing the
southern strategy—by standing firm against open housing, school

desegregation, and even the program that Nixon's administration had helped create, affirmative action.[57]

The Nixon strategy succeeded in bringing many northern urban workers into the Republican fold. In the end, the Nixon administration recognized and legitimated the category of white ethnic but in rhetoric rather than in policy. Instead, his policies and rhetoric directed ethnicity down the narrow channel of the politics of resentment. Rather than bringing ethnics into the civil rights coalition by including them in affirmative action programs, Nixon officials capitalized on white ethnics' animosity over the "special treatment" of blacks. Rather than investing in urban neighborhoods, Baroni-style, they stoked white fears of busing, housing integration, and crime, while disinvesting from black and white communities alike. Rather than developing labor and trade policies to stabilize wages and provide for greater employment security for the working class (black and white), they reinforced the redefinition of white working-class identities in ways that fostered a sense of cultural difference. The result of the Nixon efforts, for the creation of a conservative majority, was smashingly successful. But for the working class—white and black—whose incomes have stagnated and whose communities have remained largely separate and hostile in the period since the 1970s, it was a missed opportunity.

CHAPTER 10

The Conservative Struggle
and the Energy Crisis

MEG JACOBS

The energy crisis of the 1970s marked the end of an era—the end of the post–World War II prosperity, the end of the country's obsession with the big gas-guzzling cars of the 1950s and 1960s, and the end of America's standing as an economic superpower. During the Arab boycott of 1973–1974, the Organization of Petroleum Exporting Countries (OPEC) cut oil shipments to the United States and raised prices sharply. Prices at the pump doubled and then tripled. Gas lines that snaked for miles appeared as a constant reminder of what seemed like the nation's imminent decay and decline. A second oil shock struck in 1979 in the wake of the Iranian Revolution, once again making Americans feel vulnerable. In his Pulitzer Prize–winning novel *Rabbit Is Rich,* written at the end of this tumultuous decade, John Updike captured the doomsday mentality. Published in 1979, the novel begins: "Running out of gas, *apocalyptic fear* Rabbit Angstrom thinks . . . The people out there are getting frantic, they know the great American ride is ending."[1]

To the nation's young conservative policymakers, just assuming positions of influence inside Washington, the energy crisis, as it turned out, marked an important beginning. For these anti-government

193

reformers, the energy crisis posed a serious challenge: how to govern, especially amid a crisis, without increasing the power of the federal government. Up until the 1970s, almost all modern crises, from war to depression to inflation to labor unrest to civil rights, increased the power, prestige, and regulatory authority of the federal government. The response of many Americans to the energy crisis was in favor of more government, not less.

But conservatives, who came to power under Richard Nixon, sought to fight against the impulse for a big government solution to a national crisis. A new breed of Washington policymakers and intellectuals, these young conservatives saw themselves more as crusaders than as policy wonks, as anti-bureaucrat ideologues working against establishment elites, even as they occupied the very seats of government power. Their historic challenge, as they understood it, was to transform the crisis in oil into a crisis of governance—that is, the challenge was to use the crisis as a way to discredit government activism and to renew faith in the free market.

Theirs was not an easy job. The Arab embargo brought into sharp relief the hesitating, halting nature of the nation's rightward turn. It proved hard to purge Americans of their expectations that Washington would come to the rescue, especially in moments of economic crisis. In 1973, many Americans were old enough to remember how the federal government had helped Americans through the Depression, defeated the Nazis, built the nation's highways, and sent a man to the moon. Just as a car that is running out of gas, New Deal liberalism came to a slow, sputtering halt; indeed, at moments, even after it appeared to have no more life in it, liberalism could continue running on fumes. Though twice winning election on promises of scaling back government, Republican Richard Nixon himself was willing to flirt with new forms of government intervention.

This chapter explores how, in the face of a crisis, conservatives fought liberalism from inside the corridors of power. If they did not fully succeed, then at least they understood the challenge and began to devise new strategies, both ideological and political, for the battles ahead.

When Richard Nixon took office in 1969, liberalism was far from dead. Under Nixon's watch, the years that preceded the energy crisis witnessed anything but a rightward turn, with the 1960s leading to an enormous increase in government regulation of the economy. As corporate profits boomed in the 1960s, liberal activists won wide popular support for the idea that companies could afford to end poverty, make safer products, pollute less, protect their workers more, and still make a profit. Congress enacted a flurry of bills to mandate corporate social responsibility, and the environmental and consumer movements were at their peak.[2] In April 1970, 20 million Americans turned out for the inaugural Earth Day. The oil industry, long seen as the embodiment of corporate malfeasance and having recently scandalized the general public with a deadly spill off the coast of Santa Barbara, hardly escaped the regulatory avalanche. In that same year, Nixon signed the Clean Air Act Amendment and the Environmental Protection Act, both of which would saddle petroleum producers and refiners with costly and invasive regulations.

From the point of view of oil executives, the country was hardly shifting right in the early 1970s. They not only faced new threats, but in this charged political climate, they now worried about losing old privileges. Since 1926, the industry had been the beneficiary of the oil depletion allowance, an arcane, though very contentious, provision in the tax code that gave oil companies annual tax breaks worth billions of dollars to drill for new wells. For decades, oilmen spread money around to politicians to maintain the depletion allowance, funneling funds to oil-state senators to use for their own campaigns and to enhance their power by distributing donations, in turn, to other candidates in exchange for their political support. The nation's oil producers watched in horror when President Lyndon

Johnson, a friend of the industry during his days as a Texas politician, took the first stab at trimming oil's tax breaks. In 1969, even with Republican Richard Nixon in the White House, the much hated depletion allowance was finally scaled back.

Oil representatives cried that this legislative attack on the industry came at the worst possible moment. While much of the economy was booming in the late 1960s, the oil industry was running up against real geological constraints. In 1970, the American oil industry reached its peak of domestic production. American reserves were plenty, but never again would the daily number of barrels pumped out of the ground increase. Even as supply declined, the price of this increasingly scarce commodity remained fixed. The Federal Power Commission, a regulatory holdover from the New Deal, had continued its charge under both Democratic and Republican administrations to keep natural gas prices low, which in turn held down oil prices. In the summer of 1971, the Nixon administration imposed price controls directly on oil, as well as on other industries, in an effort to battle the inflation that was beginning to besiege the economy. Regulated U.S. prices, oilmen argued as they watched world prices begin to rise, prevented the accumulation of capital necessary for domestic exploration and alternative energy research. In 1971, the American Petroleum Institute spent $4 million on its television and newspaper campaign to warn the public of an impending energy crunch and to push for deregulation: "A country that runs on oil," it cautioned the nation, "cannot afford to run short." Oil executives, meanwhile, gave Nixon $5 million, which amounted to 10 percent of all donations, for his 1972 campaign war chest.[3]

On the eve of the Arab embargo, how, then, did Richard Nixon see oil politics? Supporting oil interests bolstered his electoral strategy of trying to capture the South from Democrats and appealed to newly rising southern Republicans like George H. W. Bush of Texas, who had been an independent oilman, served as a congressman in the late 1960s, and then became the Republican national chairman. Promoting domestic oil interests also seemed vital for American national security. Between 1970 and 1973, American imports doubled and accounted for one-third of the U.S. energy supply. Just as domestic oil production began to decline, OPEC production levels soared. And so, too, did OPEC's willingness to use its market power to influence American foreign policy, particularly on the question of Israel. Through its control of oil, Arab leaders could disrupt Western economies and dictate foreign policy demands. In the wake of Vietnam, with the country constrained in its use of military force, it appeared that the United States could do little to exert its national interest.

Within the White House, the oil industry found friends who shared their growing concerns. A sympathetic young Kenneth Lay, who would later achieve fame, fortune, and disgrace as head of Enron, was then deputy secretary of energy. "Our problem," he told Richard Nixon as oil supplies fell, "has resulted from outmoded Government policies, from excessive tinkering with the time tested mechanisms of the free market." George Bush echoed Kenneth Lay. America would once again become self-sufficient in energy only if the federal government got out of the way. "The freer the market," said Bush, "the better." For foreign policy and domestic political considerations, Nixon was inching closer to the oil industry's point of view.

Then, in October 1973, the Nixon administration's worst fears were realized when the Arab-Israeli War (also known as the Yom Kippur War) began. On October 6, Egypt and Syria launched a surprise attack on Israel, and in retaliation for American support of Israel, OPEC cut off oil exports to the United States. The embargo lasted until March 1974 and led to a 10 percent decline in the nation's fuel supply. The energy crisis was dynamite. It reached into every home and workplace. As energy supplies dwindled and prices shot skyward, schools closed, factories shut down, and gas lines grew long and ugly. Station attendants began packing pistols for self-protection while fistfights broke out among angry customers. A Miami Amoco dealer complained, "If you can't sell them gas, they'll threaten to beat you up, wreck your station, run you over with a car."[4] The most disruptive display of frustration came when the nation's 100,000 independent truckers staged a violent strike in February 1974, shutting down the country's highways for eleven days and leaving supermarket shelves bare as they demanded that the government roll back prices at the pump.

Nixon was in a bind. On the one hand, this shrewd politician devoted his time in office to creating what contemporaries called a "New Majority," one that would bring the white South into the Republican Party while also winning support from ethnic blue-collar Democrats in the North. Nixon successfully appealed to this "Silent Majority" in his landslide reelection in 1972 by promising to scale back expansive and intrusive government social programs, such as busing and welfare, that many white Democrats had come to resent. Nixon also appealed to millions of Americans who had taken a cultural turn to the Right, believing that it was time to rein in women's liberation, the sexual revolution, and the student protest movement against the Vietnam War. On the other hand, the idea that government should protect the public from corporate excesses, especially in hard times, still had a strong hold on American politics, particularly among working-class Democrats who had only recently and hesitantly come into Nixon's New Majority. Ever the political strategist, Nixon understood that the political loyalties of average Americans, from the small businessman in Peoria to the working-class housewife in Dayton—key members of Nixon's Silent Majority—were still up for grabs. In spite of the 1972 landslide, the New Majority was not fully cemented, and amid economic crisis, the white ethnic working-class Democrats might defect.

In the early weeks of the crisis, the president leaned to the Right. Addressing the nation, Nixon unveiled his Project Independence, a centerpiece of conservative reform, which was an ambitious deregulatory program designed to stimulate domestic production, eliminate oil imports by 1985, and push back against environmental reforms Nixon had once supported. The very name suggested American independence from Arab oil and also business independence from government regulation. America's survival, the president declared, required the deregulation of natural gas prices, the acceleration of offshore drilling, and the construction of a Trans-Alaska pipeline. Now more than ever, it was essential to lift environmental restrictions. "If you are going to freeze to death," the president told the nation's governors, "it doesn't matter much whether or not the air is clean." To achieve self-sufficiency in energy, the government had to move out of the way. "We can't fight the economics of the market place," said Nixon.[5]

But this kind of small government conservatism was a hard sell as the energy crisis coincided and contributed to the biggest economic catastrophe since the Great Depression. In the 1970s, the American economy simultaneously experienced stagnant growth and rising prices, a new phenomenon contemporaries called *stagflation* and one that policymakers did not know how to cure. The energy crisis was not the sole cause of these economic woes, but energy prices compounded inflation, and to the public, the gas lines were emblematic of a declining economy, complete with a cast of villains to blame and hold accountable. The vast majority of Americans believed that Big Oil companies artificially engineered the crisis to jack up prices. Consumer advocate Ralph Nader called the shortage "the most phony crisis" in the nation's history while rumors swirled about oil tankers waiting offshore until prices went even higher. The public demanded that the government "do something" to check what was popularly perceived as excessive and corrupt corporate greed. The problem, it seemed, stemmed not from a shortage of gas but from a shortage of effective government leadership. From a rural village in North Carolina, a citizen wrote to the

White House, expressing a newly commonplace state of alarm: "People are spending every waking hour worrying over the gasoline situation."[6]

Nixon would have a difficult time ignoring this growing discontent. As *Newsweek* reported, "the American people seem on the verge of psychic rebellion." The prominent pollster Daniel Yankelovitch laid out the problem for the White House: "No issue has such a potential for producing social instability of the magnitude of the depression as does the energy crisis. This crisis entails a radical change . . . Their lives will be disrupted and altered at the gut level." This issue, Yankelovitch warned the president's top advisers, would "either make him or break him." "If people get the impression that no one is in charge, or that there is no advance planning, or that they are being asked to make sacrifices while the oil industry raises big profits, they are going to get very angry and this issue will destroy Nixon." A Maryland citizen summed up the public mood: "We the American people are tired of the lack of competent and effective leadership."[7]

So what would Nixon do? This longtime politician was, above all, an opportunist, which in the early seventies meant the occasional lurch toward New Deal solutions when he was in trouble. At times, he could not escape support of some liberal programs, from environmentalism to minimum wages. Perhaps the greatest act of opportunism came with the president's imposition of wage and price controls in the summer of 1971 to clamp down on inflation. With inflation in check, he was then free to increase federal spending to prop up the economy before the 1972 election. As journalist and former Nixon adviser William Safire explained, "When his back is to the wall, Mr. Nixon tends to adopt the economic suggestions of his Democratic opponents, and with a vengeance." What infuriated those to his right, explained Safire, was the "President's willingness to make economic decisions for political reasons—that is, to listen to the populist demand to 'do something!'" As Safire was writing, a Democratic-sponsored windfall tax bill was working its way through Congress as was legislation requiring oil companies to roll back prices at the pump.[8]

Democratic senator Henry "Scoop" Jackson from the state of Washington took the lead on the energy situation. On foreign policy he was to the right of the Nixon administration, opposing détente (see Chapter 12 in this volume) and fighting for an increase in the military budget. But Jackson was also a New Deal liberal. Steeped in Depression-era liberalism, he believed that the federal government had to solve the energy crisis. A presidential aspirant, he also recognized he could tap into and fan populist sentiment; this crisis, in the hands of everyone to Nixon's left, from Jackson to the AFL-CIO's George Meany to Ralph Nader, followed a familiar narrative. For Jackson, Big Oil played a starring role as the profit-seeking villains, the suffering small independent oil refiners and gas dealers appeared as the virtuous little man being squeezed out of the market by the seven Big Oil major corporations, and the angry victimized public was the script's heart and soul. Casting himself as the hero, Jackson called for government to step in. Top on his list was a ten-year $20 billion research and development program for alternative fuel, which he likened to the Manhattan Project or the 1960s Apollo space program. Jackson also fought to have the government roll back gas prices while forcing the major oil companies to sell their scarce products to independent retailers, whose historically lower prices served as competition to the majors' own gas stations.

As soon as the embargo began, Scoop Jackson, with the help of other leading Democrats, went on the warpath. He subpoenaed top oil executives to a televised Senate hearing, accusing them of conspiring against the American public and of reaping "obscene profits." This so-called cheat probe made good nightly news theatrics and kept pressure on the administration and its Republican allies. As conservatives feared, the cut in oil supply put intense pressure on Nixon as momentum gained for governmental action. Liberal

Democrats, especially those from the heavy oil-consuming states of the northeast, formed an alliance with representatives from regions, mostly in the Midwest and the Plains states, with a higher proportion of independent refiners and dealers, who were being driven out of business by the majors. Both political groups were eager to make the major oil companies pay. In November, Jackson got a mandatory allocation bill passed with overwhelming support, 93 to 3 in the Senate and 348 to 46 in the House, effectively putting the oil industry under government control; an amendment to the act requiring a World War II–style nationwide federal rationing program fell only eight votes short in the Senate. For the rest of the decade, the government would set the price of oil. A newly created Federal Energy Office would oversee these new bureaucratic regulations.[9]

As much as the political winds on the Hill and at the grassroots pushed him to the Left, Nixon also came under strong pressure from a new group of conservative advisers committed to scaling back government activism. The Nixon administration was only the second Republican administration since the New Deal. In contrast to the administration of Dwight D. Eisenhower, who as a military bureaucrat and supreme commander in Europe during World War II had presided over the single greatest moment of state building in American history, the Nixon administration had different ambitions. Eisenhower's advisers came from the ranks of big business, many of whom had accommodated themselves to a world of New Deal regulation. Nixon's people had a different ideological makeup: they were Californian entrepreneurs, Wall Street buccaneers, and independent oilmen from Texas. Nixon himself came from a lower-middle-class California grocer family and grew up with deep resentment for the establishment elite. From his earliest political days, he ran against New Deal government bureaucracies, including the wartime Office of Price Administration, where he developed his anti-government disdain while serving in the tire-rationing department. Like Assistant Treasury Secretary William Simon, who was soon to become the nation's chief energy bureaucrat and had made millions as a Wall Street bond trader, many of Nixon's appointees cut their teeth in businesses that were very different from such big bureaucracies as General Motors, AT&T, and the U.S. Army. By the time Nixon took office, the Chicago school of free-market economics was in the ascendance, as was clear in the appointment of Herbert Stein, trained at the University of Chicago and recommended by Milton Friedman, as chairman of the Council of Economic Advisers. To be sure, there were others in the Nixon administration who came out of a New Deal world, like the labor mediator John Dunlop, who was in charge of wage and price controls, and even Nixon himself, who had after all served in the Office of Price Administration. But a big-government vision, while pushed opportunistically by some, was facing increasing competition from Nixon's own brain trust.

Inside government, there was a core ideological group who saw as their mission the undoing of the regulatory world that had been in place since the New Deal. Chief among them was Roy Ash, a longtime Nixon supporter who served as his budget director and had benefited from the booming Cold War economy of Southern California as cofounder of Litton Industries, a Beverly Hills–based multinational conglomerate and defense contractor. Ash made sure to bolster the president's resolve, telling Nixon that the energy situation was more of an ongoing problem, and not, in Ash's words, "a Presidential crisis." Ash therefore recommended that Nixon "avoid overreacting by getting government into activities that can and will be better done by private industry . . . What the government can most usefully do is remove impediments it has constructed, provide some incentives, and keep out of the way . . . *In short, this is not primarily a government problem.*" Instead, Ash told Nixon, this was a job for the private sector. "We must, of course, establish the perception of Federal leadership . . . but we should recognize the problem as essentially a market phenomenon."[10] All the president's top advisers, including Ash, recommended that Nixon veto any bill to roll back prices.

Beyond his ideological sympathy with these anti-government arguments, the Watergate investigation was also pushing Nixon to the Right. In the winter of 1973, as the Watergate scandal escalated, Nixon faced a complicated political landscape. As the investigation drew closer to the president, it weakened Nixon's capacity to take independent action. His declining popularity made him cleave to the Right as he searched for political friends and loyal allies. In 1976, the fallout from Watergate would damage the electoral chances of the Republican Party, but in this instance, Nixon turned in a more conservative direction as he sought to shore up political support. Within the White House, the most ideologically committed policymakers had the greatest influence. As the Watergate investigations gained momentum, Nixon adopted a bunker mentality, surrounding himself with and soliciting advice from only the most dedicated. Someone like Roy Ash was one of Nixon's core supporters, loyal to him even at a personal level. His wife wrote "Support RN" on all her Christmas cards, bills, and letters, while thirty other top-level wives sold "Get Off His Back" stickers. William Simon's wife, Carol, displayed one on her Mercedes. In words that echoed those of his sympathizers, Nixon affirmed his resolve to resist calls for a federal response, telling his top aides, "Let's not lose sight of our goal to keep government out of people's pockets and off their backs."[11]

Yet, as Ash had counseled, the president had to create the perception of government leadership. On December 4, 1973, Nixon announced that William Simon would become the head of a newly created Federal Energy Office. It was set up explicitly as a temporary office to manage an immediate problem and to avoid institutionalizing a permanent role for government. Simon was the nation's most unlikely energy czar. He had no first-hand knowledge or experience in the oil industry; as a former Wall Street whiz kid,

Simon was fiercely committed to market solutions and had little faith in Washington bureaucrats. As he commented to chief of staff Alexander Haig, "It is really quite an experience to work in a place that has more horses' assess than horses." His appointment came from the support of his key allies, Secretary of the Treasury George Shultz and the Council of Economic Advisers' Herbert Stein, whom together William Safire had dubbed the "free market mohicans." All shared the belief that only higher prices, by stimulating domestic production, would end the energy crisis.[12]

Over the next few decades, conservatives mounted their campaign against government intervention from within the halls of power. In spite of his political beliefs, Simon, a proponent of the free market, sat atop a new government agency with vast regulatory powers given him by a Democratic-controlled Congress. Yet, much like foxes sent to guard a henhouse, these conservatives assumed control of the very institutions they sought to discredit. Exxon president John Jamieson told Simon, "I can sleep better each night knowing you are the energy czar." They would undermine the legitimacy of the twentieth-century state, if by a thousand self-administered cuts.

Here the political scuffle over rationing demonstrates the expansion of an increasingly hollow state. Unable to completely retrench the American state that had emerged in the New Deal and Great Society, conservatives learned that they would have to work at limiting and containing government by controlling the levers of power. During the 1970s, conservatism was transformed from an opposition ideology premised on radically eliminating government to an ideology of officeholders who struggled to contain and gradually undermine the government they so vehemently mistrusted. As the situation at gas stations grew increasingly chaotic, Democratic leaders, organized labor, consumer activists, liberal intellectuals, and every other political force to the left of the administration demanded that the federal government institute a nationwide system of rationing to stop the mad scramble and long lines at the gas pumps. Under pressure, the president ordered Simon to print up monthly rationing booklets, each entitling its holder to thirty-five gallons. "Maybe that will shut them up," said Nixon. But Simon was careful in how he designed the program, making it function much like a market. Citizens could sell their unused coupons for whatever someone was willing to pay, thereby undermining the purpose of rationing and price controls. Even if this program would allow prices to rise as high as the market would bear, Simon had no real intention of allowing rationing to go forward. Instead, the White House urged Americans to save gas voluntarily. In the 1970s, environmentalists and anti-growth advocates often made the loudest calls for conservation. When Nixon and other conservatives asked Americans to change their "wastrel ways," they were adopting the message of the ecological Left, but for a larger political purpose. If individuals cut back on energy use, those voluntary efforts might help diminish the need for government to create an enormous bureaucracy to mandate conservation.[13]

Even as they presided over the regulatory institutions foisted on them by a Democratic Congress, these conservatives argued that the market, not the government, was the solution to national crisis. Simon took a leading role in discrediting the state's ability to act, crystallizing and articulating a free-market argument from the center of the state regulatory apparatus itself. The tools he had to combat the energy crisis, including allocations and price controls, were classic regulatory measures generated by a Democratic Congress and New Deal statecraft. But as they reluctantly deployed these statist measures, these anti-government conservatives repeatedly told themselves and the public that they were illegitimate. By his own account, Simon was a "rotten bureaucrat." In fact, as he explained, he was an "*anti*bureaucrat." Set up in reaction to a crisis, the Federal Energy Office was an "outrage." If Simon had his way, he would "abolish the agency and close its doors tomorrow." As he put it, "No group of men could be attacking the problem more sensibly than we are, but . . . no group of men, we or anyone else, could ever replace the free market."[14]

According to conservatives, the gas lines were but the most obvious symptom of liberalism's failing. The allocation measures designed by Congress were awkward and stifling, and price controls discouraged more gasoline from coming onto the market. When Simon stalled on rationing, states implemented their own programs by which owners of cars with license plates ending in even numbers could buy gas on even calendar days, and vice versa for odd-numbered plates. Fifteen states and the District of Columbia had alternating fuel purchase days, and nine other states drew up plans. But these were blunt instruments not well suited to the complexities of gasoline use. Without an elaborate bureaucracy—the Office of Price Administration employed over 100,000—to enforce equity, this improvised system seemed bungling at best. Whereas the automobile had once been the symbol of American preeminence, these long lines of cars with half-filled tanks were now a sign of the country's evident weakness, which the government seemed to be making worse rather than better.[15]

Conservatives in this era were feeling their way forward. They needed to solve pressing political problems while keeping in view their larger vision of smaller government. They would get there, but it would take time. And thus Nixon and his team, despite their ideology and efforts, did not succeed in thwarting the intrusion of government into energy markets. By the spring of 1974, Watergate was sapping his strength day by day, and the Democrats, with their commanding majorities, were making political hay. On May 7, 1974, Nixon signed legislation to extend controls and allocations for two years and to establish the Federal Energy Administration (FEA) to oversee these regulations. Six weeks later, the House Judiciary Committee passed three articles of impeachment against the president, and a newly released tape, the so-called smoking gun, implicated Nixon directly in the Watergate cover-up. To avoid impeachment, Nixon resigned on August 9.

The FEA would live on. The conservatives were right: once controls were in place, they were hard to remove. Nixon's successor, Gerald Ford, who was even more committed to the market, surrounded himself with a coterie of young ideological advisers like Dick Cheney, Donald Rumsfeld, and Alan Greenspan. To them, freeing energy markets was essential both as a marker of conservative ascendance and as the key to a revitalized foreign policy. Unless the United States achieved energy independence, it would be hamstrung in its efforts to assert its will not only in the Middle East but even among its Western allies. Yet Ford came under the same political pressure for governmental action as had Nixon, with a public unwilling to accept higher prices at the pump. After a protracted and unsuccessful political battle championed by his conservative staff, Ford signed legislation to extend the life of the FEA for three more years.[16]

The plan had not worked out exactly as these conservatives had hoped. When Richard Nixon had created the Federal Energy Office, Secretary George Shultz said to William Simon, "I'm so glad it's you who's heading up the energy bureaucracy. That way it will go out of business, and you'll be able to keep the damage in check." But it did not turn out that way. As Simon recalled with regret in 1976, "Well, I didn't keep the damage in check—it outlasted me. 'We' are all out now, 'they' are all in now, and 'our' detestable bureaucratic creations, devised by 'their' standards, are in place, waiting to be used for purposes 'we' privately deplore." Indeed, these conservatives had thought that if they were in charge, they could chart their own course, discrediting the government from within while restoring the free market. But, as Simon concluded after Jimmy Carter had taken office, "It is obvious to me that one does not acquire virtue by becoming a 'better type' of prostitute. Nor, obviously, does one win votes." For the moment, the hens had chased the foxes out of their henhouse.

And yet, the energy crisis taught these conservative reformers a valuable lesson: fighting liberalism was hard. Trench warfare over energy policy made clear that reforming government and changing popular expectations were no easy tasks. Out of office during the Carter years, they continued to refine their anti-government arguments. Their message was simple: the only solution to the energy crisis was less government, not more. As Milton Friedman, who would soon win the Nobel Prize in Economics, explained, if the Federal Energy Office shut down, as Simon had hoped it would, oil would flow freely and gas station attendants would once again wash customers' windshields. In 1977, Ronald Reagan, who would soon assume the conservative mantle and mobilize grassroots support for a rightward turn, announced, "Our problem isn't a shortage of oil. It's a surplus of government." It would not be until 1981, when Reagan came to power, that an ideologically conservative administration could finally decontrol the regulatory apparatus built up over half a century and chart a new conservative course.

198 - running over station attendants

199 - if you're going to freeze to death,
    it doesn't matter how dirty
    the air is -

20 - what came of Scoop Jacksons
    televised senate meeting
    accusing oil executives?

CHAPTER 11

Turnabout Years

Public Sector Unionism
and the Fiscal Crisis

JOSEPH A. McCARTIN

As the 1970s began, one of the least appreciated social movements spawned in the previous decade was just beginning to hit its stride, undaunted by the political upheavals of 1968 or the election of Richard M. Nixon to the presidency. Government workers at all levels—local, state, and federal—had begun organizing unions during the 1960s, and they were determined to exert their political power as the 1970s began. Between 1955 and 1975, the number of organized public sector workers rose tenfold. Public sector unions entered the 1970s with an ambitious agenda, confident that they would continue their near-exponential growth, and believing that their increasing power could provide the impetus for a broad revival and expansion of liberal politics. But the 1970s proved to be a decade of disappointed expectations for government workers' unions. By the decade's end, not only had they lost their growth momentum; they had become a political lightning rod whose alleged influence on the Democratic Party sent former allies scurrying for political cover, and whose strikes, legislative initiatives, and contractual

210

demands provided an effective target of opportunity for the rising conservative movement. The story of this surprising reversal reveals how central the fiscal crisis of the mid-1970s and related struggles for workplace power were to the conservative realignment of American politics in the dawning Reagan era.

For public sector labor, the decade of the 1970s can be divided neatly in two, with the first half of the decade characterized by aggressive expansionism and rising expectations, and the second half by defensiveness and disappointed dreams. The years between 1970 and 1975 saw the movement enjoying a heady expansion that union leaders likened to the industrial union upsurge of the 1930s. Teachers, sanitation workers, firefighters, police officers, postal workers, social workers, and others flocked into unions, turning once-sleepy organizations like the American Federation of State, County, and Municipal Employees (AFSCME) into robust and increasingly militant unions. Indeed, with 500,000 members by 1973, AFSCME became the fastest growing union in the AFL-CIO.[1]

The conjunction of three factors in the 1960s had ignited this expansive phase. First, the ranks of government employees rose significantly in the postwar decades, going from 5.5 million to 11.6 million, with about 85 percent of that growth taking place at the state and local level. By 1970, public employees constituted 18 percent of the nation's workforce. Second, Democratic allies changed public policy in ways that facilitated government union organization. Democratic mayors Robert Wagner Jr. of New York and Joseph Clark of Philadelphia began bargaining collectively with municipal unions in the 1950s, inspiring others to follow suit. Wisconsin's Democratic governor Gaylord Nelson signed the nation's first statewide collective bargaining bill in 1959, and by the early 1970s more than two dozen states had enacted similar laws. And in 1962, President John F. Kennedy brought a limited form of collective bargaining to the federal service through Executive Order 10988, dramatically expanding the ranks of unionized federal workers. Third, the civil rights movement of the 1960s inspired public sector workers (many of whom were African Americans or women) to organize for rights in their workplaces.[2]

As the 1970s began, continued government growth, the support of Democratic allies, and the ongoing influence of the rights revolution contributed to a positive outlook for the movement. And through the middle of the decade, at least three other indicators suggested that public sector union growth might continue unabated. First, the politics of these years seemed to favor public sector labor. Once public sector unions began to grow, Republican leaders seemed unwilling to challenge them head on. Indeed, moderate Republicans sought to build alliances with the unions. Governor Nelson A. Rockefeller of New York made efforts to associate himself with some municipal and state workers' organizations, while on the national level President Nixon issued a 1969 executive order that strengthened collective bargaining procedures in the federal service. The Nixon administration also took a moderate approach to federal labor militancy. When 180,000 postal workers and approximately 3,000 air traffic controllers staged illegal walkouts in 1970, Nixon did not authorize mass firings, although the law allowed him to do so. Instead, he signed the Postal Reorganization Act, which allowed mail handlers to bargain over their compensation for the first time, and later his administration extended exclusive recognition to the controllers' union, the Professional Air Traffic Controllers Organization (PATCO).[3]

A second indicator of public sector union vigor in the first half of the 1970s was the rising level of labor militancy. Before the mid-1960s, government workers' strikes were a rarity, and neither federal nor state governments recognized the right of public workers to strike. But as government workers organized, they chafed under such strike bans. Illegal walkouts by New York City transit workers in 1966 and by Memphis, Tennessee, sanitation workers in 1968 signaled the growing willingness of public sector workers to

Civil disobedience

defy the law in order to secure just treatment. That willingness obviously grew between 1965 and 1975, as strike rates rose tenfold among government workers during these years.[4]

Finally, the growing labor militancy convinced an increasing number of experts and politicians that liberalization of public sector labor laws would provide the best method of bringing order to government labor relations. Four states legalized public employee strikes in the early 1970s, and others began to consider doing so. William Usery, whom President Nixon appointed to head the Federal Mediation and Conciliation Service, urged an end to strike bans and passage of laws that would make it easier for workers to organize and bargain. Representative William Clay (D-MO), a former AFSCME organizer, drafted one such legislative proposal. In 1971, Clay introduced the National Public Employee Relations Act (NPERA), which promised organizing rights to all state and local workers in the United States, extended strike rights to most of those workers, and offered unions stronger dues checkoff and union security provisions than those in the Wagner Act (which covered only the private sector). The bill received the warm endorsement of key Democratic leaders. While Republican leaders of course opposed the Clay bill, momentum seemed to be swinging against them. In 1974, President Nixon signed a law extending the wage and hour protections of the Fair Labor Standards Act (FLSA) to state and local government workers for the first time. By doing so, Nixon effectively undermined the main argument then wielded by opponents of NPERA: the notion that the federal government could not constitutionally regulate the labor relations practices of state governments. With opposition to NPERA thus weakened, and larger Democratic majorities returned to Congress as a result of the post-Watergate 1974 mid-term elections, labor strategists believed that Clay's bill or some variant of it would soon be law. Confident of victory, labor allies mapped out other objectives, including the repeal of the hated 1939 Hatch Act, which prohibited federal workers from engaging in most political activity.[5]

what about states' sovereignty?

As 1975 dawned, public sector unions felt that they were on the verge of making some critical breakthroughs. By the end of that year, however, government unions were on the defensive. The reason for this turnabout is not hard to find. In 1975, the U.S. economy suffered a triple shock: the nation's gross domestic product plunged by 1.3 percent, inflation hit a postwar high of 9.1 percent, and unemployment rose to 8.5 percent. Before the year was out, the economic turmoil created by these developments sent state and local governments all over the nation into the red. Hardest hit was New York City, which nearly went into default. This fiscal crisis decisively altered the political terrain upon which public sector unions had been thriving. Growing deficits made it harder for governments to meet the demands of their workers, inflation encouraged taxpayers to scream for relief even as it also prodded government workers toward militant efforts to win wage increases, and private sector unemployment fueled resentment against public sector workers, whose job security was less sensitive to economic downturns. These developments began to open up a breach between public sector unions and erstwhile allies in the Democratic Party.[6]

Government officials at all levels dealt with the crisis by slashing budgets, freezing hiring, and adopting a hard line in union contract negotiations. In many cases, Democratic administrations once allied to the public sector union movement were forced to take the lead in instituting austerity measures. In 1975, Pittsburgh mayor Peter F. Flaherty cut city payrolls by one-third, California governor Edmund G. Brown Jr. scaled back planned wage increases for state workers, and Massachusetts governor Michael S. Dukakis announced layoffs. In the new environment created by "stagflation" (see Chapter 10 in this volume) and budget deficits, Democrats like these had to show that they were able to "stand up to" public sector unions in order to escape attacks from their right. The problem of inflation was particularly vexing. The average annual inflation rate during the 1960s, when the public sector labor movement began to gather steam, was 2.3 percent. That figure jumped to 7.1 percent in the 1970s. This had a perverse effect on public sector labor relations. On the one hand, inflation fed the militancy of public sector workers whose wages began to lag behind spiraling prices. On the other hand, inflation contributed to worries about "tax bracket creep" and declining purchasing power among increasing numbers of voters, which in turn stiffened politicians' resolve to resist government workers' demands. As the new era took shape, one AFSCME official revealingly complained that "everybody is bargaining harder than in the past."[7]

The new dynamics were becoming quite clear by July 1, 1975. On that day, three revealing battles between government workers and Democratic elected officials came to a head in New York City, Seattle, and across the Commonwealth of Pennsylvania. Taken together, these struggles illustrate how starkly the political context was changing. The New York conflict erupted when thousands of sanitation workers went on strike to protest layoffs ordered by Democratic mayor Abe Beame in response to the city's fiscal crisis. The language of the workers was militant: "Christ Almighty is not going to stop this [strike]," sanitation union president John DeLury announced. That day 76,000 Pennsylvania state workers also went on strike when Democratic governor Milton Shapp, who had pledged to hold down taxes, refused to meet their demands for a wage increase. Meanwhile, voters went to the polls in Seattle on July 1 in a recall election that had been brought about through the efforts of Seattle's firefighters' union, which was determined to oust Democratic mayor Wes Uhlman after Uhlman cut some fire department jobs in response to a budget deficit.

In all three of these cases, the unions made short-term gains. Most of the New York municipal workers laid off by Beame were rehired within weeks in a deal brokered by Democratic governor Hugh Carey. In order to end the strike in Pennsylvania, Governor Shapp agreed to an 11 percent wage increase for state workers.

And to help Uhlman fight off the recall effort, Seattle officials restored many of the cuts that had angered the firefighters' union. But in all three settings, these short-term union wins came at a steep cost. In each setting, the fiscal crisis crystallized growing anger against the power of public sector unions. In the aftermath of the New York strike, the *New York Times* railed against what it called the "union-ruled city." Following the AFSCME strike, the *Philadelphia Inquirer* wondered whether Pennsylvania was "run by a labor union or by its elected officials." In Seattle, Democrat Wes Uhlman beat back the recall effort by attacking the power of the public sector workers. If the firefighters' union ousted the mayor, Uhlman's press secretary warned, then no mayor would ever be able to stand up to municipal labor unions again. This tactic rescued Uhlman. At the beginning of the recall effort, his prospects appeared dim. But once voters perceived Uhlman as resisting unreasonable city employees, they rallied behind him and he easily retained his seat.[8]

These three conflicts, and others like them that erupted in the mid-1970s, signaled a sharp shift in the politics of public sector unionism. During 1975, rising public anxiety about the economy pushed elected officials, including erstwhile Democratic allies, into conflicts with unions that for their part were trying to fend off budget cuts and layoffs. As unions mobilized to defend their members' interests, the strike rate among government workers spiked by 24 percent in 1975. But in mid-decade, labor militancy met a less sympathetic audience than it had in the early 1970s. Polls showed a significant decline in support for public sector strikes between 1974 and 1978.[9]

By the fall of 1975, with Democrats tempering their support for public sector union demands, Republicans began to seize the initiative. Federal workers were among the first to feel the results, when President Gerald R. Ford won an important victory against federal workers' unions in October 1975. Ford refused to support an increase in federal workers' salaries by more than 5 percent, even though his own pay agent had recommended an 8.66 percent increase in order to allow federal workers to keep pace with inflation. Outraged federal unions lobbied Congress to reverse Ford's action. When Nixon had tried a similar tactic in 1973, unions were able to get Congress to override him. But even though Democratic margins were greater in 1975, a motion to restore the pay agent's recommended pay increase failed badly in both houses. That defeat was "a stunner" to labor lobbyists. "These guys were voting under orders from their constituents and the orders said: 'We want you to strike out at big government, at high pay, at those loafers in government, and at everything about this big government that is on our backs," explained one analyst. The AFL-CIO's chief lobbyist, Ken Young, admitted that "many of our liberal friends in Congress are voting like conservatives."[10]

The growing fiscal crisis also influenced how the U.S. Supreme Court viewed public sector labor laws. When Richard Nixon signed the extension of the FLSA in 1974, he had good reason to believe that the Court would uphold the law, for in 1968 it had seemingly endorsed the principle that the federal government could regulate state and local government labor relations in the case of *Maryland v. Wirtz.*[11] Still, the National League of Cities challenged the constitutionality of the FLSA extension, arguing that Congress had overstepped the bounds of federalism. When the Court heard arguments in the case in 1975, many observers felt that it would uphold the FLSA extension under the Wirtz precedent. But by the time the Court finally ruled in 1976, it delivered a 5–4 decision that rolled back federal power to regulate state and local government labor relations, in effect overturning *Maryland v. Wirtz.* In the end, the fiscal environment and rising labor militancy influenced how justices read the case. The *National League of Cities v. Usery* decision delivered a death blow to the NPERA. If Congress did not have the power to mandate wage and hour protections for state and local government workers, then surely it also lacked the power to protect their right to organize unions. Consequently, Democratic leaders all but abandoned the NPERA, whose passage had seemed a near certainty only a year earlier.[12]

The changing political terrain of the mid-1970s not only weakened Democratic support for public sector union demands; it also encouraged the rise of grassroots conservative organizations that specifically targeted public sector union power. By 1975, the conservative movement, which had reeled before the sudden rise of public sector unions in the 1960s, finally began to counterattack. Key to that response was a new organization, the Public Service Research Council (PSRC), which had been launched in 1974 by activists affiliated with the anti-union National Right to Work Committee. The PSRC was created specifically to combat the growing influence of public sector labor. Its goals were radical. The views of its members were strongly influenced by Wake Forest University law professor Sylvester Petro, who had long championed the repeal of the Wagner Act and other labor laws. In Petro's mind, the introduction of unions in the public sector was an especially dangerous development. Petro claimed that there was "an absolute and ineradicable incompatibility" between government sovereignty and public sector collective bargaining. By bargaining with unions of their workers, governments abdicated their claim to sovereignty, Petro asserted. If allowed to expand, public sector collective bargaining would eventually make all governments the captives of labor bosses, undermining democracy itself.[13]

The labor upheavals and fiscal crisis of 1975 opened the door to the PSRC's emergence as a significant political force. When mainstream papers like the *New York Times* and the *Philadelphia Inquirer* and Democratic elected officials like Seattle mayor Wes Uhlman began to accuse unions of trying to control government, the views of the PSRC suddenly seemed more mainstream and its message began to resonate more widely. With the help of direct mail fundraiser Richard Viguerie, the organization began to attract tens of thousands of supporters. PSRC leaders used this support to circulate a pamphlet that became profoundly influential in conservative circles. *Public Sector Bargaining and Strikes,* which was first issued in 1974, then updated and reissued biannually for the rest of the decade, charged that public sector collective bargaining laws promoted strikes. The charge challenged a central contention of the government unions and their allies: that the extension of collective bargaining to government would foster labor peace and improve government efficiency. The PSRC's charges thus struck a nerve. As the public sector strike rate rose in 1975, so too did the PSRC's fortunes.[14]

During that tumultuous year, the PSRC promoted a sensational book purporting to be an exposé of arrogant public sector union power. The book, *Let Our Cities Burn* (1975), was written by journalist Ralph de Toledano, who had embraced conservatism after meeting Whittaker Chambers in the early 1950s. The book took its title from a statement that AFSCME president Jerry Wurf allegedly made during a 1974 Baltimore strike. Its argument was that union leaders were out to take control over government. De Toledano especially feared labor's drive to pass the NPERA. In his eyes, Representative Clay's bill was a "massive assault on the American system" that had to be repulsed. If enacted, de Toledano warned, the bill would reduce the constitution "to a scrap of paper."[15]

The arguments of the PSRC and de Toledano soon found an echo among the most conservative Republicans in the Congress. Senators Jesse Helms (R-NC) and Jake Garn (R-UT) endorsed de Toledano's arguments and conservative Republican representatives repeated them on the House floor. In mid-July 1975, Representatives John H. Rousselot (R-CA) and Philip Crane (R-IL) were among those who took to the floor vowing to defeat the NPERA and roll back collective bargaining in government. "We are bound to have strikes by public employees," Rousselot insisted, as long as governments "bargain with union organizers as co-equals."[16]

The PSRC worked tirelessly to spread its message in the second half of the 1970s. It launched an academic journal called the *Government*

Union Review; published a biweekly newsletter, the *Government Union Critique;* and created a lobbying arm called Americans Against Union Control of Government. Before the end of the decade, the ideas of Sylvester Petro and his circle, once deemed part of a right-wing fringe, were not only circulating broadly in conservative circles, but were receiving attention from mainstream politicians and the press.

Slow to grasp how decisively the public mood was shifting, union leaders unwittingly helped legitimize the PSRC during this period. Two decisions by labor leaders in 1975 were especially important in this regard. The first occurred when the American Federation of Government Employees (AFGE) announced its intention to organize members of the U.S. military in August 1975. Unveiling the initiative, the union's president joked that the "AFGE might negotiate a shorter work week . . . so we'd have shorter wars." The ill-timed initiative raised such a storm of opposition that the AFGE quickly dropped it. But before the short-lived idea could be jettisoned, it reaped a windfall of new PSRC members and contributors and allowed Strom Thurmond (R-SC) to win passage of a law barring unions in the uniformed military by a huge margin in the Senate. The second controversy erupted when delegates to the AFL-CIO's October 1975 convention went on record supporting the right of all government workers to strike. Labor leaders saw the resolution as an affirmation of a basic human right. But the action only contributed to public fears about the potential for strikes by firefighters, police officers, and others who protected the public safety. AFL-CIO secretary-treasurer Lane Kirkland only reinforced public apprehension when he told a gathering of federal sector union leaders in October 1975 that even federal workers had the right to "protest and strike, despite unjust laws."[17]

How much political currents were shifting against public sector labor became clearer to the unions after the election of Democrat Jimmy Carter in 1976.[18] With Democrats in control of the presidency

and both houses of Congress for the first time since the early phase
of public sector union growth, the unions understandably hoped
for several legislative victories, including the repeal of the Hatch
Act (which Carter had pledged he would sign if it reached his desk).
But when the Hatch Act bill came to the House in the spring of
1977, the PSRC and the *Wall Street Journal* launched a campaign
against it, charging that "union bosses" were engaged in a raw
"power grab" that would "throw open the doors of public service
to partisan politics and political coercion." Many rank-and-file
House Democrats became so skittish that they initially joined Republicans in gutting the reform bill. Only when union lobbyists and
Democratic leaders applied pressure were they able to get the bill
through the Democratic House of Representatives. President
Carter offered no help. Indeed, he worked behind the scenes to ensure that the bill was bottled up in the Senate. Carter breathed a
sigh of relief when Senator Abraham Ribicoff (D-CT) refused to
bring the bill to a vote in committee: The president had no desire to
see the deeply controversial Hatch Act reform debated before he
had a chance to push through his sweeping reform of federal civil
service laws.[19]

Yet Carter's promised reform of civil service and collective bargaining laws in the federal service itself proved to be a deep disappointment to labor. Since John F. Kennedy's 1962 executive order,
federal workers' union rights had rested on a series of presidential
directives. Unions had long hoped to concretize and broaden federal workers' rights through legislation that might grant them the
power to bargain over wages and even the right to strike under certain conditions for some workers. The Carter administration also
wanted to put federal workers' rights on a legislative footing, but
not in the way that many public sector unionists had hoped. When
the administration drafted the Civil Service Reform Act of 1978, it
stressed the need for greater efficiency and flexibility in the federal
workforce. The bill did include some improvements in federal

workers' rights, but these fell far short of the dreams entertained by union leaders in the early 1970s. Federal workers did not achieve the right to bargain over compensation or to strike. Instead Carter praised the bill by arguing that it would "mean less job security for incompetent Federal employees." When Representative Morris K. Udall (D-AZ) defended Carter's bill before a convention of federal workers, he was showered with boos. To help win passage of the bill in the face of such opposition, Carter promised to support a resurrection of the Hatch Act reform bill. Yet he never delivered. After Carter won civil service reform, the Hatch bill remained bottled up.[20]

Carter was not alone in disappointing public sector labor in the latter half of the 1970s. State- and local-level Democrats were increasingly resisting union demands by the time a second wave of inflation-driven public sector militancy pushed strike rates up by 18 percent in 1978. "We're going to see more of these strikes," warned W. Howard McClennan, of the International Association of Fire Fighters. "We are tired of being made the scapegoat of the plight of the cities." But Democratic politicians were in no mood to give in to labor militancy. When 260,000 New York state employees entered into negotiations with New York's Democratic governor Hugh Carey in 1978, union leaders feared "the roughest [negotiations] in a long time" because the climate was "not conducive to large settlements." Atlanta's Democratic mayor Maynard Jackson proved even tougher than Carey. When sanitation workers, whose union had helped elect Jackson as Atlanta's first black mayor in 1973, demanded long overdue pay increases in 1977, Jackson took a hard line with them. "The employees deserve a pay increase," Jackson admitted, "but we don't have it." He vowed that "elephants would roost in trees" before he let the city's budget go into deficit. When the sanitation workers went on strike in April 1977, Jackson gave them forty-eight hours to return to work. When they did not end their strike, he fired them and began hiring replacements.

Only when the union surrendered unconditionally did Jackson relent and begin to rehire some fired strikers. Jackson's hard line inspired several other Democratic mayors to follow suit.[21]

Ironically, the more Democratic politicians resisted public employee union demands in the latter half of the 1970s, the more they helped legitimize the charge of the PSRC and other conservative groups that public sector unions were too powerful. Indeed, Democrats had helped give that argument credibility. In Seattle, Wes Uhlman had charged firefighters with attempting to put the mayor under their thumb. In Atlanta, Maynard Jackson warned that sanitation strikers were singling him out because of his liberal credentials. Jackson warned that if he gave in, then other black mayors would also face unreasonable union demands. Future U.S. senator Dianne Feinstein advanced her career on the San Francisco Board of Supervisors by urging the city to resist power-hungry municipal unions. And in New York, Mayor Ed Koch, a fiscal populist, took a belligerent tone toward public employee unions. In the short run, these politicians and other Democrats who followed this tack enhanced their personal political appeal among voters who worried about inflation and taxes. But in the long run, they fed a perception that the rising cost of government was due to union demands, a perception that conservatives were ultimately better positioned to exploit.[22]

Indeed, conservatives effectively parlayed that perception into support for the "tax revolt" of the late 1970s. In the midst of the wave of public sector labor militancy in 1978, California voters went to the polls in the first major skirmish of that revolt, ratifying Proposition 13, which mandated drastic reductions in property taxes across the state. Howard Jarvis, who engineered the Proposition 13 campaign, later attributed its success to the voters' desire to send the message to labor. The message was this: "public employee unions are not . . . entitled to run the country." The argument obviously resonated: Jarvis boasted that even a majority of private sector union members, who themselves were worried about high taxes, supported Proposition 13. The liberal analyst Nicholas von Hoffman lent some credence to Jarvis's contentions, arguing in 1978 that public opinion had "turned so ferociously against striking civil servants that non-governmental union members won't even support them." Although this claim was overstated, there was at least some element of truth in it for the Jarvis formula proved eminently exportable even to states with high union densities. The liberal state of Massachusetts enacted its own tax-cutting referendum, Proposition 2½. And one worried Michigan legislator warned that the voters were "out for blood" in 1978, as anti-tax sentiment grew in one of labor's most highly organized states.[23]

As concerns about public employee union power, high taxes, and the cost of government merged in the minds of an increasing number of American voters, a self-reinforcing political dynamic had taken hold by 1980. Democrats saw Republicans convincingly position themselves as more frugal and responsible stewards of the public purse in part because the latter were seen as less beholden to public employee unions. Having themselves recently characterized public sector unions as unreasonable, Democrats found it increasingly difficult to counter GOP charges of union overreaching. Even when Democrats did take hard-line positions against their allies in government workers' unions, they rarely reaped a lasting benefit from these actions. Critics contended that Democrats' tough talk was merely a ritualistic effort to reassure voters. When the dust settled after individual confrontations between government unions and Democratic executives, conservatives charged, it was business as usual, with Democrats buying off the unions with higher wages and improved benefits at the taxpayer's expense. Even when Democratic mayors fired workers who struck illegally, argued the critics, those mayors tended to rehire the law breakers once the conflicts were settled, as happened after Atlanta's sanitation strike. "Each time public servants strike in violation of court orders, laws or contractual agreements, officials warn that the strikers will be punished, usually by fines or firings or both," *Washington Post* columnist Bill Gold pointed out in 1979. "But in almost every case, the warnings prove to be without substance," Gold contended. It was time for politicians to draw the line, Gold argued.[24]

Ronald Reagan pledged to do just that. By the time Reagan catapulted into the presidency in 1980 by promising to get "government off our backs," Republicans had become adept at manipulating fears of public sector union power. Reagan exploited that issue to the fullest in his first year in office. In August 1981, he faced a walkout by 12,000 federal air traffic controllers, members of PATCO, the union Richard Nixon's administration had granted recognition to less than a decade earlier. Reagan did not respond by merely threatening to fire PATCO strikers. He made good on the threat, permanently replacing the striking air traffic controllers. The move sent shock waves through the entire U.S. labor relations regime. Following Reagan's lead, emboldened private sector employers successfully replaced strikers in a series of high-profile labor conflicts in the 1980s, strike rates plummeted, and union power sharply declined, inaugurating a harsh new era for American unions. Ironically, those Democrats who sought during the 1970s to portray themselves as defenders of the public interest against overweening union power had helped fashion the hard-line tactics and rhetoric that Ronald Reagan used so effectively in 1981 to undermine the Democrats' labor allies.[25]

Ultimately, the PATCO strike did not just legitimize private sector union busting in the 1980s; it also further weakened the once-aggressively expansive public sector movement, ensuring that the 1970s would be remembered as a disappointing decade for labor. Democrats and their public sector union allies had entered the 1970s believing that their alliance could work to their mutual advantage and spark a liberal labor resurgence. But the fiscal crisis of the 1970s undermined these hopes, pitted many Democrats against government unions, and opened the door to a conservative revival. To be sure, the Reagan Revolution did not end public sector union power. Despite the PATCO debacle, public sector unions generally retained the gains they had made in the early 1970s. Moreover, Reagan's ascendance helped re-cement the once-strained ties between Democrats and public sector unions in the 1980s. But by the early 1980s, it was clear that the era of public sector labor's expansion was over, and a new conservative era had dawned.

How could Dem's abandon the unions rights, especially with how synonomous they are with civil rights. even abolitioning slavery was essentially the fed gov over stepping sovereignty, but w/ a greater purpose.

[handwritten annotation: conservative activists, most notably the former actor + CA governor Ronald Reagan, started to break into the foreign policy community through attacks on détente.]

Détente and Its Discontents

JEREMI SURI

By 1972, Henry Kissinger had become the dominant foreign policy figure of his era. Through a mix of adroit diplomatic maneuvers, bluster, and secrecy, he gave shape to the floundering efforts of his predecessors. Kissinger personally managed the negotiation of the first agreement with Moscow to limit the growth of Soviet and American nuclear arsenals (the Strategic Arms Limitation Treaty [SALT I]), he opened relations for the first time between the United States and the People's Republic of China, and he began the bloody extraction of American military forces from Vietnam. The concept of "détente" became associated with Kissinger as a turn toward stability, cooperation, and order in international politics after years of perpetual crisis. Détente would not replace the Cold War, but it would make it more livable, more normal.

President Richard Nixon was, of course, largely responsible for many of these policy shifts in the early 1970s. Kissinger, however, cultivated the imagination of diplomats and citizens alike. He was the figure most closely associated with détente. The genius and mystery of his activities, particularly the initial cloak-and-dagger contacts with the Chinese, made this portly German Jewish immigrant the most unlikely of celebrities.

227

Oriana Fallaci, a famous Italian writer, captured the early 1970s allure of détente and Kissinger, in her revealing interview with the American policymaker:

Fallaci: Dr. Kissinger, how do you explain your incredible super-star status, how do you explain that fact that you have become almost more famous and popular than a president?

Kissinger: China was an important element in the mechanics of my success. And yet, that isn't the main point . . . The main point stems from the fact that I've always acted alone. Americans ad-mire that enormously. Americans admire the cowboy leading the caravan alone astride his horse, the cowboy entering a village or city alone on his horse. Without even a pistol, maybe, because he doesn't go in for shooting. He acts, that's all: aiming at the right spot at the right time. A Wild West tale, if you like.[1]

Kissinger's words highlight the personalized nature of his for-eign policy and the aspiration of détente to bring leadership to a world on the frontier of chaos. Within only eight years, however, the public image of both détente and Kissinger had changed radi-cally. The early 1970s superstar came under attack from Demo-crats and Republicans for sacrificing American ideals in the pursuit of international stability. Human rights activists and em-boldened conservatives similarly condemned the moral vacuous-ness of détente as evidenced in alleged American appeasement of the Soviet Union and China, ignominious defeat in Vietnam, and U.S. support for brutal dictators throughout Latin America, Africa, and the Middle East. In the aftermath of the Iranian Revo-lution of 1978 and the Soviet invasion of Afghanistan a year later, many of Kissinger's former admirers believed that he had placed the country on the wrong side of history.

In 1976 and 1980, both Ronald Reagan and Jimmy Carter used Kissinger as a political punching bag. He had quickly mutated from a celebrity hero into a notorious villain. Talking at the end of the decade with former Israeli ambassador and prime minister Yitzhak Rabin, Kissinger gave up the cowboy self-image and adopted the position of a prophetic martyr: "The most recent internal crises in the United States during the last decade have created, in the past few years, an American foreign policy that gave up vital geopolitical positions and allowed the Soviets to expand their sphere of influence without a fear. In the U.S. there is an atmosphere of exaggerated opposition to an active American involvement outside the continent."

Commenting on this discussion with Kissinger, Rabin observed: "As we sit in Kissinger's office in Washington, wrapped in memories from the great days of the late 1960s and the early 1970s, gloom pervades the outside atmosphere. America was brought to its knees in different corners of the world. The television news is filled with vivid and depressing broadcasts about the state of the nation; tens of thousands of hysterical demonstrators in Tehran shout in front of the cameras and burn flags."[2]

The international stability and American leadership that détente fostered in the early 1970s proved both superficial and self-defeating. In direct relations between the United States and the Soviet Union, it reinforced the status quo, discouraging attempts to overcome international divisions around Germany and the Korean peninsula. In other areas, it failed to prevent, and in fact encouraged, violence and conflict. Particularly in Africa, foreign intervention, political turmoil, and warfare became more common during this period. Détente created a hollow peace.[3]

Widespread criticism of American intervention in Vietnam, and of Cold War foreign policy in general, placed enormous pressure on leaders to offer a scheme that limited direct U.S. commitments overseas and promised new forms of international cooperation. As Kissinger admitted, "This administration came into office when the intellectual capital of U.S. postwar policy had been used up and when the conditions determining postwar U.S. policy had been altered." "We had to adjust our foreign policy," he continued, "to the new facts of life." Domestic upheaval in almost all of the most powerful states encouraged embattled leaders, like Kissinger, to seek a "new international settlement—which will be more stable, less crisis-conscious, and less dependent on decisions in one capital."[4]

Détente provided Kissinger with new political leverage at home and abroad, but it also inspired powerful opposition. In jettisoning traditional American claims about democracy and justice, Kissinger ceded the moral agenda to others. Human rights activists criticized détente for neglecting the basic needs and wants of citizens, particularly in countries like Chile, where the United States cooperated with an oppressive anti-Communist regime. Advocates of a more aggressive ("hard-line") foreign policy that challenged Communist governments condemned détente for its weakness and its willingness to accept the enemy on its own terms. According to this argument, détente was a surrender to Soviet power.

Human rights activists and hard-liners shared a strong moral critique of détente for abandoning basic American ideals. They also shared a belief that the United States should do more to change the world, rather than to accept it as it is. Most important, both groups looked to new leaders who could replace Kissinger's emphasis on settlement with a more positive and hopeful agenda. By the late 1970s, Kissinger symbolized an old and discredited Cold War *Realpolitik*.

Détente's achievement in providing some basic international stability empowered these criticisms. This is one of the central ironies of the period. A reduction in prior fears of nuclear holocaust and major war in Europe allowed more attention to issues of human rights and basic ideals. The broader international contacts encouraged by détente facilitated the formation of human rights organizations (like Amnesty International) and conservative networks (like the Committee on the Present Danger). These groups were the children of détente and also the primary poles of opposition—on the

Left and the Right—to American foreign policy in the 1970s. They drew popular support away from the political middle ground that Kissinger attempted to occupy. The early successes of détente sowed the seeds of its demise at decade's end.

Détente was a source and a target of attacks on American foreign policy. It nurtured high expectations among initial supporters that quickly evolved into frustration and disillusion. By the end of the decade, it became a "useful adversary" for advocates of political transformation.

Despite the international setbacks for the United States in the late 1970s, the challenges of a decade earlier proved far greater. The late 1960s, in fact, marked the most contentious and troubled moment for American foreign policy since the first years of the twentieth century. The conflict in Vietnam became more self-defeating for the United States with every additional deployment of soldiers and every promise that there was "a light at the end of the tunnel." By 1968, the war had decimated a large section of Southeast Asia, alienated Washington's closest allies, divided Americans on the proper role for their nation in the world, and destroyed a presidency. Public protests made Lyndon Johnson a virtual hostage in the White House. In this context, American foreign policy was paralyzed, and the future promised more setbacks at home and abroad. Observing these developments from London, British foreign minister Michael Stewart recorded a common foreboding outlook about the future in his personal diary: "The 10:pm television news presents a depressing picture . . . The great difficulty of the world is the moral deficiencies of what should be the free world."[5]

Stewart followed this diary entry with a desperate hope that détente would restore American leadership, alliance solidarity, and public confidence that government could "devise something truly better" for international relations.[6] This was the sentiment that the newly elected president, Richard Nixon, and his special assistant for national security affairs, Henry Kissinger, tapped when they promised to reassert American leverage over the world by replacing the paralysis of the late 1960s with new foreign policy overtures. In particular, the incoming administration pledged to reduce U.S. troop commitments in Vietnam while building an indigenous anti-Communist replacement ("Vietnamization"), to strengthen regional allies with fewer losses of American life (the "Nixon Doctrine"), and to establish peaceful East–West relations through trade and diplomacy. Détente referred specifically to East–West relations, but it came to embody the new administration's efforts to offer a fresh beginning after years of turmoil and despair.

Kissinger's fame as the daily manager of détente rose as hopes for diplomatic success reached a crescendo in 1972. During that extraordinary year, he and President Nixon traveled to China in February and the Soviet Union in May. The announcement of the planned "opening" to China, and of Kissinger's secret preparatory trip, "shook the world."[7] This was not an exaggeration. The images of Nixon and Kissinger conversing with Mao Zedong in his cluttered study signaled a new era of Sino-American friendship, after more than two decades of estrangement and conflict. The joint statement of the U.S. and Chinese governments that concluded Nixon's visit on February 28, 1972 (the "Shanghai Communiqué"), endorsed peaceful relations between the two countries as well as cooperation in settling regional disputes. Despite its deep ties to the anti-Communist regime in Taiwan, the Nixon administration accepted the Chinese Communist Party as the only legitimate government on the mainland. This crucial shift in diplomatic recognition set the basis for the People's Republic to assume the "Chinese" seat in the United Nations for the first time and to establish "normal" diplomatic relations with the United States a few years later. Sino-American détente, rather than traditional Cold War animosity, promised stability in Asia and new leverage for

Washington in its relations with North Vietnam and the Soviet Union.

Moscow's leadership was indeed shaken by Nixon and Kissinger's visit to China. Anatoly Dobrynin, the Soviet ambassador to the United States at the time, recalled that his government "had not even considered . . . a possibility of rapprochement" between Washington and Beijing. "No one was more surprised and confused than the Kremlin when it received the news of Nixon's plan to go to China even before, as it finally turned out, he would meet [Soviet general secretary Leonid] Brezhnev at the summit in Moscow."[8]

The Soviet Union and China competed against one another for international influence and dominance of their long, disputed border. They nearly went to war over a series of boundary skirmishes in 1969. In this context, despite increased American bombing of Moscow's ally in North Vietnam, the Soviet Union pressed for a visible improvement in its relations with the United States to counteract potential Chinese advances. Nixon and Kissinger's trip to Moscow in May 1972 produced the first superpower treaty (SALT I) to curtail the future expansion of nuclear arsenals, an agreement (the ABM Treaty) to limit the deployment of anti-ballistic missile systems, and a public pledge to international cooperation. The Moscow summit marked a clear turn away from the Cold War belligerence that inspired so much international and domestic division during the 1960s.[9]

Kissinger and his Soviet counterparts drafted an agreement, creating a cornerstone of détente, on "basic principles" that would assure "mutual understanding and business-like cooperation" between the superpowers in order to "remove the threat of war" and to "create conditions which promote the reduction of tensions."[10] In contrast to the aggression associated with American actions in Vietnam, the United States would now take a leadership role in establishing "rules of conduct" to govern an "age in which a cataclysm depends on the decisions of men."[11] The new rules included mutual consultation between the superpowers, respect for national sovereignty, and increased contact through trade and person-to-person exchanges. If the visit to China opened an era of Sino-American cooperation, the Moscow summit initiated a period of U.S.–Soviet coordination on arms control, economics, and crisis management. Recognizing the diplomatic and political value of Kissinger's "basic principles," the leaders of the superpowers signed the final version of the text at the conclusion of their meetings on May 29, 1972.[12]

Détente, as enshrined in the "basic principles" agreement, promised to replace Cold War conflict with a peaceful international order. It also attempted to restore America's asserted international role as a proponent of progress and enlightenment. The continuation of the Vietnam War at the same time, however, undercut this position. In mid-1972, the United States still had about 70,000 soldiers fighting in Southeast Asia. In response to the "Easter Offensive" initiated by North Vietnamese forces, Nixon and Kissinger launched the largest series of American aerial bombardments and related attacks on enemy forces in the region. Within six months, the United States had carpeted the landscape with more than 125,000 tons of bomb materièl. The combined ferocity of the fighting on the ground and the bombardments from the air produced more than 150,000 casualties, recorded in the horrifying pictures circulating throughout the American media of fleeing families and scorched children. Although public protests against the Vietnam War diminished in their intensity during this period (at least in comparison to the demonstrations between 1968 and 1970), the escalating brutality in Southeast Asia belied the peaceful promises of détente. The expansion of the conflict made it appear that the United States was using improved relations with China and the Soviet Union to further its military aims rather than to pursue peace.[13]

The final piece of the détente puzzle, therefore, involved a full American withdrawal from Vietnam. Nixon and Kissinger sought to extricate the United States from this conflict with minimal damage to the credibility of American power. They feared that if the United States looked weak in Southeast Asia, that would encourage challenges to American power elsewhere. Preserving the image of strength required the fiction of "Vietnamization"—the illusion that Washington's allies in South Vietnam would take over the fight against the Communists. This policy began with a gradual drawdown in American soldiers fighting on the ground. It also included a broader transformation in the structure of the U.S. military. In 1973, the Nixon administration eliminated the draft and created a smaller all-volunteer force that would, at least in theory, fight more professionally and effectively. The U.S. government also worked to isolate the military from the intensely politicized environment at home, hoping that a self-contained corps could remain a credible threat, despite domestic dissent.[14]

The logical end of "Vietnamization" was a departure of American battlefield troops from the region and their transfer to support activities for indigenous forces through the use of air and sea power, in particular. Nixon and Kissinger claimed, perhaps dishonestly, that this shift would prevent defeat for America's allies. After months of intensive and often secret negotiations with Communist representatives from the government of North Vietnam and the National Liberation Front for South Vietnam, in January 1973 Kissinger concluded the Paris Peace Accords, which assured the withdrawal of the last American soldiers in the next year. Along with his North Vietnamese interlocutor, Le Duc Tho, Kissinger received the Nobel Peace Prize for bringing an end to direct American participation in the Vietnam War and for delivering on détente's promise.

President Nixon declared that he and Kissinger had achieved "peace with honor"—an end to America's longest, bloodiest, and most controversial Cold War conflict.[15] Kissinger's popular allure derived largely from his central role in this endeavor. He had, in some eyes, saved the nation from a continued hemorrhaging of lives and treasure.[16]

In April 1975, however, the rapid collapse of Washington's South Vietnamese allies led many to question whether Kissinger had really achieved anything in his negotiations. Some critics, often associated with the Democratic Party, argued that the Nixon administration prolonged the Vietnam War needlessly, achieving the same withdrawal and defeat in 1975 that it could have attained in 1969—without the death and destruction of the last six years. Other critics, frequently connected to an insurgent element within the Republican Party, accused Nixon and Kissinger of conciliating weak-willed protestors and treacherous Communist enemies— accepting a virtual surrender of American efforts in Vietnam. Kissinger, in fact, adopted this latter argument in his criticism of the U.S. Congress for cutting off all aid to South Vietnam in 1974. He proclaimed his own commitment to achieving an honorable peace that strengthened America's international position.[17]

Debates about the "lessons" of Vietnam dominated the discussion of foreign policy in the United States during the second half of the 1970s. Was the American withdrawal from Vietnam crucial to securing peace, stability, and international leadership for the nation, as Kissinger claimed? Did the lateness of the departure undermine the deeper prospects for peace and cooperation, as Democratic detractors argued? Or was the withdrawal and collapse of South Vietnam an indication of détente's cowardice, as Republican critics like Ronald Reagan asserted?

The Cold War entered a period of détente with the conclusion of the China opening, the Moscow summit, and the American withdrawal from Vietnam. Unlike the years between 1961 and 1969 (when John Kennedy and Lyndon Johnson occupied the White House), the years between 1969 and 1977 (when Richard Nixon and Gerald Ford were commanders-in-chief) witnessed no major foreign policy crises threatening war between the United States and either of its main Communist adversaries. The flow of trade, ideas, and people across societies increased by virtually all measures, especially in Europe and Asia.

Kissinger was both the hero and the villain of this historical moment. He orchestrated many of the moves that made détente possible, but his achievements raised new and difficult questions about America's role in the world. Advocates of human rights on one side and defenders of tough-minded anti-Communism on the other attacked Kissinger for the troubling limitations of détente. Leaving office in 1977, the former special assistant for national security affairs and secretary of state felt that his critics unfairly made him a victim of his own successes.[18]

In encouraging increased person-to-person contacts across societies, détente facilitated the formation of transnational political movements. This was particularly true for groups advocating human rights. Between 1974 and 1976, Amnesty International, one of the most prominent examples of these groups, experienced an astronomical expansion, from 3,000 to 50,000 members.[19] Grassroots attention to human rights spread through publicity about notorious abuses in countries like Chile, Argentina, Czechoslovakia, and the Soviet Union. Citizens across societies, including many Communist-dominated nations, became more comfortable associating themselves with calls for political reform. The participants in Amnesty International and other similar organizations shared information and resources in their efforts to expand universal citizen protections. Their efforts helped to create the rudiments for a common recognition about the importance of human rights. Even violent dictators felt pressure to claim, falsely, that they were meeting basic standards of conduct. By the end of the decade, the transnational mobilization of activists had made human rights a recognized and powerful part of international politics.[20]

Nixon and Kissinger felt the sting of human rights activism at home and abroad. Many critics of the Vietnam War turned their attention to the regional tyrants that the United States aided through its détente policies. The U.S.-supported coup in Chile on September 11, 1973, and the rise to power of a brutal dictator, Augusto Pinochet, became a strong inspiration for popular condemnations of Nixon and Kissinger. Chilean and other South American dissidents who escaped the domestic terror played an especially influential role in drawing attention to the consequences of the coup and to Washington's responsibility. With a less threatening Soviet Union and the widespread flow of information about the atrocities committed by U.S. allies, American citizens grew skeptical (and frequently angry) about the undemocratic consequences of détente.[21]

Popular revulsion at the human rights violations in Chile and other countries drove congressional efforts to restrict the foreign policy power of the president. In 1975, the Senate and the House of Representatives initiated extensive investigations (through the Church and Pike committees, respectively) into abuses of covert action by the White House. The committees sought to open the secretive world of foreign policymaking to closer public scrutiny, especially for those who had lost loved ones at the hands of America's allies. Congress uncovered evidence of CIA interventions in Latin America, the Middle East, and other parts of the globe. The Church and Pike committees prohibited U.S. intelligence agencies from conducting targeted assassinations in the future, and they required more public reporting. The investigations of 1975–1976 diminished the capabilities of the White House. They affirmed a set of humanitarian limitations on the uses of secrecy and force.[22]

Senator Henry "Scoop" Jackson, a Democratic presidential hopeful from Washington State, channeled the moral outrage directed at American intelligence activities into calls for assistance to repressed groups within the Soviet Union, particularly Jews. Jackson accused Kissinger of reinforcing Soviet tyranny by signing a "basic principles" agreement that offered the regime Western trade and legitimacy without any stipulations about improving the treatment of its citizens. He focused on Russian Jews because they were an active and visible minority suffering under Soviet oppression. They also had wealthy and influential supporters among the Jewish population in the United States. In 1974, Jackson and his colleague in the House of Representatives Charles Vanik (D-OH) successfully amended American legislation to prohibit most-favored-nation trade status with the Soviet Union and other countries that did not permit the free emigration of minorities (this was the content of the "Jackson-Vanik Amendment").

Public human rights mobilization had very quickly produced legislative restrictions on Kissinger's détente maneuvers. The Soviet leadership predictably objected to the Jackson-Vanik Amendment, and to human rights criticisms in general, as an interference in its sovereign domestic sphere. Kissinger also condemned Jackson and other activists for threatening the global order that he had built: "American-Soviet relations were turning fragile under the impact of an ideological crusade conducted without adequate regard for the long-term international consequences." Kissinger pointed out that Soviet restrictions on Jewish immigration actually increased in response to the Jackson-Vanik challenge.[23]

Human rights critics opposed détente not in theory but in its practice in the Nixon administration. Supporters of Amnesty International and other groups agreed with Kissinger on the need for a more stable world with increased cooperation among leaders. That was not enough, however. They wanted to see evidence that cooperation among leaders served higher principles, not just the political status quo. They wanted evidence of progress toward a better world, not just a stable one.

In this context, advocates of a more principled approach to East–West relations pushed for new policy alternatives. Operating through the Conference on Security and Cooperation in Europe (CSCE)—which included the European states, the Soviet Union, Canada, and the United States—a small group of politicians and activists, mostly from outside the United States, attempted to revise the nature of détente. They called for the freer movement of all peoples (not just Russian Jews), for protections for basic human dignities defined in political and economic terms, and for improvements in social welfare. In place of the stability guaranteed by nuclear deterrence, CSCE participants sought to build assurances for peace through deeper interpenetration between societies and through strong assertions of moral principle. Étienne Davignon, a member of the Belgian Foreign Ministry, was most eloquent in his articulation of this position. He argued that a "United Europe must be founded on a common patrimony of respect for liberty and human rights."[24]

Davignon's words implied a growing division between the American government's position on détente and that of its allies in Europe. Kissinger recognized this phenomenon and its connection to the turmoil of the late 1960s: "The problem of the western countries right now is that the nature of authority in all of them is in the process of redefinition. The nature of their national purposes is in redefinition because all of them are going through domestic crises, including we [sic]."[25]

By early 1975, Kissinger and President Gerald Ford (who succeeded Nixon on August 9, 1974) understood that they could not resist this growing human rights pressure. Despite their doubts, they endorsed a provision in the emerging CSCE treaty that affirmed the "universal significance of human rights."[26] Enshrined as "Basket 3" of the Helsinki Final Act, signed by both superpowers and their European allies on August 1, 1975, this statement made détente conditional on improvements in the treatment of citizens.

It subordinated geopolitical order to moral principles. Most significant, it inspired and legitimized the further mobilization of human rights activists—East and West—to challenge the secrecy and elitism at the core of détente policy, as initially formulated by Kissinger.

Détente, in this sense, was a precondition and an opponent of the political movements that formed in the 1970s and ultimately undermined the Cold War. Although Nixon and Kissinger sought to minimize the influence of human rights claims on policy, the international stability and cooperation they nurtured made these claims difficult to resist. The U.S. government's continued support for inhumane regimes meant that it would become a primary target for the very human rights claims it had enabled. Détente shifted the human rights agenda out of American control.

Ronald Reagan, the B-grade movie actor and General Electric spokesman turned politician, reacted against this loss of American moral prestige. He was the anti-Kissinger of the 1970s and early 1980s. He championed a return to American assertiveness against the very adversaries Kissinger conciliated through détente. Instead of arms control agreements with the Soviet Union, Reagan demanded a military buildup to challenge Communist positions, especially in Eastern Europe. Instead of emphasizing a new opening with Communist China, he argued for a strengthening of the U.S. relationship with the regime in Taiwan. Instead of accepting a negotiated settlement in Indochina that allowed for the North Vietnamese to overrun the peninsula, Reagan called for an international outcry against the horrors of Communist aggression. Attacking both the détente policies of Kissinger and the human rights rhetoric of many of his opponents, Reagan condemned the "hypocrisy" of elite opinion makers "in the town of Babel on the Hudson": "We express concern that human rights are being denied to some in Rhodesia, South Africa and Chile. But where are the indignant voices protesting the hundreds of thousands of South Vietnamese, Laotians, and Cambodians who are dying of torture and starvation in North Vietnam's concentration camps?"[27]

In 1976, Reagan challenged and nearly defeated Gerald Ford for the Republican Party's presidential nomination. His criticisms transformed détente from a badge of honor into a political expletive. The Ford campaign went so far as to ban its public use of the term. Reagan also popularized the viewpoints of a small bipartisan group of intellectuals and former policymakers—"the Committee on the Present Danger"—that argued for an immediate American rearmament: "The Soviet military budget is 40 to 80% more per year than our own in real terms. Our secretary of defense has described the situation as the fable of the tortoise and the hare. We sat back deceived by the belief that we had 'overkill' capacity. We cut our military budgets by half while the Soviets increased theirs . . . The American people are clearly in favor of regaining the military position of number one but like the hare, officialdom is still sleeping under the tree."[28]

Kissinger, human rights activists, and many mainstream American officials contested both Reagan's facts and his general argument. Nonetheless, the majority of the American people believed Reagan's words. In the aftermath of the social turmoil of the early 1970s, the humiliating retreat from Vietnam, the Soviet invasion of Afghanistan, and the prolonged frustration of the American hostage crisis in Iran, voters wanted to believe that the nation could make a comeback. Reagan effectively blamed the foreign policy "establishment"—embodied by Kissinger—for contributing to the nation's predicament, and he promised to bring a new populist approach to the White House. He would combine a return to comfortable old anti-Communist and exceptionalist American themes with a new sense of energy and hope.

After his election in 1980, Reagan followed through on his promises to dismantle détente. He initiated one of the largest military buildups in American history. He also refused to conduct amicable relations with Soviet leaders until they changed their behavior at home and abroad. He was particularly concerned with the Kremlin's treatment of religious and political dissidents. Reagan held superpower relations hostage to evidence of human rights improvements in the Soviet Union—a position that even advocacy groups like Amnesty International found unwise. Mainstream human rights activists pursued reform through East–West cooperation. Reagan believed reform would occur only when Communist regimes faced forceful pressure, including threats of war.

These policies became intensely controversial in the United States and Europe, inspiring accusations that a reckless and ignorant president was bringing the world to the precipice of nuclear annihilation. He had rejected years of established diplomatic precedence. Instead of focusing on how to make peace with the Soviet Union, Reagan asked how to use threat and force against Communist adversaries. He presumed change through conflict, not cooperation. Reagan's policies evolved during the 1980s, but his positions were unequivocal when he entered office.

Détente had advocated stability and coexistence between East and West. After the late 1970s, international relations entered a period of uncertainty, belligerence, and low-scale warfare between the largest states. Rewriting Kissinger's script, Reagan largely authored this shift. Although this revolutionary transformation did not bring an end to the Cold War, as some of his admirers claim, it did set the stage for major changes in the nature of Soviet–American relations. Reagan's policies tore apart the geopolitical status quo upon which Kissinger had built the edifice of détente.[29]

Looking back on his years in office, Kissinger claimed that "there was no significant conceptual difference among the various assessments of the international environment by the Nixon, Ford, and Reagan administrations."[30] Nothing could be further from the truth.

The 1970s was a decade filled with serious and wide-ranging debates about the conduct of American foreign policy. Kissinger's concept of détente brilliantly set the terms of discussion. He advocated American international leadership through stability, cooperation, and improved relations with former adversaries. Although he always accepted the superiority of American democracy and freedom, Kissinger sought to limit their use as guides for foreign policy.[31]

Kissinger's successes in the early part of the decade empowered those who focused on the costs of his policies. Human rights advocates and conservative anti-Communists attacked the efficacy and morality of Kissinger's basic assumptions. With each passing year, these condemnations gained ground among voters. By 1980, the critics of détente had come to dominate American politics, and they have retained this position ever since. Kissinger's rise and fall as a heroic public figure tracks the rise and fall of détente. Reagan's emergence, in place of Kissinger, highlights the self-confidence and self-assertion that have defined American thinking about the world since the 1970s.

Détente helped to preserve, and even enhance, American international power. It also motivated a renewed desire for moral clarity, rather than diplomatic subtlety, in U.S. policy. Ronald Reagan and the political Right drew on Kissinger's commitment to the exercise of American power, but they added a faith in the universal applicability of American ideals that Kissinger lacked. Kissinger provided the tools for men with Reagan's aims.

Two decades after Reagan left office, his successors have forgotten this important historical lesson. They have adopted Reagan's moralistic rhetoric and his expansive international aims, but they have neglected the diplomacy, compromise, and flexibility that allowed him to act effectively. They have pursued a hollow crusade for global democracy without the consensus building and international stability that only détente could provide. Success in transforming the Middle East, modeled on the defeat of the Soviet

Union in the 1980s, requires both cooperation and force, diplomacy and moral clarity. Henry Kissinger's influence in the White House after the first year of the Iraq War reflects this recognition—though perhaps too late. The next president will have to craft a more consistent mix of détente and idealism—a combination of Kissinger and Reagan.[32]

the inability of Democratic leaders to respond to the challenges raised by Vietnam created a huge vacuum that conservatives exploited.

CHAPTER 13

Carter's Nicaragua and Other Democratic Quagmires

DEREK N. BUCKALOO

Jimmy Carter's 1976 presidential campaign was perfectly modulated for its times, for Washington had rarely looked so tawdry and misguided. Richard Nixon had resigned in disgrace in August 1974 and was replaced by the unelected Gerald Ford, who pardoned his predecessor just weeks later. These Republican sins of Watergate were coupled in foreign affairs with the end of the Vietnam War, a conflict that had concluded anticlimactically in North Vietnamese victory in April 1975. Seizing this opportunity, Carter avoided staking policy positions while seeming to offer the greatest of departures: the promise of honesty. In this context, his lack of national experience became an asset, for the candidate could argue that he was untainted by the sins of Washington's recent past. In foreign affairs, Carter promised to reground American policy by returning it to the American people themselves, telling cheering crowds on the campaign trail that "what we seek is . . . a foreign policy that reflects the decency and generosity and common sense of our own people."[1]

Such rhetoric was surely attractive on the campaign trail, for it congratulated the electorate for its common sense while seeming to

246

put forward a future that few could oppose. By 1976, few Americans wanted more Vietnams. However, that broad agreement sat unstably atop profound disagreements over just what the phrase "no more Vietnams" meant. Faced with American failure in Southeast Asia, Americans divided over what was to be avoided. Conservatives argued that the United States should never fail militarily again and placed blame on the media and the antiwar movement for undermining the troops overseas. Mainstream liberals rued the choice to fight in Vietnam and urged that Americans look with finer discernment at which international situations required which tactics. And further to the Left, in a space that many Democrats were moving to as they pondered what the United States had done in Vietnam, many viewed the Vietnam War as evidence that the United States had become, or always had been, an aggressive, expansionist power. In this case, the lessons were about ends as much as tactics: only by redefining what the United States should oppose could one avoid the tumble into future Vietnam-like wars. This dissensus on American foreign policy replaced the Cold War consensus that had led into Vietnam. How to finesse these divisions while putting in place a defensible and politically popular foreign policy would be among Jimmy Carter's challenges as he took office in the post–Vietnam War moment.

If anything, that moment becomes all the more significant as we look back from the post-9/11 world, in which the George W. Bush administration's war in Iraq has churned up charged debate over analogies between the Vietnam War and present policy while Democrats struggle consistently with the charge of weakness on foreign policy. How is it that, over time, Democrats were saddled with weakness, rather than credited with principled wisdom, in responding to the legacy of the Vietnam War?

The Carter administration, as the first post-Vietnam presidency, is a crucial place to begin to understand this development, for it was Carter's White House that had the first opportunity to redefine how the United States would relate to the world after the Vietnam War, as well as how the Democratic Party would be perceived on foreign policy and national security. The Vietnam War had raised unprecedented questions about the American relationship to the rest of the world as a "superpower," and with the Cold War consensus ended, the question of what would underpin American foreign policy could not be avoided. In responding to this question, there can be little doubt that the Carter administration made an earnest rhetorical attempt at regrounding American foreign policy on a basis of human rights, a recognition of limits, and a pledge to avoid Vietnam-like military interventions. However, when put into practice, as in the case of the Sandinista Revolution in Nicaragua, such a regrounding foundered on Central American realities and the unwillingness of the Carter administration to accept and defend the logical result of its rhetoric—local change in the developing world.

In the case of Nicaragua, Jimmy Carter attempted a mainstream liberal response to the lessons of the Vietnam War. In terms of means, the Carter administration reacted with relative patience and a clear avoidance of a military solution; however, in terms of ends, and despite rhetoric about putting aside Americans' "inordinate fear of communism," the administration reacted from traditional Cold War fears of leftist change. In other words, the policy change of the Carter administration was more apparent than real. Looking consistently for an evolutionary course that was not there, the administration ended up fighting a Nicaraguan version of "Vietnam minus the troops," a policy that varied on tactics, but not in terms of acceptable outcomes. Without clearly redefining the proper ends of U.S. foreign policy, the Carter administration appeared weak and remained vulnerable to conservative arguments for more martial means, whether by Americans or by proxies. If leftists should be kept from power in Nicaragua, as the Carter White House believed, then quibbling over the means of doing so appeared as weakness, not principle. Such a major redefinition of U.S. foreign policy goals would have proven quite difficult, given the real divisions among Americans on what post-Vietnam foreign policy should be, but it was never tried, and without it, Democrats, from Jimmy Carter forward, were consistently forced into defensive positions in arguments over national security. And the charge of Democratic weakness on national security would serve Republicans well as they rode American politics to the Right, under Ronald Reagan and beyond.

As Jimmy Carter took office in January 1977, he knew that he did so with a slim victory margin on the one hand, but with a victory based on his personification of a "fresh start" on the other. Informed by the set of Vietnam War lessons typical of liberals, Carter believed in and spoke of regrounding U.S. policy around basic principles that Americans could put forth with pride. On Inauguration Day, Carter assured the world that the United States would "not seek to dominate nor dictate to others. As we Americans have concluded one chapter in our Nation's history and are beginning to work on another, we have, I believe, acquired a more mature perspective on the problems of the world."[2]

That "more mature perspective" revolved around two chief ideas: the need to recognize limits and the value of human rights. By arguing in his inaugural address that "even our great nation has its recognized limits, and that we can neither answer all questions nor solve all problems," Carter was both preparing the American people to face their energy problems and stating the reality he recognized in Vietnam. Not all international events could be controlled by the United States, and Americans would need to accept results overseas that ran counter to their perception of what was right. If, as Carter believed, the Vietnam War was a hubristic mistake, the first step in avoiding such mistakes would be to recognize such limits. It was crucial for the United States, when it did attempt to affect international events, to remain committed to principles of human rights. In Vietnam, the United States had fought to defend a series of dictators who, though not Communist, were hardly paragons of virtue. Only by a rededication to doing good in the world could the United States hope to accomplish it. Carter institutionalized his human rights commitment by appointing civil rights activist Patricia Derian as human rights coordinator in the State Department and then, in August 1977, elevating her to assistant secretary of state for human rights.

Carter's most prominent statement of his departure in foreign affairs came in a commencement address at the University of Notre Dame on May 22, 1977. "I believe we can have a foreign policy that is democratic, that is based on fundamental values, and that uses power and influence, which we have, for humane purposes," Carter told the graduates. The ability to craft a new diplomatic policy was based on Americans' confidence in their own democratic system. "Being confident of our own future, we are now free of that inordinate fear of communism which once led us to embrace any dictator who joined us in that fear." Vietnam was his primary example of the failure of the old ways. "We've fought fire with fire, never thinking that fire is better quenched with water. This approach failed, with Vietnam the best example of its intellectual and moral poverty."[3] Free of fear and tempered by Vietnam, Carter argued that a more confident America could recognize limits, champion human rights, and avoid future quagmires.

Nicaragua and its dictatorial leader, Anastasio Somoza Jr., seemed like prime targets for the administration's new direction. Somoza was the third member of his family to wield power in Nicaragua, a line that ran back to the presence of U.S. Marines in the country in the early 1930s. His father had inspired the famous (though likely apocryphal) Franklin Roosevelt quip that "he is a son-of-a-bitch, but he's our son-of-a-bitch," a piece of jaded wisdom that would appear to apply equally to a long list of dictators in the Cold War era. The son, like the father, brazenly terrorized his domestic opponents and ran Nicaragua almost as his personal property. Ruthless and venal, Somoza was just the sort of dictator whose rule and relations with the United States might be reconsidered under a Carter administration.

Nicaraguans themselves were rethinking their relationship to their leader. Somoza's unseemly display of profiting from relief aid designed to rebuild Nicaragua after a devastating earthquake in 1972 broadened the ranks of those opposing him. Taking the lead in opposition was the Sandinista National Liberation Front (or FSLN, from the Spanish *Frente Sandinista de Liberación Nacional*), a Left-leaning resistance movement that had been founded in 1961 and named for the homegrown rebel hero Augusto Cesar Sandino, who had led the fight against the U.S. Marines in the 1920s and 1930s. Double-crossed and killed by Somoza Sr.'s National Guard in 1934, Sandino remained a potent symbol of resistance to both U.S. imperialism and the Somozas. Transcending their beginnings as a ragtag group of rebels, the Sandinistas survived Somoza's blows against them and found broadening support from trade unionists, Catholic liberals, and even businessmen willing to support a movement aimed at ridding Nicaragua of its long-time dictator.

Nicaragua thus presented the Carter administration with a perfect setting in which to apply a new foreign policy. Somoza was a dictator with a horrendous human rights record. Nicaraguans were progressively moving into active opposition to him. The United States had an aid relationship with the government, providing the Americans with a lever to encourage change. And unlike the Shah's Iran, Nicaragua was not an oil-rich country that crucially underpinned the American economy. Although Central America, since the days of the Monroe Doctrine, had long been perceived as a vital region to American interests, it was a region in which chances could be taken. The actions of the Somozas and their American sponsors afforded the new administration the opportunity to repent plenty of past sins through the application of a policy self-consciously focused on human rights.

In the event, however, the application of this new foreign policy to Nicaragua would be distinguished more by its limits than by its achievements, for the administration would consistently fail to get in front of the revolution and make a virtue of change by coming out in favor of it. Rather than confidently regrounding its policy toward Nicaragua on human rights principles and an acceptance of change, the administration, much like its predecessors, would modify its approach piecemeal and in response to events in Nicaragua. Without such crucial reframing from the bully pulpit of the White House, Carter's foreign policy proved too easily portrayed as that of one selling out a friend, rather than of standing on principle.

In early 1977, Nicaragua was not high on the list of administration priorities, even in Latin America. Regionally, as it applied human rights policies to autocratic regimes like Somoza's, the White House was focused on the Panama Canal treaties, which it considered an important symbol of its new departure in Central America. Although the pursuits of treaties in Panama and human rights improvements in Nicaragua were logically consistent as policy, they were at cross-purposes politically on Capitol Hill and created pressure on the administration to limit its own pressure on Somoza. Conservatives in Congress, including some prominent Democrats who aided in approving and implementing the Panama Canal treaties, viewed them as a wrong-headed giveaway of American property. These were often the same congressmen who viewed the situation in Nicaragua as a simple case of violent revolutionaries trying to create "the new Cuba of the Western Hemisphere" and saw the Carter administration pressure on Somoza as inappropriate lack of support for "a long and consistent ally of the United States."[4]

The heart of this group was the so-called Nicaragua Lobby, a varied group of legislators carefully cultivated by Somoza who viewed him as a crucial figure in defending U.S. interests against a Cuban operation aimed at turning Central America into another potential Vietnam much closer to American shores. This informal lobby was led by Representative John Murphy (D-NY), a personal friend of Somoza's since childhood, who remained in close touch with the dictator to the end of the revolution. When Lawrence Pezzullo, the newly appointed U.S. ambassador to Nicaragua, entered Somoza's office to meet him for the first time in June 1979, he found Murphy sitting on Somoza's desk, ready to advise him during the meeting. Thus, the Carter administration did face formidable obstacles on Capitol Hill, but these obstacles reinforced, rather than molded, the policy that was freely chosen by the White House. Somoza, whose government was viewed as stable in 1977, would be nudged toward improvements in human rights, in the hope of allowing a slow evolution of Nicaraguan politics without risking a revolution that leaned too far left.

The problem would be applying such an evolutionary policy in the revolutionary context of Nicaragua. The Carter administration wished to liberalize Somoza, but it was never willing to turn on him completely, inasmuch as such a policy would seemingly bring on the revolutionary changes it feared. As Robert Pastor writes, "viewing the key Sandinista military leaders as Marxist-Leninists who admired Cuba and despised the United States, the administration aimed to preclude a military victory by the Sandinistas but not to support Somoza, who was seen as indefensible."[5] Simple "nonsupport" of Somoza, after years of very active American support, could hardly place the administration on the side of change in the eyes of Nicaraguans and guaranteed a minimum of influence on any new Sandinista government. And in Washington, the policy raised the ire of conservatives, with their charges of weakness, without allowing a principled defense of change in Nicaragua as the logical outcome of a new, and improved, American policy shorn of the inordinate fear of Communism.

Unfortunately for the administration, revolutionary momentum continued to build in Nicaragua, as the FSLN attracted broadening support from respectable corners of society. In October 1977, a gathering of prominent Nicaraguans calling themselves the "Group of Twelve" issued a statement warning that "there can be no permanent solution to the escalating armed conflict . . . without the participation of the Sandinista National Liberation Front."[6] Months later, in the wake of the January 10, 1978, assassination of Pedro Jouquin Chamorro Cardenal, the publisher-editor of the respected opposition newspaper *La Prensa,* Nicaraguan business leaders called for a national strike, which shut down 90 percent of the Nicaraguan economy. Despite this broadening local support for the FSLN, the Carter administration policy remained focused on keeping the Nicaraguan Left from any real power, no matter how sensible their rhetoric or how broad their support became.

Somoza responded by aggressively putting down the FSLN's October military offensive, self-righteously refusing to take part in any sort of "national dialogue," and responding in the United States with savvy public relations. Labeling the Sandinista movement as "100 percent Communist," a letter from his press secretary in the *New York Times* charged that those opposed to Somoza "find it impossible to abide by the democratic climate which exists in our country. They are bent on trying to destroy it in order to replace it with a Marxist-Leninist regime—it is as simple as that."[7]

Certainly, members of the Nicaragua Lobby would have agreed with such charges, but the Carter administration remained caught in the middle. Armed with its human rights commitments and distaste for Somoza, the White House wanted to move Somoza toward an openness to political change, a move that would serve human rights goals and hopefully win Nicaraguan hearts and minds without affecting the economic realities that underpinned both his regime and the revolution overtaking it. But politics and economics are two sides of the same coin. A more gentle approach by Somoza would undermine his ability to fight the insurgents without removing the sources of the insurgents' fight. In the Nicaraguan context, human rights policy logically led to change that went beyond cautious political liberalization. Without forewarning Americans of this, while defending that outcome as known and acceptable, the Carter White House risked the appearance of an unwelcome revolutionary change brought on by its policies, rather than the fall of a human-rights violator who had lost the support of his own people. Thus, the White House remained caught between competing desires to apply human rights policies without fear and to avoid the revolutionary change that followed from such policies.

Although Carter's strict nonintervention policy hardly put the administration in open opposition to Somoza, it did allow Nicaraguans to take that position. "With Nixon in the White House and a pro-Somoza ambassador here, this [January 1978] strike simply would not have taken place," opined William Baez Sacasa, the manager of the Nicaraguan Development Institute. "No one was prepared to take on both the Somozas and the United States."[8] To this extent, conservative critics of Carter were right to suggest that his policy was contributing to the unrest, but this explanation ignores the fundamental socioeconomic realities in Nicaragua and simply defines revolutionary change to overthrow Somoza as a problem. The White House had not worked to redefine Somoza's revolutionary removal as a solution earlier, and it continued to refuse to do so, even as its distaste for Somoza grew.

Somoza continued to respond defensively to human rights pressures from Washington by criticizing both the policy and its source, stating that "those who historically have beaten up blacks and kept Indians as second-class citizens have nothing to teach us."[9] However, the dictator was far too savvy to let his anger toward Jimmy Carter, "that Baptist," as he called him, get in the way of his survival instinct.[10] Instead, Somoza played the public relations game, refusing to arrest members of the Group of Twelve, promising to allow the Inter-American Human Rights Commission to visit and to consider signing the American Convention on Human Rights, and declaring amnesty for political prisoners. In response, one of the more infamous letters in recent U.S. history was drafted. Jimmy Carter routinely sent letters to encourage progress on human rights and, impressed by the appearance of movement, asked for such a letter to Somoza. The substance and tone of the June 30, 1978, letter was a measured show of support for Somoza's promises, described by Carter as "important and heartening signs." But the symbolism proved much more important than the substance, for it seemed to show Carter's support for the dictatorship, even in the face of increasing reports of brutality by Somoza's National Guard. On August 1, the letter was leaked from the State Department and was splashed across the front page of the *Washington Post,* where it was described as giving "Somoza an encouraging pat on the back." The administration tried to clarify the letter's purposes, but failed. Carter had inadvertently associated himself with Somoza. The letter, too, brought genuine administration focus to the Nicaraguan situation for the first time and moved it from "the bureaucratic context of the human rights policy" to a full-fledged "political-security crisis" in which "the Human Rights Bureau was excluded from the central deliberations."[11] Faced with a typical Cold War choice between security concerns and human rights principles, the administration chose the former, muting its talk of necessary reforms in the hope of staving off a leftist victory. The Americans remained interested in talking human rights, but the situation in Nicaragua was changing too fast for this approach to work. As promising as Somoza's announcements appeared in Washington, they were seen in Nicaragua, quite correctly, as public relations moves designed to undercut the revolution.

In the fall of 1978 and in response to the increasing bloodshed of guerrilla attacks and brutal government retaliation, the Carter administration departed from its policy of strict nonintervention and called for mediation, a tactical move designed to remove Somoza as early and peacefully as possible, in order to frustrate the Left. Hope for the plan's success was based on Somoza's acceptance and the assumption that the Sandinistas could still be marginalized. "The longer Somoza remains in power, the greater (the FSLN's) claim to a share of power in any successor regime," wrote Cyrus Vance to the president. "Were Somoza replaced in the near future by an independent government—even a conservative one," Vance continued, "the Sandinistas would probably lose their basic appeal and become a marginal splinter group." Such advice spoke to the liberal faith of the Vietnam years that if a government could be "reformed enough," the Left would be marginalized and the United States would not lose the struggle for liberal democratic reform. But even with time of the essence, the administration would not turn on Somoza. As Vance put it, "we do not now contemplate asking Somoza to step down," though he granted that mediation might eventually require that.[12] The American balancing act, tilted against the Left, would continue under the heading of "mediation."

Publicly, the White House put the emphasis on stability and reducing the "suffering" of the Nicaraguan people from the war. In a September 22 interview, Carter stated that the United States was trying "to put an end to the suffering . . . in Nicaragua. We want a stable government there. We don't want to intervene in the affairs of a sovereign country."[13] But such sentiments amounted to little more than hopeful wishes. The Carter administration would not send in troops, but it offered mediation in Nicaragua as a peaceful alternative to similar ends. This "new" policy ignored root causes as surely as American policy in Vietnam had, for taking such causes seriously pointed to the leftist victory that the administration still strove to resist.

The Americans, hopeful yet for mediation, succeeded in getting the approval of the Organization of American States (OAS) and in talking Somoza into accepting it. The Commission of Friendly Co-operation and Conciliation, complete with a name to make Orwell smile, was formed by representatives of Guatemala, the Dominican Republic, and the United States. Mediation was the process, but maintaining the Nicaraguan status quo was the goal, for the instructions to William Bowdler, the U.S. representative to the commission, "were to promote and assist negotiations between Somoza and the FAO [*Frente Amplio Opositor*, or Broad Opposition Front, a Nicaraguan anti-Somoza coalition] and to preserve the National Guard." The significance of this was not lost on the Nicaraguan opposition. The Group of Twelve, seeing the goals of mediation as preserving "the core of the system . . . with the goal of isolating the Sandinista Front," pulled out of the effort in late October, and other groups soon followed.[14] From Washington's perspective, this was fine, for keeping the Left from real power was a paramount goal of the process. But on the other hand, a process that excluded them was unlikely to succeed, and this one did not. After buying weeks of time to build up his National Guard, Somoza rejected key parts of the emerging plan. The mediation, denounced by the Sandinistas as an effort to have "Somocismo sin Somoza," the system minus the dictator, was dead.

By this point, Washington, too, was running out of patience. Somoza had to go, and the sooner, the better. As Defense Secretary Harold Brown phrased the consensus of the Policy Review Committee (PRC) meeting on January 26, 1979, "the longer Somoza stayed in power, the higher the chances were of a radical takeover. The only question was when the Sandinistas would assume power."[15] Accordingly, on February 8, 1979, the administration announced the full termination of previously suspended military aid, the withdrawal of the American Military Group and Peace Corps workers, and the slicing of the embassy staff from 82 to 37. In addition, no new aid would be considered. The significance of these moves was more symbolic than real, however, since Somoza had found other countries to outfit his military. Carter could have gone further, by supporting an international arms boycott, investigating American mercenary activities, and cutting Nicaraguan import quotas. In reality, even as the administration was "getting tough," it was Somoza who benefited most from the time he had bought during mediation. The National Guard had been rearmed, and the sanctions merely made manifest an American position that Somoza had understood for months.

Less understanding were the members of the Nicaragua Lobby, who made clear their displeasure. Representative Murphy wrote Carter that Somoza had taken "an overly concessional approach" and that Carter should reconsider.[16] And from the other side of the aisle, Representative George Hansen (R-ID) demanded "an immediate end to our bullying of Nicaragua."[17] Liberals on the Hill, however, including Ted Kennedy, Alan Cranston, and Republican senators Mark Hatfield of Oregon and Jacob Javits of New York, supported Carter in his "recent actions to dissociate the United States from the Somoza government in Nicaragua" and proceeded to list further political and economic steps that could be taken if Somoza remained unmoved.[18]

The Carter administration was not inclined to take further steps, and in reality, the February 8 announcement reduced the American ability to modulate the transition in Nicaragua. The issues were moving back to the battlefield, where American abilities to either head off the leftist insurgency or influence Somoza were decidedly limited. In effect, the Carter administration was replaying American policy in Vietnam minus the use of military power and hoping that "reform" would keep the revolution at bay. Not liking any of the alternatives, even as it wished for a third option that would remake Nicaragua on an American model of stable reform, it found itself without useful ways of blunting the Nicaraguan-made revolution. And by not reframing such change as a logical, and acceptable, result of its policies, it faced a policy failure.

On May 29, the FSLN began its "final offensive," which Washington was again slow to recognize for what it was. Even as FSLN guerrillas gained increasing control of Nicaragua, the administration searched for alternatives. In a memo drafted in preparation for the PRC meeting on June 11, Robert Pastor posed the question that had animated Carter's policy all along: "Can we find a strategy to preserve and strengthen the middle . . . in a region spiraling downward in violence toward political polarization?"[19] Thus, even months removed from concluding that Somoza had to go, the administration was unwilling to make a virtue of necessity and accept revolutionary change in Nicaragua, unwilling, in fact, to put aside the "inordinate fear of communism" that Carter had identified in American policy in Vietnam. Without actively framing the Nicaraguan revolution as local change that the United States could accept and live with, the administration was left with what appeared to be a frightening Cold War setback taking place on its watch. A truly novel policy would have placed emphasis on the inevitability of change, the crimes of Somoza, and the justice of the Nicaraguan people removing him. Instead, the White House, sharing the fear of revolution with the Right, was mired in an ineffectual policy that was an easy target for conservatives using old language about embattled friends and evil Communists. In effect, the White House ceded the high ground because of its unwillingness to enter the debate on the side of change. Like the Truman administration's accommodation to the Red-baiting of the 1940s and 1950s, the Carter administration implicitly allowed conservatives devoutly suspicious of its human rights policy to frame the Nicaraguan crisis, leaving Carter with the blame for "selling out an ally to the communists," rather than with the credit for allowing Nicaraguans to remove their dictator. The United States could hardly be expected to lose its "inordinate fear of communism" if the president and his men still remained so fearful.

As the revolutionary end neared, the administration continued its vain search for alternatives. Secretary of State Cyrus Vance called for the formation of an OAS peacekeeping force, but was unprecedentedly turned down by that body. National Security Adviser Zbigniew Brzezinski made a spirited case for unilateral intervention, but Carter ruled that out, remaining true to his sense of the lessons of Vietnam, even though that choice was tantamount to allowing "the loss of Nicaragua."[20] The administration turned to the insurgents, hoping to use Somoza's agreement to resign as a way of tempering the resulting change. On July 10, U.S. diplomat William Bowdler issued an ultimatum, telling the Junta to expand its membership, accept the National Guard, and agree to a ceasefire and elections. The Junta, with momentum on its side, rejected such ideas.[21] It remained willing to negotiate with the United States, but it would hardly give up the fruits of victory at the moment of triumph. As the *New York Times* editors put it, "it is a little late in the day, after four decades of involvement with the Somoza dynasty, for the United States to insist that any successor to President Somoza's regime must now meet Washington's test of moderate democracy."[22] Even in terms of its own policy history, which reflected its relentless, though nonmilitary, fight against an FSLN triumph, the Carter administration could hardly expect the Junta to listen. Dictating to Latin American countries with American force had worked before, but efforts to dictate to Nicaraguans without that stick had no chance now.

The end came quickly over several days in July, with Somoza flying into exile on July 17 and the Junta entering Managua and taking power on July 20. Despite Somoza's intransigence and a concerted effort by the Carter administration, the FSLN had effected a revolution and become the government of Nicaragua. The Carter administration, having to its credit avoided military intervention, now endeavored to put the best face on its failed policy. Asked at a press conference about "the danger of another Cuba," the president opted to draw clear distinctions that had eluded him in the preceding months: "It's a mistake for Americans to assume or to claim that every time an evolutionary change takes place, or even an abrupt change takes place in this hemisphere, that somehow it's the result of secret, massive Cuban intervention. The fact in Nicaragua is that the incumbent government, the Somoza regime, lost the confidence of the Nicaraguan people."[23] Finally, but too late to influence the Nicaraguans or make it a point of principle, the administration was willing to accept the revolution wrought by Nicaraguan effort to solve a local problem. By then, any opportunity present in America's post–Vietnam War moment was passed.

In the 1976 campaign, Jimmy Carter had offered himself as a clean break from the soiled past of Watergate and Vietnam and appealed to the confidence that Americans should have in their democratic way of life. Indeed, 1977 was dominated by presidential proclamations of just such principles. But when it came to applying these principles, as in the case of Nicaragua, the Carter administration lacked the courage of its rhetorical convictions. A true reframing of American foreign policy on principles of human rights and confident patience in American relations to the third world logically required a willingness to accept potentially radical change in places like Nicaragua. Only a reframing of both means and ends could render such results politically defensible. Given the very different lessons that Americans drew from the Vietnam War experience, criticism from the Right was inevitable, but a possible, if politically challenging, opportunity did exist to best it with a forthright explanation of such change as the acceptable, and preferable, outcome of a more enlightened policy. A president who followed up his rhetoric about transcending America's "inordinate fear of communism" with policy change might have succeeded in building this new consensus and marginalizing right-wing criticism as old ideas inappropriate to the new world of post–Vietnam War foreign policy.

In reality, however, the Carter administration acted on a very limited understanding of the change it was forging. Carter did not want to "dominate or dictate," but he still perceived the stakes in the same way as his predecessors and wanted the results of American foreign policy to remain similar. He altered tactics with the Vietnam experience in mind and, significantly, refused to send the Marines to Nicaragua. But the administration refused to defend change forged in the local context by the Nicaraguans themselves as the logical result of its tactical choices until after the revolution. Instead, it fought local change as long as it could, defying the reality on the ground while continually searching for a middle way of evolution, rather than revolution. When these efforts failed, the Carter White House found itself wide open to criticism from the political Right and from Americans in general, for the measures of its success were the old ones. From this angle, Carter foreign policy was ineffective rather than principled, weak rather than wise, charges that continue to be leveled at Democrats in the conservative echo chamber of television and radio, with millions of Americans nodding along in agreement.

By the time Ronald Reagan won election in 1980, Carter's foreign policy of human rights and patience was but one more piece of the Republican argument that American weakness was the cause of the long list of problems that Americans faced, from leftists in the third world to hostages in Iran to the troubled economy. And the party associated with that weakness was that of the Democrats. The American public would remain wary of the Reaganites' more martial impulses, as Reagan's own experience with Nicaragua makes clear, but without a clear articulation of an argument for accepting governments like the Sandinistas', the door remained open for a movement rightward in American foreign policy, and liberal Democrats would be left with only the political cover to fight rearguard actions against more muscular Republican policy, rather than offering a defensible alternative policy of their own. Without a convincing redefinition of American "national security" and what it properly requires, the possibility of another

Vietnam, or Nicaragua, or Iraq is always with us. In the wake of the U.S. failure in Vietnam, which at least opened the possibility for an argument to reorient U.S. foreign policy toward the developing world, the Carter administration did not offer this redefinition, and the national Democratic Party has remained in a position of self-limited means and old fears that has proven difficult to defend from charges of weakness. Sometimes, in politics, the rewards go to the bold. And when was the last time that word was used to describe Democratic foreign policy?

CHAPTER 14

Conservatives, Carter, and the Politics of National Security

JULIAN E. ZELIZER

The new year of 1980 was not a happy one for President Jimmy Carter. On December 27, the Soviet Union invaded Afghanistan. When Carter heard the reports, he blurted out, "there goes SALT II." The invasion seemed to confirm everything that conservatives had been saying about the president, his national security policies, and the weakness of the Democratic Party. The president's wife, Rosalynn, had never seen him more upset. "We will help to make sure that Afghanistan will be their Vietnam," the shaken Carter vowed to his spouse.[1] In the coming weeks, the president imposed a grain embargo against the Soviet Union, endorsed substantial increases in defense spending, and announced the United States' boycott of the Moscow Summer Olympics.

The invasion of Afghanistan and its political aftermath ended a decade-long quest among Democrats and moderate Republicans for a centrist national security agenda. During the 1970s, all three American presidents had responded to the aftermath of Vietnam by promoting national security agendas that avoided extreme positions toward the Soviet Union. Earlier in the decade, the Republican version of centrism, *détente* (see Chapter 12 in this volume), had revolved around arms and trade agreements with the Soviet Union and China. Although President Richard Nixon enjoyed significant success with this policy, he came under attack from two factions in the burgeoning conservative movement: "neoconservative" Democrats, who had become disaffected with the leftward drift of their party, and hawkish Republicans. President Gerald Ford continued the policy of détente since he believed it to be one of the more successful inheritances from his predecessor. Ford, though, discovered that Watergate had tarnished everything associated with Nixon, détente included. And Ford did not possess the skills needed to fend off the pressure from the Right to adopt a more hawkish posture. In 1976, with the support of the conservative movement, Ronald Reagan nearly defeated Ford in the primaries and signaled the future of the GOP.

This chapter examines how the conservative movement capitalized on President Jimmy Carter's struggles to redefine and champion centrism. When Carter struggled politically and the Soviet Union undertook actions that undermined the promise of détente, conservatives took advantage of the situation. Following the national security problems encountered by Nixon and Ford, Carter both added a human rights component to détente and moderated the military aspects of foreign policy to form a Democratic Party vision of centrism. He, unsurprisingly, courted moderates. The conventional wisdom in the 1970s stipulated that presidents should try to please voters who occupied the political center. The forces that would soon push politics toward the extremes, such as a reformed primary system that privileged party activists, had not yet fully taken hold. The memory of Barry Goldwater's defeat in 1964 compounded by George McGovern's loss in 1972 loomed large as proof that voters preferred candidates who eschewed extremist rhetoric. In the 1970s, congressional moderates in both parties continued to enjoy powerful positions. The electoral forces that had tended to push politicians toward the center, such as southern Democratic voters, were still fulfilling their traditional role.

During the 1976 primaries, Democrats selected Georgia governor Jimmy Carter as their candidate. Throughout his campaign, Carter presented himself as an outsider who could restore trust in government. In contrast to the other Democratic candidates, his southern upbringing offered the possibility of appealing to core Democratic voters. Carter conducted an effective primary campaign that played into this perception while retaining the trust of enough core Democratic voters to win the nomination. Regarding national security, Carter was hard to pin down. He endorsed most of the policies of détente, although he criticized the secrecy through which the policies had been conducted under Kissinger. When asked, Carter was hesitant about allying directly with such Democrats as Senator Henry "Scoop" Jackson. Yet he ran a campaign that appealed to their critique of foreign policy as he sought to distance himself from how mainstream Democrats were handling international relations. Carter also promised to promote a human rights policy. As his speechwriter explained, a human rights policy was "seen politically as a no-lose issue. Liberals liked human rights because it involved political freedom and getting liberals out of jail in dictatorships, and conservatives liked it because it involved criticisms of Russia."[2]

The memories of Richard Nixon and Watergate haunted Gerald Ford's campaign. The one-two punch of economic stagnation and high inflation left citizens disillusioned with economic expectations that had been widespread since World War II. Ford's economic policies had failed to curb the rapid decline of the U.S. economy in the 1970s. Comedic depictions of Ford as a klutz did not help. Ford also made mistakes that reinforced the poor impressions many Americans had about him. The criticism about détente from the Right continued to plague him. For instance, during his second debate with Carter, Ford said that Eastern Europe was not under the control of the Soviet Union. When advisers implored him to apologize, Ford refused.

Carter defeated Ford by one of the narrowest margins in U.S. history, receiving 50.1 percent of the popular vote and 297 electoral votes to Ford's 48 percent of the popular vote and 240 electoral votes (Ronald Reagan received 1 vote). Democrats retained control of Congress. Although Carter won the general election, one of the most important developments in the campaign with far-reaching national consequences was the shift within the GOP in 1976. When Ford ended his presidency, so too ended the centrist foreign policy agenda that Republican presidents had pursued since 1968.

Despite Carter's victory, conservatives were re-energized soon after the election by an independent study that was commissioned by the CIA of its own intelligence. Official CIA data had come under criticism from the Right for underestimating the military strength of the Soviet Union. The study's staff included Lieutenant General Daniel Graham; Harvard historian Richard Pipes; former deputy secretary of defense Paul Nitze, who had been a main author of NSC-68, a secret 1950 State Department report that called for a huge increase in defense spending; and State Department official Paul Wolfowitz.

Team B, as the commission was called, concluded that the CIA's National Intelligence Estimate on Soviet Strategic Objectives had downplayed the strength of the Soviet military. Just as conservatives had been warning, the commission found that the world's strategic balance of power was threatened as a result of Soviet advances in the development of intercontinental missiles and other weapons. The Soviets, they said, had abandoned the concept of parity, which was the bedrock of Mutual Assured Destruction, in pursuit of military superiority.[3] Although scholars would later find that Team B had overstated Soviet advances, at the time the findings were dramatic. The commission's report constituted a watershed moment for many conservatives by confirming their worst fears about the effects of Vietnam and détente on the national security establishment, which in turn galvanized them.

Inspired by this report and related arguments, a group of policymakers sympathetic to the claims from Team B formed the Committee on the Present Danger. The committee, which included such prominent Democrats as Nitze, Eugene Rostow, Richard Perle, and Georgetown professor Jeane Kirkpatrick, aimed to produce an intellectual counterweight to détente. Expressing the committee's mission, Kirkpatrick complained that the "Vietnam syndrome" (which she defined as the fear among policymakers to authorize military operations as a result of Vietnam) had nurtured a "culture of appeasement, which finds reasons not only against the use of force, but denies its place in the world."[4]

But in contrast to the rightward drift of Team B, during his transition to the presidency Carter hoped to develop a different set of policies that transcended Left/Right divisions and achieved more than merely containing Communism.[5] While resisting pressure from the Right in early 1977, Carter refused to ally with the liberal wing of his party. There was still more than enough reason for him to believe that a national security center was politically attractive. After all, Carter had defeated Ford, and Democrats controlled Congress. Thus, Carter pursued all the hallmarks of détente, including arms negotiations, trade agreements, and territorial compromises. He dismissed the findings of Team B and promoted a more optimistic vision of what could be achieved in negotiations with the Soviets.

Unlike his Republican predecessors, as he started his presidency Carter elevated the issue of human rights to the center of his policies. Conservatives had used human rights to attack détente's efficacy. For Carter, supporting human rights and practicing détente could be compatible policies. He thought he could demand that the Soviets and their allies improve their human rights records while simultaneously negotiating arms agreements to reduce the possibility of nuclear war. In unstable regions such as Africa, he felt that the recognition of majority rule was essential to countering the appeal of the Soviets and Cubans.

Besides Carter's ideological commitment to the issue, the political logic behind his stance was simple. With human rights integral to his agenda, critics would not be able to charge the administration with downplaying the importance of democratic and civil liberties in pursuit of arms and trade agreements. Human rights offered political advantages in addition to ideological appeal. Most important, the administration thought the strategy had the potential to unite neoconservatives and liberals in the Democratic Party. Crafting a foreign policy that advanced human rights, Carter explained in 1977, required policymakers to overcome the "inordinate fear of communism, which once led us to embrace any dictator who joined us in that fear."[6]

During the first months of his administration, conservatives in both parties joined liberals and moderates in praising Carter's human rights efforts. Before the specific direction of his human rights initiatives became clear, there was enough reason for neoconservative Democrats, and even some Republicans, to believe that they might not be that far apart from the president on this particular issue. On May 14, the neoconservative Coalition for a Democratic Majority sent the president a letter congratulating him on his decision to make human rights a diplomatic issue, which they said had "reminded us what our foreign policy is supposed to be about: protecting our own interests, to be sure, but primary among these interests the defense and preservation of freedom in the world."[7] The appointment of Zbigniew Brzezinksi—a Columbia professor who was seen as extremely sympathetic to the arguments of neoconservative Democrats—as national security adviser counteracted some of Carter's more dovish appointments, such as Cyrus Vance as secretary of state. Senator George McGovern became concerned that "the Carter [human rights] policy looks like a reincarnation of

John Foster Dulles's attempt to bring Communism down by encouraging dissent and revolt in Eastern Europe."[8]

By embracing human rights, Carter built on a strong base of preexisting congressional and interest group support. In addition to support from the neoconservatives, Carter found allies among a liberal human rights lobby that included such legislators as Tom Harkin of Iowa.[9] Other supportive organizations included the Human Rights Working Group of the Coalition for a New Foreign and Military Policy, Amnesty International, and Freedom House. President Carter even went so far as to institutionalize his priority of human rights. For example, he established a Bureau of Human Rights and Humanitarian Affairs in the State Department.

But over time, the administration failed to achieve a consensus. The contradictions in the policy proved to be problematic. Despite early enthusiasm, conservatives quickly started to complain that most of Carter's human rights initiatives targeted right-wing governments in Latin America or Africa rather than governments allied with the Soviets. Neoconservative Democrats and conservative Republicans thought that the focus of human rights had to be the Soviet Union above any other authoritarian regime, on the grounds that the Soviets were the worst and most dangerous violators of these principles. Another dilemma that Carter encountered was the difficulty of avoiding the tensions that existed between simultaneously propounding human rights and practicing détente with the Soviets. When Carter explained to Soviet ambassador Anatoly Dobrynin that he did not intend to interfere with the internal affairs of the Soviets or to embarrass them for their human rights record, the Soviet ambassador angrily suggested that in return the Soviets might point out the human rights failures of the United States, such as with the nation's treatment of African Americans.[10]

The difficulty of combining human rights rhetoric with détente became apparent in the debate over Soviet dissidents in the summer of 1978. Just as Carter was negotiating the Strategic Arms Limitation

Treaty (SALT) agreements, the Soviets initiated trials against dissidents such as Alexander Ginzburg and Anatoly Scharansky. Human rights official Jessica Tuchman feared that the trials were a "turning point" that could undermine the administration's initiatives in this area. "If we do not respond," Tuchman wrote, "the Soviets will feel free to crack down even harder, and it will not be difficult for US press and public opinion to draw the obvious connection."[11] In July, Carter announced that the United States would limit the sale of oil and computer technology to the Soviets. After the trials of the dissidents, though, Carter shifted his attention away from the Soviets and focused his human rights efforts on other governments, a decision that opened him up to criticism.[12]

The situation in Congress made things even more difficult. Carter immediately had trouble working with the Democratic leadership on Capitol Hill given that Congress, as a result of 1970s reforms, had become highly unpredictable. The reforms weakened the authority of committee chairs, decentralized power, and opened more proceedings to the public and press.[13] The president began his term expecting harmonious relationships with the legislative branch and loyalty toward his administration. The reality was quite different.

As the president tried to complete the types of international agreements pursued by Nixon and Ford earlier in the 1970s, he found himself snarled in the same web as his predecessors. Soviet aggression did not make things easy for Carter. Like Nixon and Ford, Carter had to defend détente at the same time that the Soviets seemed to become more expansionist. In 1977 and 1978, a war between Somalia and Ethiopia offered evidence to conservatives that the Soviets, as well as the Cubans, were committed to expansion and could not be trusted to negotiate over an arms limitation agreement. The Soviets and the Cubans supported Ethiopia in this war. Carter admitted that Soviet policies in Somalia would weaken public confidence in détente. Most members of the administration perceived the Horn of Africa as a test of whether the Soviets were willing to take actions that they understood to be damaging to détente. Zbigniew Brzezinksi feared that the Soviets were trying to secure control of the area around Saudi Arabia—and its oil.[14] "SALT lies buried in the sands of Ogaden," he later wrote.[15]

The most contentious issue in President Carter's relationship with conservatives turned out to be the Panama Canal. Carter decided that, given the anger that had developed in Panama about continued U.S. control of the canal, returning authority over the canal was essential to securing regional peace in Latin America. There had been sizable protests within Panama about America's continued presence. Panama, according to Carter, could serve as a symbol that the United States was prepared to take bold steps to ease tensions in regions turned "hot" by the Cold War and to back off from policies that had been criticized as imperialistic.

Carter understood the political risks of tackling this issue. When he proposed the treaties in August 1978, polls showed that 78 percent of Americans opposed returning the canal. One White House official noted that the challenge was to "mobilize middle-of-the-road public support for a SALT Treaty, while avoiding a left-wing vs. right-wing fight [over the Panama Canal] reminiscent of the Sixties. If we fail to act promptly, well-established peace organizations will take the lead, and the anti-disarmament forces will have an opportunity to label us as 'soft.' "[16] They were worried that peace organizations would claim this issue and make it appear that the treaties were a demand of America's left wing rather than a part of Carter's centrist agenda.

And the opposition was energized. According to White House adviser Hamilton Jordan, conservatives considered the fight over Panama to be a "dry run" for the upcoming debate over SALT II. Republicans, he said, were planning to "use the Treaty as a partisan issue" and to embarrass the Democratic president.[17] While there were some genuine fears about how a diminished U.S. role in Panama could pose a security threat in the region, the Panama Canal was an issue that could serve the conservatives' larger political interest in building support for their organizations and attacking Democrats. "It's patriotism, and that's the issue we do the best with," explained Howard Phillips, head of the Conservative Caucus.[18]

As expected, conservatives attacked through a variety of lobbying groups, including the American Conservative Union, the Conservative Caucus, the Committee for the Survival of a Free Congress, the American Security Council, and the Young Americans for Freedom. The conservative lobby that formed against the treaties sent out a "truth squad" of prominent figures, including Ronald Reagan and Senator Paul Laxalt, to speak in major media markets.[19] They argued that the Soviets would use American withdrawal to gain a stronger foothold in Latin America by expanding Communist influence.

For conservative activists, a victory on the treaties was less important than using Panama to expand the movement's political and financial base and to publicize their movement, which they accomplished. Although Carter and allied liberal interest groups fought hard for the treaties, they were not as organized and they lacked a grassroots force. The most effective tactic that Carter employed was lobbying senators personally. Carter also turned to old-fashioned horse-trading and took advantage of divisions within the conservative movement to garner support for his Panama treaty.

These tactics were sufficient for the president to win the battle over the treaties. In March 1978, the Senate ratified the first Panama treaty by one vote (68 to 32, with two-thirds of the Senate needed for ratification) and ratified the second treaty in April 1978 with the same vote.

Carter saw the treaties as an important success. But conservatives emerged in 1978 with renewed vigor, organizational strength, and disciplined opposition. Carter had cashed in most of his political chips over the Panama Canal.[20] Public opinion about the treaties remained tepid. Carter's popularity plummeted.

Carter confronted conservatives for a second, charged time in 1978 when he initiated negotiations over SALT II. The president based his support for a new arms control agreement on a sunnier view of America's military position than the one held by neoconservatives. And he gave Soviet leaders the benefit of the doubt on their desire to reach an agreement.

Although polls indicated public support for an arms limitation agreement, the administration realized that the domestic path to SALT II would be rough. Many Americans who supported the goals of SALT II doubted that the Soviets could be trusted to keep their end of the bargain.[21] Based on Ford's experience, Carter's advisers concluded that the legislative support for SALT II was thin. These were serious problems for the president, who did not have the hawkish background of Nixon to assuage conservative anxieties.[22]

Throughout the debates in 1978, conservatives demonstrated that they were better prepared to challenge SALT II than the administration was ready to defend it. The anti-SALT forces had strong representation at all levels. In Congress, a well-prepared group that included reputable senators like Scoop Jackson made it difficult for Carter to depict his opponents as extremists. Unlike with the Panama treaty, Republicans were unified on SALT II.

No one in the Senate leadership strongly supported SALT II. Majority Leader Robert Byrd (D-WV) had little trust of the Soviets and greatly respected, and feared, the hawks in his party. Early on, Senate Minority Leader Howard Baker (R-TN) decided that he could not consent to another controversial Carter initiative. Moderates in both parties were skeptical about negotiations. While the administration remained cautious in making any statements for fear of jeopardizing negotiations, Senator Jackson and the right wing showed no hesitation in leveling accusations about the dangers of negotiating with the Soviets and thus received much more press attention than

Carter.[23] The "anti-Soviet climate on the Hill," according to congressional liaison Frank Moore, was also making an agreement difficult to achieve.[24] Conservatives were gradually broadening their support in the Senate thanks to the battles over the Panama treaties. Soviet actions did not help either. As with the Ethiopia–Somalia war, Soviets again added fuel to the fire with their decision to deploy on their borders intermediate range missiles, called SS-20s, that were capable of striking Western Europe. Although Carter considered SALT II to be his most important policy objective because he thought it would lessen the possibility of nuclear war, he could not garner enough senatorial support. Whereas Panama brought Carter an immediate policy victory with significant political costs, the fight for SALT II did not produce any benefit for the president.

The conflicts between Carter and the conservative movement were important to the congressional elections of 1978. Although Democrats retained control of both chambers (59–41 in the Senate and 277–158 in the House), Republicans increased their numbers in the House by fifteen seats and in the Senate by three seats. Five liberal Democrats on whom Carter was counting to vote for SALT II, including one influential member of the Senate Armed Services Committee, were defeated by conservatives whose electoral support included opponents of the Panama treaties. "There are as many interpretations of the mid-term congressional elections as there are interpreters," noted the *Economist,* "but as the dust settled one conclusion seemed even clearer: in the area of foreign policy, the United States Senate has moved significantly to the right."[25] Conservative Republicans from the South and Southwest—who won support from former Democrats—were the most notable victors.

The new Republican legislators, such as Representative Newt Gingrich of Georgia, were not interested in compromising with Democrats. They believed that the GOP needed to embrace the conservative movement as a way to take control of government. Strengthening America's military presence abroad and cutting taxes were their prime concerns. If Carter's policy battles with conservatives had not convinced the president that he faced a serious threat on the Right, the 1978 elections made this threat real and impossible to ignore.

What made matters even more trying for Carter was that he had never developed a strong working relationship with the Democratic leadership in Congress. Most congressional Democrats personally disliked Carter and his Georgia advisers. Speaker Tip O'Neill (D-MA) felt that "Carter rode into town like a knight on a white horse. But while the gentleman leading the charge was capable, too many of the troops he brought with him were amateurs. They didn't know much about Washington, but that didn't prevent them from being arrogant."[26] Legislators were also troubled by media reports about ongoing tensions between Brzezinski and Secretary of State Cyrus Vance. Whereas Brzezinski agreed with neoconservative positions, Vance tended to oppose military operations and focused more heavily on negotiations. The stories of strife created the impression that the president did not fully control his own White House.

Following the elections of 1978, Carter shifted his rhetoric and policies. After two years of holding the line on military budgets, the president called on NATO members to increase defense spending by 3 percent above the rate of inflation each year. On February 28, 1979, Brzezinski outlined a new national security framework centering on the Persian Gulf. The "return to militarism," as one historian called it, was under way.[27]

By the time that the "crisis years" began for Carter, his administration was grappling with tremendous political challenges. Administration policies had come under intense fire from the conservative movement. "To the Communists and those others who are hostile to our country," Ronald Reagan wrote, "Carter and his supporters in the Congress seem like Santa Claus."[28]

Carter had one reason to be optimistic in 1979 as he helped broker a historic peace agreement between Israel and Egypt. Despite a series of compromises made to reach agreement, the handshake between Anwar Sadat and Menachim Begin on March 26 received international acclaim. The agreement stipulated that Israel would remove its troops from the Sinai. Egypt would recognize Israel and open diplomatic channels. The agreement left out the issue of Jewish settlements around the Palestinian territories as well as the status of the West Bank. All three American networks covered the event live. While in the cities of Jerusalem and Tel Aviv Israelis flooded the streets to dance to folk music and sing nationalistic songs, most Arab countries opposed the treaties. Many conservatives in the United States feared that the agreement signaled diminished support for Israel, but given the strong public enthusiasm for the accord, most of them remained quiet.

But political problems quickly pushed this peace agreement out of the limelight. Four events between the summer and winter of 1979 created the perception that America was in crisis and that the Cold War was heating up: a revolution in Nicaragua, the revelation of a Soviet brigade in Cuba, the Iran hostage crisis, and the Soviet invasion of Afghanistan.

The first crisis took place in Nicaragua, when the authoritarian regime of Anastasio Somoza collapsed in July. The regime was overthrown by a left-wing revolution under the leadership of the Sandinista National Liberation Front. Prior to the revolution, Carter had refused to support Somoza's Western-friendly regime because of its violation of human rights. Conservatives saw the revolution as proof that the administration was not interested in preventing the spread of Communism in this region (for further analysis of this event, see Chapter 13 in this volume).[29]

The second explosive incident involved the revelation of a Soviet brigade in Cuba. After Leonid Brezhnev and President Carter signed the SALT II agreement in Vienna in June 1979, the president sent the treaty to the Senate for ratification. At the signing ceremony, Carter infuriated conservatives by embracing Brezhnev in front of the cameras. Shortly after, Senator Richard Stone (D-FL) and Senator Frank Church (D-ID), chair of the Senate Foreign Relations Committee and presidential aspirant, revealed that intelligence reports had uncovered a Soviet brigade of about 2,000 men stationed in Cuba. For Church, a famous Vietnam opponent who had supported the Panama Canal treaties, this revelation offered him an opportunity to appear tough on foreign policy and to appeal to the conservative electorate of his state. Church had run into trouble in the 1978 elections when conservative organizations purchased ads that superimposed his face next to Fidel Castro. The other senator who publicized the presence of the Soviet brigade, Richard Stone, had taken a tough stand against Cuba since entering the Senate. When the media picked up on the revelation in July, the neoconservative Senator Scoop Jackson immediately called for every Soviet aircraft in Cuba to be removed.[30]

Most military experts agreed that the brigade did not really threaten national security. On September 7, Carter told reporters that the United States had a right to ask that the brigade be removed but that the forces did not represent a danger to the country because they were primarily used to train proxy armies for Africa. "Politics and nuclear arsenals do not mix," the president said.[31] The speech did not change Republican minds or their agenda.[32] A group of bipartisan security experts agreed that regardless of its accuracy, the release of the information had placed SALT in jeopardy by spreading evidence that suggested that the Soviets could still not be trusted.[33]

Conservative legislators called the brigade further proof that the Soviets had not abandoned their expansionist aims. Many senators who were wavering on SALT II withdrew their support. The agreement remained unratified.

A third crisis arose in early November when militant Iranian students took American diplomats hostage in Tehran. The troubled history of U.S.–Iranian relations dated back to 1953. The Eisenhower administration had authorized the CIA to mount a coup against the democratically elected government of Muhammad Mossadegh, which had moved to nationalize its oil supplies, and to install a regime that would be sympathetic to Western interests. The new regime ended up being that of Shah Pahlavi, with whom the United States had a strong relationship into the 1970s. Many Iranians despised the shah because of his efforts to modernize the country, his authoritarian regime, and his brutal secret police. The human rights lobby had been extremely critical of the shah. Despite his support of human rights and his concerns about the shah, Carter defended his economic support for Pahlavi.

In August and September 1978, revolutionaries in Tehran attacked the government. The revolution included secular intelligentsia and Islamic fundamentalists who were loyal to the Ayatollah Ruhollah Khomeini. Most members of the administration believed that the crisis was part of the Cold War.[34] Some were scared that Khomeini was supported by the Soviets while others feared that any instability opened up opportunities for the Soviets to influence the region. Brzezinski warned of the "Arc of Crisis" that threatened the Persian Gulf—with the arc extending from Afghanistan to the Horn of Africa.

Carter struggled over his response when the shah requested permission in 1979 to enter the United States to receive medical treatment for cancer. Admitting the shah was a choice that worried the president, as the political fallout could be grave. These concerns were outweighed, however, by the fact that the shah had many influential American supporters. Carter finally decided to allow the shah to enter the United States for treatment in October.

Iranian rebels were furious upon receiving news of the decision. It seemed to many of them that the United States was protecting the shah. On November 4, 1979, students stormed the American embassy in Tehran with fears that the events of 1953 would happen all over again. The Iranians took fifty-two soldiers and diplomats hostage. In their view, the United States was protecting a tyrant by allowing him to avoid trial in his home country. Khomeini praised the "ten thousand martyrs" who had led the revolution. He demanded that "the Great Satan Carter" send the shah back to Iran so that he could stand trial and that the United States return the money that the shah had taken from the Iranian people.[35] Although Americans had seen a series of terrorist incidents in the 1970s, none hit so close to home and none demanded so much attention as the hostage crisis.[36]

Things got worse. In the month after the hostages were taken, the Soviets invaded Afghanistan. The Soviets had maintained close ties to the government of Afghanistan. But Muslim fundamentalists had formed alliances with various tribal leaders to fight against the divided Afghan Communist leadership. The conflicts in Afghanistan caused tremendous concern for the Soviets, who decided to invade and reestablish control in this troublesome country on its border. Brzezinski told the president that the Soviets were trying to achieve their "age-long dream" of direct access to the Indian Ocean. The United States was even before this event already involved. Following the 1979 assassination of the U.S. ambassador in Kabul, Carter had secretly sent support to Muslim guerrillas fighting the Afghan Communists.

Despite this history and the U.S. involvement, President Carter was genuinely shocked when on December 27 Soviet troops crossed the border, moving for the first time into a country that was not part of the Warsaw Pact. The invasion appeared to confirm the gravest warnings of conservatives: the Soviets were committed to reckless expansionism and did not care how the world interpreted their actions. The neoconservative Ben Wattenberg wrote supporters of his Coalition for a Democratic Majority that "people keep saying 'all those lies you've been telling us—are true!' "[37]

"This is the most serious international development that has occurred," Carter wrote in his diary on January 3, 1980, "since I have been President, and unless the Soviets recognize that it has been counterproductive for them, we will face additional problems with invasions or subversion in the future."[38] On January 3, the president requested that Senate Democrats delay further discussions of SALT II in the Senate. The administration concluded that it was not advisable to bring the treaty up for a vote at the time.

It did not take long for these international issues to bubble up and pervade domestic politics. Republicans dismissed the president's change of tone. They blamed Carter by saying that the Soviets had been emboldened to invade Afghanistan as a result of the administration's foreign policies. In early January, Republicans launched a political offensive against the president. Bill Brock, director of the Republican National Committee, put Democrats on notice. On *Good Morning America,* he stated that "the policy of patience" is the "policy of weakness."[39]

Yet these attacks did not deter the president. During his State of the Union address in 1980, he outlined his "Carter Doctrine" in which he announced a formal U.S. commitment to protect the Persian Gulf Region from Communism. He called for a large increase in defense spending (a 4.5 percent annual increase for five years) and an aggressive response to Soviet activities. "The Soviet attack on Afghanistan and the ruthless extermination of its government," Carter announced, "have highlighted in the starkest terms the darker side of their policies—going well beyond competition and the legitimate pursuit of national interest, and violating all norms of international law and practice."[40]

Throughout the year, and as the presidential election season heated up, Carter strove to demonstrate his toughness on defense. In July 1980, he signed a national security document (PD-59) that endorsed further increased defense spending and planning for targeted nuclear attacks against strategic Soviet sites. The president also convinced Congress to pass legislation that required all males when they reached the age of eighteen to register for a draft— should a system be reinstated. The previous year, Carter officials had resisted this move, despite pressure from the military. While it was good to separate politics from policy, one staffer had said, Democrats Jerry Brown or Massachusetts senator Ted Kennedy would capitalize on such a decision in the 1980 primaries to portray Carter as too much of a hawk.[41] Just in September 1979, after receiving reports on the dire state of the army, the House had killed a proposal for registration by a vote of 2 to 1.

After Afghanistan, however, Carter went so far as to consider reinstating the draft. He was dissuaded from doing so by Vice President Walter Mondale and domestic policy adviser Stuart Eizenstat on the grounds that it would be a political disaster. Nonetheless, with true fears of a full-scale crisis as America struggled on multiple fronts, the president insisted on a registration system owing to his concern that the all-volunteer forces were not up to the job. Since the termination of the draft in 1973, the all-volunteer forces had suffered. Enrollment levels remained low, while pay and bonuses were inadequate. Secretary of Defense Harold Brown had also convinced the president that registration would send a strong message to the Soviets. Even liberal senators who had opposed the draft and registration, such as Alan Cranston (D-CA), said they were willing to consider registration.[42] In the end, Carter concluded that a registration system would be necessary, sufficient, and the most he could realistically obtain. Reagan, who opposed the draft and was Carter's most outspoken foe, said that registration would do nothing for national security.

Carter's most important symbolic move was his announcement that the United States would boycott the Moscow Olympics, an action that conservatives had promoted since 1976. After the invasion of Afghanistan, Carter and his advisers agreed. "There is no single action we could take," said Marshall Brement of the National Security Council, "which could have a greater effect in the Soviet Union."[43] Carter believed that a boycott would punish the Russians and constitute a declaration of moral principle. Carter sent a letter to the president of the Olympic Committee asking for the Games to be moved to a different site if the Soviets did not withdraw within a month. Although critics warned that the boycott would not have a major economic impact on the Soviet Union, proponents believed that a boycott would damage the prestige of the Soviets.

Olympic officials were shocked that any nation would consider boycotting the Games, let alone calling for them to be transferred. The U.S. Olympic Committee claimed that the boycott would punish athletes unfairly. Nonetheless, Carter found public support for the boycott to be strong, including among sportswriters and athletes (although there were many athletes who were upset that Carter was mixing politics and sports). One poll found that the public supported the boycott by more than two to one.[44] Strong congressional support existed for the boycott.[45] Democratic and Republican leaders together wrote the Olympic Committee that "we must not let the Olympics be prostituted by the Soviets."[46]

When the International Olympic Committee denied the request to change the venue, the U.S. Olympic Committee voted by a 2–1 margin to endorse the boycott. The majority of the committee did so reluctantly because they were under significant pressure from the president and Congress. After tense negotiations, sixty countries agreed to boycott the events, although many American allies, including Britain, France, and Italy, decided to participate. The Soviets warned the European nations, such as Germany, that the success of the Moscow Olympics was essential to the continuation of détente.

By this time, the forces of anti-Communism were growing around the globe. In Rome, Pope John Paul II mobilized the Catholic Church around the cause of anti-Communism, focusing on the anti-Soviet forces that had emerged in his original home of Poland. In 1979, Margaret Thatcher became the prime minister of England and drew on sharply conservative rhetoric, more akin to Reagan than to Ford, for her harsh words against Communism.

Carter's shift to the Right occurred as the 1980 presidential election was gathering momentum. Before the general election, Carter first had to fend off a primary challenge. Many Democrats thought the party should move left, not right. Throughout the 1970s, politicians such as George McGovern and Frank Church had supported budget cuts in defense spending along with stern regulations on national security operations, both at home and abroad. Like proponents of détente, these Democrats endorsed negotiations with the nation's adversaries, called for policymakers to distinguish between nationalist movements that experimented with socialism and those that were Communist, and endorsed aggressive efforts to reach agreements on the reduction of the world's nuclear arsenal. Senator Kennedy, who supported many of these positions, announced his candidacy in 1979. During his campaign, Kennedy lashed out at the president for lacking focus on national security and for unleashing a dangerous, militaristic rhetoric.

The deteriorating crisis in Iran did not help Carter. By January 1980, CBS News anchor Walter Cronkite was ending each broadcast by reminding viewers how long the hostages had been in captivity. When Carter finally decided to use military force to attempt to free the hostages, it was a failure. Without telling Secretary of State Vance, Carter authorized a military rescue attempt on April 24. But the two helicopters crashed in a sandstorm, leaving eight American soldiers dead. With the hostages still captive, the incident turned into a grotesque embarrassment.

In the meantime, Republicans had nominated Ronald Reagan to run for president. From the start of his campaign, Reagan focused on and skewered Carter's national security record. The Iran hostage crisis and Afghanistan served as potent symbols of an administration that had lost control. Reagan also attacked the inefficiencies of such domestic programs as welfare, and he called for steep tax reductions. As the campaign took shape, according to pollster Patrick Caddell, the situation did not look good for the president. Caddell believed that the president was in "jeopardy of losing the center to Reagan." Independent candidate John Anderson (a former Republican from Illinois) was also eating away at Carter's "natural liberal base."[47]

Hawkish Republicans passionately supported Reagan. They saw him as embodying the type of politics that their wing of the GOP had promoted since the late 1940s. Although many neoconservatives were torn about how to express their anger toward Carter, a large number would vote for Reagan and begin their break from the party.

The Carter campaign could not figure out a way to overcome Reagan's charisma. The former actor's campaign of renewal and hope contrasted starkly with the image of Carter as an inept president who could not respond to international crises or economic decline. "Our President's admission the other day that he at last believes that the Soviets are not to be trusted would be laughable," Reagan wrote, "if it were not so tragic. Even as he said it, he acknowledged that he would probably be willing to trust them in the near future when he will once again take up the SALT II treaty."[48] While Reagan gave speeches calling for Americans to believe in their country again, Carter delivered speeches about limits. Reagan offered shining optimism, Carter sobering realism.

In the end, Carter's efforts failed to create a stable political majority at home. When crises struck in 1979, centrism was already in political trouble. The president's weakness as a politician and contradictions in his policies had exposed him to domestic attack. Soviet aggression in Somalia, and then Afghanistan, undermined his ability to deliver on the promise of détente. Politicians allied with the conservative movement took advantage of Carter's vulnerability and moved national security politics toward the right.

The defeat of the center in national security politics during the 1970s was a defining moment in the history of modern conservatism. After a tough three-decade struggle against liberal internationalism, right-wing isolationism, and moderates in both parties, hawkish Republicans allied with the conservative movement captured the White House, Senate, and the GOP in 1980.

In one important respect, the 1970s marked the end rather than the beginning of an era for conservatism with regards to national security. The 1970s was the last moment when the movement was an oppositional force rather than one with formal power and responsibilities. Conservatives now needed to demonstrate that they could marshal the same type of political success while governing. Either in the White House or Congress, conservatives would hold positions of influence throughout the next two-and-a-half decades. Along the road to power, conservatives had made crucial decisions that helped them to win on the campaign trail, such as the decision to promote an ambitious vision of what America's national security institutions could achieve. These choices would present major challenges when conservatives were in power.

After the 1970s, American politics would look very different: sustaining moderate positions in national politics would be extremely difficult. When politicians, including President Bill Clinton, adopted this strategy, they did so with thin legislative and party support. By 2000, President George W. Bush and his top strategist Karl Rove would decide to ignore moderate voters on the grounds that Republicans could achieve bigger gains by pleasing the right wing and increasing their voter participation on Election Day. Campaign consultant Matthew Dowd outlined this strategy in a memo that showed how only a minute fraction of the electorate consisted of swing voters.[49] The electorate, Rove and Bush concluded, had become so divided that there were only a limited number of voters who could be persuaded to change their voting patterns. As was evident in national security, the shift was not just a product of institutional or demographic changes, as social scientists argue, but also of a concerted effort by younger conservatives and liberals to defeat the bipartisan center, on national security and other issues, which they felt had stifled politics for too long.

Epilogue

BRUCE J. SCHULMAN

JULIAN E. ZELIZER

"Now comes the revolution." The day after President George W. Bush won reelection in 2004, conservative activist Richard Viguerie, an architect of the New Right in the 1970s, confidently prophesied the ultimate victory of the conservative movement that he had helped to construct a generation earlier. Viguerie and his fellow movement conservatives noted that "conservative Christians and 'values voters' won this election for George W. Bush and Republicans in Congress." One did not have to be a die-hard activist to reach the same conclusion. Even if the New Right organizer had exaggerated, the fact remains that Bush won three-quarters of white born-again Christian voters, while ballot measures forbidding gay marriage in eleven states helped the president win the popular majority that had eluded him four years earlier. "If you don't implement a conservative agenda now," Viguerie wondered aloud, "when do you?"

Just two years later, however, Democrats put a "thumpin'," in the president's pungent language, on Republicans in the 2006 midterm elections. Twelve years after the Republican Revolution in Congress had appeared to complete the conservative ascendancy,

289

Democrats defied most predictions and retook control of the House and Senate. Americans loudly voiced their opposition to the president's handling of the war in Iraq and to Bush's larger foreign policy vision. In so doing, voters expressed discontent with the conservative national security policy that, as Jeremi Suri, Derek Buckaloo, and Julian Zelizer show in this volume, took root in the 1970s right-wing critique of Cold War centrism.

At the same time, the 2006 elections exposed the limitations of conservatism at home. Across the country, support for embryonic stem cell research energized liberal candidacies and contributed to Democratic victories in Wisconsin, Missouri, Maryland, New Jersey, Arizona, and Ohio.[1] And even with President Bush in the White House and Republicans dominant on Capitol Hill, the federal government—that central bugaboo of the conservative movement— had grown ever larger, costlier, and more powerful. Frustrated by the Bush administration's failure to fulfill the conservative agenda, Viguerie himself published a scathing attack on the administration and the Republican Party. Its title said it all: *Conservatives Betrayed*.[2] This was just one of many books in 2006 and 2007 in which conservatives voiced their frustration about the phenomenon of "Big Government Conservatism." The cover of *Time* magazine featured a picture of President Ronald Reagan shedding a tear.[3]

In many ways, this incomplete revolution defines contemporary American public life. On the one hand, conservatism has entrenched itself with a vigor that even the most committed New Right activists would not have imagined in the 1970s. Looking much different than the famous Age of Aquarius, conservative institutions now crisscross the American landscape: the pioneering conservative churches, foundations, think tanks, colleges, businesses, and media outlets that Paul Boyer, Alice O'Connor, Joseph Crespino, and Bethany Moreton describe in this anthology have become familiar and influential players in the national arena. Conservatives have ensconced themselves in the federal judiciary, and their policy agenda continues to shape national debate. On foreign policy, stem cell research, restrictions on greenhouse gases, and gun control, the conservative movement that coalesced in the seventies has left its imprint on American society.

Meanwhile, the continued expansion of evangelical Christianity testifies to the economic vitality and cultural influence of conservative values. Whereas country music was once populated by pot-smoking, beer-drinking anti-establishment figures such as Willie Nelson, Waylon Jennings, and Johnny Cash, the Nashville country music establishment and most country radio stations united in opposition to the Dixie Chicks after the chart-topping trio's lead singer criticized President Bush. Some organizations even sponsored bonfires into which protestors hurled the group's CDs. The family values campaigners that Matthew Lassiter and Marjorie Spruill chronicle in this volume have much to be pleased about.

But not too much. Abortion remains legal despite decades of concerted effort, stem cell research has wide public support, and more and more Americans approve of civil rights for homosexuals. Despite resistance to taxation, voters continue to look to the federal government for increases in the minimum wage, protection for their medical care and retirement, and relief from natural disasters and economic downturns. When President Bush made a major push to privatize Social Security, he discovered, like Ronald Reagan in the 1980s, that government often turns out to be far more popular than conservatives suggest. It was one thing to talk about the virtues of private accounts and investor choice, but quite another to eliminate the safety net that millions of elderly citizens depend upon. Meanwhile, issues such as the Iraq war, domestic surveillance, global warming, deficit spending, and immigration split the conservative coalition and left it vulnerable to electoral defeat. The 2006 elections highlighted those very fissures and inconsistencies.

Turn on a television or open a Web browser and you find airwaves full of violence, sexuality, edgy humor, and the very secular values conservatives have long derided. The nation's liberal cultural elite, among them the singer/songwriters that Bradford Martin describes, largely gave up their countercultural aversion to mainstream party politics and have become a potent political force. For the past decade, the Hollywood Left has furnished financial muscle and cultural cachet to liberal Democrats. In 2007, the Los Angeles–based Recording Academy conferred its prestigious "Record of the Year" Grammy on the Dixie Chicks. Recognizing the defiant anthem "Not Ready to Make Nice," the industry thumbed its nose at the activists who had boycotted the Dixie Chicks.

"We're in the political equivalent of a world without the law of gravity," Republican strategist and former Christian Coalition chief Ralph Reed told *Time* magazine in 2007. "Nothing we have known in the past seems relevant."[4]

Sincere as Reed's confusion and the frustration of many of today's conservatives may be, the essays in this book demonstrate that the past has much to say about the contemporary condition. The incomplete revolution conservatives directed in the 1970s makes the problems they face today deep rooted and difficult to overcome. Contrary to the conventional wisdom, conservatism will not be easily remade simply with a new person in the White House or fresh leadership on Capitol Hill. Frustration remains a defining feature of a movement that has been so sweeping and powerful politically, yet limited in what it could accomplish and transform. As the essays by Thomas Sugrue and John Skrentny, Meg Jacobs, Joseph McCartin, and Suleiman Osman vividly document, conservatives often benefited from larger economic and social forces, but they also succumbed to them sometimes. The challenges of international relations, the established institutions and policy preferences built into American governance, and the tides of popular culture have often beaten against the conservative movement. That several 2008 Republican presidential contenders are admitted adulterers with multiple marriages, that conservatives divide bitterly over the

Iraq war, that John McCain passed up the 2007 Conservative Political Action Conference for an appearance on the David Letterman show—all these reveal deep-seated forces, products of the struggles of the 1970s, that constrain even so powerful a force as American conservatives have been since the emergence of the New Right in the 1970s.

The problems that contemporary conservatives face did not emerge in 2006; they go back three decades. America turned right in the 1970s, but it was not as a result of a political sweep. As the conservative movement took shape and expanded its influence, it faced a series of challenges, a persistent struggle between mounting conservative political power and liberal social change. As the chapters in this book show, that struggle defined the rightward turn in the seventies, and it lingers today.

Notes

Introduction

1. "The GOP's Spending Spree" (editorial), *Wall Street Journal,* November 25, 2003.

2. Among the most important contributions to this scholarship are Thomas J. Sugrue, *The Origins of the Urban Crisis* (Princeton, N.J.: Princeton University Press, 1996); Kevin Kruse, *White Flight* (Princeton, N.J.: Princeton University Press, 2005); Michael Flamm, *Law and Order* (New York: Columbia University Press, 2005); Robert Self, *American Babylon* (Princeton, N.J.: Princeton University Press, 2004); Julian Zelizer, "The Uneasy Relationship: Democracy, Taxation, and State-Building since the New Deal," in *The Democratic Experiment: New Directions in American Political History,* ed. Meg Jacobs, William Novak, and Julian E. Zelizer (Princeton, N.J.: Princeton University Press, 2003), 276–300; John McGreevy, *Parish Boundaries* (Chicago: University of Chicago Press, 1996); and Alan Brinkley, *The End of Reform* (New York: Alfred A. Knopf, 1995).

3. See for example Lisa McGirr, *Suburban Warriors* (Princeton, N.J.: Princeton University Press, 2001); Donald Critchlow, *Phyllis Schlafly and Grassroots Conservatism* (Princeton, N.J.: Princeton University Press, 2005); Jonathan Schoenwald, *A Time for Choosing* (New York: Oxford University Press, 2001); John Andrew, *The Other Side of the Sixties* (New Brunswick, N.J.: Rutgers University Press, 1997); Catherine Rymph, *Republican Women* (Chapel Hill: University of North Carolina Press, 2006); and George Nash, *The Conservative Intellectual Movement in the United States since 1945* (New York: Basic Books, 1976).

4. For growing interest in the 1970s, see Philip Jenkins, *Decade of Nightmares: The End of the Sixties and the Making of Eighties America* (New York: Oxford University Press, 2006); Andreas Killin, *1973 Nervous Breakdown: Watergate, Warhol and the Birth of Post-Sixties America* (New York: Bloomsbury, 2006); Edward Berkowitz, *Something Happened: A Political and Cultural Overview of the Seventies* (New York: Columbia University Press, 2005); Julian E. Zelizer, *On Capitol Hill: The Struggle to Reform Congress and Its Consequences, 1945–2000* (New York: Cambridge University Press, 2004); David Farber and Beth Bailey, eds., *America in the 1970s* (Lawrence: University of Kansas Press, 2000); Bruce J. Schulman, *The Seventies: The Great Shift in American Culture, Society, and Politics* (New York: Free Press, 2001); David Frum, *How We Got Here: The 70's—the Decade That Brought You Modern Life—For Better or Worse* (New York: Basic Books, 2000).

1. Inventing Family Values

1. *1979, God Fights Back* (Alexandria, Va.: PBS Video, 1999); "Prophets and Advisors," episode 4 of *With God on Our Side: The Rise of the Religious Right in America* (Alexandria, Va.: PBS Video, 1996).
2. Stephanie Coontz, *The Way We Never Were: American Families and the Nostalgia Trap* (New York: Basic Books, 1992), 14–20.
3. Richard M. Nixon, "Acceptance Speech," August 8, 1968, in *Campaign Speeches of American Presidential Candidates, 1948–1984,* ed. Gregory Bush (New York: Frederick Ungar, 1985), 153–163; "Man and Woman of the Year: The Middle Americans," *Time,* January 5, 1970, 10–17; "The American Family: Future Uncertain," *Time,* December 28, 1970, 34–39.
4. *New York Times,* December 10, 1971; "Teen-Age Sex: Letting the Pendulum Swing," *Time,* August 21, 1972, 34–40.
5. *An American Family* (New York: Educational Broadcasting System, 1973); "An American Family," *Newsweek,* January 15, 1973, 68; Susan J. Douglas, *Where the Girls Are: Growing Up Female with the Mass Media* (New York: Times Books, 1994), 196–209.
6. Jeffrey Ruoff, *An American Family: A Televised Life* (Minneapolis: University of Minnesota Press, 2002); "An American Family," *Newsweek,* January 15, 1973, 68; Abigail McCarthy, "An American Family and the Family of Man," *Atlantic Monthly* (July 1973): 72–76;

Anne Roiphe, "Things Are Keen but Could Be Keener," *New York Times Magazine*, February 18, 1973, 8–9, 43–53; "The Broken Family: Divorce U.S. Style," *Newsweek*, March 12, 1973, 47–57; " 'Throwaway Marriages': Threat to the American Family," *U.S. News and World Report*, January 13, 1975, 43–45; Paul Friggens, "If You Spoil the Marriage, Spare the Child," *Reader's Digest* (June 1975): 155–158.

7. James Dobson, *Dare to Discipline* (Wheaton, Ill.: Tyndale House, 1970), quotations 22, 54; Barbara Ehrenreich, *Fear of Falling: The Inner Life of the Middle Class* (New York: HarperPerennial, 1990), 57–96.

8. James Dobson, *Hide or Seek* (Old Tappan, N.J.: Fleming H. Revell, 1974), 49, 128–130; James Dobson, *The Strong-Willed Child: Birth through Adolescence* (Wheaton, Ill.: Tyndale House, 1978), 226–230.

9. Phyllis Schlafly, *The Power of the Positive Woman* (New York: Jove Publications, 1977, 1978), quotations 86, 179, 206; *New York Times*, July 30, 1980. Anti-ERA flier reproduced in Ruth Murray Brown, *For a "Christian America": A History of the Religious Right* (Amherst, N.Y.: Prometheus Books, 2002), 40.

10. "What Next for U.S. Women," *Time*, December 5, 1977, 19–26; Rebecca E. Klatch, *Women of the New Right* (Philadelphia: Temple University Press, 1987), 119–142.

11. "Gays on the March," *Time*, September 8, 1975, 33–43; *New York Times*, January 18, March 28, June 5, 8, 19, 27, 1977, October 15, 1979; *Washington Post*, April 28, 1979; Schlafly, *Power of the Positive Woman*, 112; Jerry Falwell, *Listen, America!* (Garden City, N.Y.: Doubleday, 1980), 185.

12. White House Conference on Families, *Listening to America's Families: Action for the 80's* (Washington, D.C.: U.S. Government Printing Office, 1980), quotations 13, 167; Marvin Stone, "Focus on the Family," *U.S. News and World Report*, May 5, 1980, 88; James Dobson interview, *Christianity Today*, May 7, 1982, 19; William Martin, *With God on Our Side: The Rise of the Religious Right in America* (New York: Broadway Books, 1996).

13. *New York Times*, July 30, 1980; *Washington Post*, October 13, 1980; Falwell, *Listen, America!*, 121, 266; Jerry Falwell, ed., *The Fundamentalist Phenomenon: The Resurgence of Conservative Christianity* (Garden City, N.Y.: Doubleday, 1981), 188.

14. Coontz, *The Way We Never Were;* White House Conference on Families, *Listening to America's Families,* 18–19; Cal Thomas and Ed Dobson, *Blinded by Might: Can the Religious Right Save America?* (Grand Rapids, Mich.: Zondervan Publishing House, 1999), 23.

15. Falwell, *Listen, America!,* 126; Dobson interview, *Christianity Today,* 15–19; Ronald J. Sider, *The Scandal of the Evangelical Conscience: Why Are Christians Living Just Like the Rest of the World?* (Grand Rapids, Mich.: Baker Books, 2005); James Dobson, "In Defending Marriage—Take the Offensive!" *Focus on the Family Newsletter* (April 2004), http://www.focusonthefamily.com (accessed April 15, 2007). On the links between the instability of capitalism and the scapegoating of gays and lesbians, see John D'Emilio, "Capitalism and Gay Identity," in *Powers of Desire: The Politics of Sexuality,* ed. Ann Snitnow, Christine Stansell, and Sharon Thompson (New York: Monthly Review Press, 1983), 100–113.

2. The Evangelical Resurgence in 1970s American Protestantism

1. *Newsweek,* October 25, 1976; D. G. Hart, *That Old-Time Religion in Modern America: Evangelical Protestantism in the Twentieth Century* (Chicago: Ivan R. Dee, 2002), chap. 2, "The Formation of an Evangelical Subculture," 54–83. Distinctions among the terms *evangelical, fundamentalist, Pentecostal,* and *charismatic* have spawned much debate. For the purposes of this chapter, I will generally use *evangelical* to cover a diverse array of doctrinally conservative Protestant groups. For a helpful discussion, see Larry Eskridge, "Defining Evangelicalism" (1995, rev. 2006), Institute for the Study of American Evangelicals, Wheaton College, at www.wheaton.edu/isae/defining_evangelicalism.html.

2. Martin Marty, "Herberg's Relevance," *Sightings,* University of Chicago Divinity School, May 9, 2005, www.sightings_admin@listhost.un chicago.edu; Harvey Cox, *The Secular City: Secularization in Theological Perspective* (New York: Macmillan, 1965); Robert Bellah, "Civil Religion in America," *Daedalus* 99 (Winter 1967): 1–21. For a critical discussion of Bellah in this context, see Walter H. Capps, *The New Religious Right: Piety, Patriotism, and Politics* (Columbia: University of South Carolina Press, 1990), 195–198.

3. George M. Marsden, *Fundamentalism and American Culture: The Shaping of Twentieth-Century Evangelicalism, 1870–1925* (New York:

Oxford University Press, 1980), 118–123; Grant Wacker, *Heaven Below: Early Pentecostals and American Culture* (Cambridge, Mass.: Harvard University Press, 2001), 1–6.

4. Paul Boyer, *When Time Shall Be No More: Prophecy Belief in Modern American Culture* (Cambridge, Mass.: Harvard University Press, 1992), 86–100.

5. Marsden, *Fundamentalism and American Culture*, 31, 98, 119; William Vance Trollinger Jr., *God's Empire: William Bell Riley and Midwestern Fundamentalism* (Madison: University of Wisconsin Press, 1990); David Osielski, reference archivist, Wheaton College, personal communication to author, August 25, 2006.

6. William Martin, *A Prophet with Honor: The Billy Graham Story* (New York: William Morrow, 1991).

7. Brenda E. Brasher, ed., *Encyclopedia of Fundamentalism* (New York: Routledge, 2001), 522–523 (Youth for Christ). For information on the NAE, see William Martin, *With God on Our Side: The Rise of the Religious Right in America* (New York: Broadway Books, 1996), 23. For more on *Christianity Today,* see Hart, *That Old-Time Religion in Modern America,* 129–130.

8. Timothy Dudley-Smith, *John Stott,* 2 vols. (Downer's Grove, Ill.: Inter-Varsity Press, 1999, 2001); "The Rev. Dr. John R. W. Stott," http://www.langhampartnership.org/john-stott/biography.

9. James L. Evans, "Billy Graham's Final Crusade," *Sightings,* The Martin Marty Center, University of Chicago, July 7, 2005; Fred C. Schwarz, *You Can Trust the Communists (to Be Communists)* (Englewood Cliffs, N.J.: Prentice Hall, 1960); Billy James Hargis, *Communist America—Must It Be?* (Tulsa, Okla.: Christian Crusade, 1960); *CCAC Newsletter,* October 1997; "Evangelist Billy James Hargis Dies: Spread Anti-Communist Message," *Washington Post,* November 30, 2004, B6, online at washingtonpost.com.

10. Winthrop S. Hudson and John Corrigan, *Religion in America,* 6th ed. (Upper Saddle River, N.J.: Prentice Hall, 1999), 385; Princeton Religion Research Report, 2002, cited in Eskridge, "How Many Evangelicals Are There?" a section of his essay "Defining Evangelicalism," cited in note 1 above. See also Roger Finke and Rodney Starke, *The Churching of America, 1776–1990: Winners and Losers in Our Religious Economy* (New Brunswick, N.J.: Rutgers University Press, 1993); and Christian Smith, *American Evangelicalism: Embattled and Thriving* (Chicago: University of Chicago Press, 1999).

11. Harvey Cox, *Fire from Heaven: The Rise of Pentecostal Spirituality and the Reshaping of Religion in the 21st Century* (Reading, Mass.: Addison-Wesley, 1995); Hudson and Corrigan, *Religion in America*, 385.

12. C. Kirk Hadaway and Penny Long Marler, "How Many Americans Attend Worship Each Week?" *Journal for the Scientific Study of Religion* 44, no. 3 (September 2005): 307–322.

13. For more on the Campus Crusade for Christ, see Brasher, *Encyclopedia of Fundamentalism*, 85–86; Dudley-Smith, *John Stott*, vol. 2, *A Global Ministry*. The prolific Stott published at least ten books in the late 1960s and 1970s, including *Christ the Liberator* (1971) and *Christian Counter Culture: The Message of the Sermon on the Mount* (1975).

14. Martin, *A Prophet with Honor*. Graham's 1970s books include *Jesus Generation* (1971); *Angels, God's Secret Agents* (1975); *How to Be Born Again* (1977); and *Holy Spirit: Activating God's Power in Your Life* (1979).

15. Billy Graham Archives display, Wheaton College.

16. For a thoughtful interpretation, see Hugh Heclo, "The Sixties' False Dawn: Awakenings, Movements, and Postmodern Policymaking," *Journal of Policy History* 8, no. 1 (1996): 34–63.

17. Jeffrey K. Hadden and Charles E. Swann, *Prime Time Preachers: The Rising Power of Televangelism* (Reading, Mass.: Addison-Wesley, 1981), 160.

18. Dean C. Kelley, *Why Conservative Churches Are Growing* (New York: Harper & Row, 1972). As early as 1956, in the inaugural issue of *Christianity Today*, Carl F.H. Henry had noted the failure of liberal mainstream churches "to meet the moral and spiritual needs of the people" (quoted in Hart, *That Old-Time Religion in Modern America*, 130).

19. James Davison Hunter, *Culture Wars: The Struggle to Define America* (New York: Basic Books, 1991), 178–180 (*The Nashville Banner*, March 1, 1980, quoted on 180).

20. For a discussion of Schaeffer's influence on the moral stance of 1970s evangelicalism, see Capps, *The New Religious Right*, chap. 3, "The Theologian, the Teacher," 58–88. For a striking example of this influence, see Tim LaHaye, *The Battle for the Mind* (Old Tappan, N.J.: Fleming H. Revell, 1980). See also Hart, *That Old-Time Religion in Modern America*, 134–143.

21. Godfrey Hodgson, *The World Turned Right Side Up: A History of the Conservative Ascendancy in America* (Boston: Houghton Mifflin, 1996), 176–178.

22. Richard Mouw, "Evangelicals and Catholics: A New Partnership," www.beliefnet.com/story/10/story_1008_1.html; Paul Blanshard, *American Freedom and Catholic Power* (Boston: Beacon Press, 1949); Hunter, *Culture Wars,* 36–37, 39–48, 61–72, 86–106, quoted passage, 47. See also William M. Shea, *The Lion and the Lamb: Evangelicals and Catholics in America* (New York: Oxford University Press, 2004), and Mark A. Noll and Carolyn Nystrom, *Is the Reformation Over? An Evangelical Assessment of Contemporary Catholicism* (Grand Rapids, Mich.: Baker Academic Books, 2005).

23. Boyer, *When Time Shall Be No More,* 5; Paul S. Boyer, "The Growth of Fundamentalist Apocalypticism in the United States," in *The Encyclopedia of Apocalypticism,* ed. Stephen J. Stein, 3 vols. (New York: Continuum, 1998), 3:140–178, esp. 166–168, on Lindsey.

24. R. Laurence Moore, *Selling God: American Religion in the Marketplace of Culture* (New York: Oxford University Press, 1994), 136–138; Paul Boyer, *Urban Masses and Moral Order in America, 1820–1920* (Cambridge, Mass.: Harvard University Press, 1978), chap. 2, "The Tract Societies: Transmitting a Traditional Morality by Untraditional Means," 22–33; Hart, *That Old-Time Religion in Modern America,* 59–60, on Paul Rader.

25. Hart, *That Old-Time Religion in Modern America,* 107 (on Graham), 175.

26. Randall Balmer, *Mine Eyes Have Seen the Glory: A Journey into the Evangelical Subculture in America* (New York: Oxford University Press, 1989), chap. 3, "On Location," 48–70, on the career of Donald W. Thompson; Hart, *That Old-Time Religion in Modern America,* 183–184.

27. Peter Horsfield, *Religious Television: The American Experience* (New York: Longman, 1984), chap. 1, "The Emergence of Religious Television"; Scott Lupo, "Televangelism," in Brasher, *Encyclopedia of Fundamentalism,* 472; "Meet Dr. Falwell," Jerry Falwell ministries Web site, www.falwell.com/meet_dr_falwell.php; Dirk Smillie, "Inside Jerry Falwell, Inc.: Prophets of Boom," *Forbes,* September 18, 2006, 118–121; Hadden and Swann, *Prime Time Preachers,* 51, 53, on viewership of *Old Time Gospel Hour* as reported by Arbitron. Falwell claimed a far larger viewership, charging that Arbitron and other rating services undercounted cable viewers.

28. Hadden and Swann, *Prime Time Preachers,* 34–37; Lupo, "Televangelism," 472; "It's Time to Pray, America! The complete original

soundtrack from the national television special" (Virginia Beach, Va.: House Top Records, 1976).

29. Lupo, "Televangelism," 472–473; Capps, *The New Religious Right,* chap. 5, "A Christian Theme Park," 127–157, on Jim and Tammy Bakker.

30. Colleen McDannell, *Material Christianity: Religion and Popular Culture in America* (New Haven, Conn.: Yale University Press, 1996), chap. 8, "Christian Retailing," 222–269; "CBA Timeline, 1950–2000," www .cbaonline.org/General/CBA_history.jsp; "Religious Items Sell," *Arizona Daily Star,* January 27, 2004, www.azstar.net.com/sn/border/7395.php.

31. Steve Rabey with additional reporting by Doug Trouten and Dean Nelson, "Age to Age," *CCM Magazine* (July 1998): 18–44, on a history of the early Contemporary Christian Music movement, available online at www.CCM.com.

32. For two diametrically opposed assessments of Dobson, see Rolf Zettersten, *Dr. Dobson: Turning Hearts toward Home* (Dallas: Word Publishing, 1989), and Gil Alexander-Moergerle, *James Dobson's War on America* (Amherst, N.Y.: Prometheus Books, 1997). The Web site of Dobson's Focus on the Family organization is www.family.org.

33. "The Great Jesus Rally in Dallas," *Life,* June 30, 1972; Rabey, "Age to Age" (Larry Norman quote). On the Jesus Movement, see also J. David Hoeveler Jr., *The Postmodernist Turn: American Thought and Culture in the 1970s* (New York: Twayne Publishers, 1996), 140–141.

34. On Calvary Chapel in the 1980s and an account of its origins, see Balmer, *Mine Eyes Have Seen the Glory,* chap. 1, "California Kickback," 12–30, quote from early convert Oden Fong, 19–20.

35. The Vineyard: A Community of Churches, "The History of the Vineyard Movement," www.vineyardusa.org/about/history.aspx.

36. Malcolm Gladwell, "Letter from Saddleback: The Cellular Church, How Rick Warren's Congregation Grew," *The New Yorker,* September 12, 2005, 60–67.

37. William C. Symonds, "Earthly Empires: How Evangelical Churches Are Borrowing from the Business Play Book," *Business Week,* May 23, 2005, 78–88; Anne C. Loveland and Otis B. Wheeler, *From Meetinghouse to Megachurch: A Material and Cultural History* (New York: Columbia University Press, 2003).

38. Charles W. Dunn and J. David Woodard, *The Conservative Tradition in America* (Lanham, Md.: Rowman & Littlefield, 1996), 7–8; Hodgson, *The World Turned Right Side Up,* 170–171.

39. Brasher, *Encyclopedia of Fundamentalism,* 315–316 (see "Moral Majority"). For Falwell's "pro-life, pro-family" quote, see William Vance Trollinger Jr., "Moral Majority," in *The Oxford Companion to United States History,* ed. Paul S. Boyer (New York: Oxford University Press, 2001), 514–515 (quote on 514). Falwell's "Get them saved" quote appeared in *Time,* October 1, 1979, 68, cited in Peter N. Carroll, *It Seemed Like Nothing Happened: America in the 1970s* (New Brunswick, N.J.: Rutgers University Press, 1990, reprint of 1982 ed.), 332.

40. See Lisa McGirr, *Suburban Warriors: The Origins of the New American Right* (Princeton, N.J.: Princeton University Press, 2002), for a study of Orange County politics; Hart, *That Old-Time Religion in Modern America,* 162–163.

41. Richard V. Pierard, "Reagan and the Evangelicals: The Making of a Love Affair," *Christian Century,* December 21–28, 1983; Hodgson, *The World Turned Right Side Up,* 179–181; John and Irene Conlan, *Beyond Nineteen Eighty Four* (Scottsdale, Ariz.: FaithAmerica Foundation, 1984).

42. Hodgson, *The World Turned Right Side Up,* 180; Carroll, *It Seemed Like Nothing Happened,* 329 (for quoted passage); Hadden and Swann, *Prime Time Preachers,* 137–139.

43. Hadden and Swann, *Prime Time Preachers,* 130–133 (for the Reagan quote, see 133); Boyer, *When Time Shall Be No More,* 142–146; Hodgson, *The World Turned Right Side Up,* 182; "Robert Billings, Religious Activist and Moral Majority Co-Founder," obituary in *The Virginian-Pilot,* June 1, 1995, www.scholar.lib.vt.edu/VA-news/VA -Pilot/issues/1995/v950601/06010439.htm.

44. Steve Bruce, *The Rise and Fall of the New Christian Right: Conservative Protestant Politics in America, 1978–1988* (Oxford: Clarendon Press, 1988), 101.

45. Paul S. Boyer, ed., *Reagan as President: Contemporary Views of the Man, His Politics, and His Policies* (Chicago: Ivan R. Dee, 1990), 166, 168.

46. Michael Cromarie, ed., *No Longer Exiles: The Religious Right in American Politics* (Washington, D.C.: Ethics and Public Policy Center, 1992); Mark Noll, *The Scandal of the Evangelical Mind* (Grand Rapids, Mich.: William B. Eerdmans, 1994), 170–172.

47. Hodgson, *The World Turned Right Side Up,* 183–184.

48. "Remembering a Supernatural Life Lived as a Slave of Jesus" (Bill Bright interview), Bright Media Foundation: Continuing the Legacy,

www.brightmedia.org/high-bandwidth/interview5.htm; "Armstrong Named President of Colorado Christian University," Colorado Christian University News Web site, June 29, 2006, www.ccu.edu.

49. David O. Moberg, *The Great Reversal: Evangelicalism versus Social Concern* (Philadelphia: Lippincott, 1977); Hart, *That Old-Time Religion in Modern America,* 148.

50. "The Lausanne Covenant," www.feb.org/lausanne_covenant.htm; "The Rev. Dr. John R. W. Stott."

51. "Chicago Declaration of Evangelical Social Concerns," November 25, 1973, www.esa-online.org/conferences/chicago/chicago.html; Ronald J. Sider, *Rich Christians in an Age of Hunger: A Biblical Study* (Downer's Grove, Ill.: Intervarsity Press, 1977); Jim Wallis, *Agenda for a Biblical People* (New York: Harper & Row, 1976). See also Craig M. Gay, *With Liberty and Justice for Whom? The Recent Evangelical Debate over Capitalism* (Grand Rapids, Mich.: Eerdmans, 1991).

52. Mark Gerson, *The Neoconservative Vision: From the Cold War to the Culture Wars* (Lanham, Md.: Madison Books, 1996); Hoeveler, *The Postmodernist Turn,* 139–140; Dan T. Carter, *The Politics of Rage: George Wallace, the Origins of the New Conservatism and The Transformation of American Politics* (New York: Simon and Schuster, 1995); Kevin P. Phillips, *The Emerging Republican Majority* (New Rochelle, N.Y.: Arlington House, 1969). Phillips's influential book focused on long-term shifts in regional and ethnic voting patterns, and especially white voter reactions to the civil rights revolution and black activism. The work paid little attention to religion except to note the decline of anti-Catholicism as a factor in determining voting behavior.

53. Thomas Frank, *What's the Matter with Kansas? How Conservatives Won the Heart of America* (New York: Holt, 2004).

54. Ibid., 68–76, 215, 216, 217, 225. Data were obtained from the following sources: for Kansas Christian radio stations, http://www.christart.com/radio/kansas; for Christian bookstores, www.cba.know-where.com/cba/region/us/us/KS.html; for Vineyard Christian Fellowships, www.vineyardusa.org/churches/church_search.aspx; for Calvary Chapels, www.calvarychapel.com/?show=churches; for Assembly of God churches, telephone information obtained September 11, 2006, from the Kansas District Council of the Assemblies of God Church; for Southern Baptist churches, telephone information obtained September 11, 2006, from the Kansas–Nebraska Convention of Southern Baptists; for megachurches, Hartford Institute for Religious Research, www.hirr

.hartsem.edu/org/faith_megachurches_database_kansas.html. While right-wing polemicists Ann Coulter, Rush Limbaugh, Bill O'Reilly, and Gordon Liddy receive a total of thirty index entries in Frank's book, there are no entries for Billy Graham, Hal Lindsey, Jerry Falwell, Charles Colson, Tim LaHaye, Bill Bright, the Moral Majority, Campus Crusade for Christ, or other leaders of politicized evangelicalism. (Pat Robertson's Christian Coalition merits two passing references, with no discussion of its overall impact.) In addition to the neglect of Kansas's evangelical churches, radio stations, and bookstores, the state's dense network of evangelical schools, colleges, and home schoolers (who are often religious conservatives) is similarly ignored or mentioned in passing. Although the book's present-minded focus makes it highly readable, the absence of much historical background further impedes the reader's ability to understand the larger context of the contemporary political realities Frank describes.

55. G. K. Chesterton, *What I Saw in America* (New York: Dodd, Mead & Co., 1922), 11–12; Alexis de Tocqueville, *Democracy in America,* ed. Phillips Bradley (New York: Alfred A. Knopf, 1945; Vintage Paperback ed.), 1:314.

3. Make Payroll, Not War

1. By contrast, the African American students similarly slain at Jackson State later that month never assumed the same iconic status for the white majority, as police action against black crowds carried quite different meanings.

2. Jack Higgins quoted in Ronald Alsop, "Capitalism 101: Programs to Teach Free Enterprise Sprout on College Campuses," *Wall Street Journal,* May 10, 1978, 1.

3. Of the four who died from the National Guard assault at Kent State, two were actively protesting; additionally, nine other students were wounded by the more than sixty bullets fired into the crowd.

4. Keith Furman quoted in Alsop, "Capitalism 101."

5. Michael L. King, "Corporations Back Campus Missionaries for Free Enterprise," *Wall Street Journal,* June 21, 1979, 1.

6. "Excerpts from Platform Adopted by Republican Convention," *New York Times,* August 22, 1984, A18.

7. Donald M. Kendall, "The Generation Gap: Economic Illiteracy [Remarks Delivered before the National Food Brokers Association Annual

Conference, New York, December 5, 1970]," *Vital Speeches of the Day* 37 (1971): 245–246.

8. William L. Bird Jr., *Better Living: Advertising, Media, and the New Vocabulary of Business Leadership, 1935–1955* (Evanston, Ill.: Northwestern University Press, 1999); Elizabeth A. Fones-Wolf, *Selling Free Enterprise: The Business Assault on Labor and Liberalism, 1945–60* (Urbana: University of Illinois Press, 1994); Kim Phillips-Fein, "Top-Down Revolution: Businessmen, Intellectuals, and Politicians against the New Deal, 1945–1964," *Enterprise & Society* 7 (2006): 686–694.

9. Dan Harrison, "A Broader Role for Business?" *Chain Store Age Executive with Shopping Center Age* 53 (February 1977): 11.

10. Henry C. Wallach, "Generation Gap," *Newsweek,* October 12, 1970, 98; Ronald Reagan, "Free Enterprise Economics [Remarks Delivered before the Annual Dinner, 77th Congress of American Industry, National Association of Manufacturers, New York]," *Vital Speeches of the Day* 39 (January 15, 1973): 196–201. See also "Reading, 'Riting, 'Rithmetic—and Profits," *Nation's Business* (May 1974): 57; William H. Hunt, "The High Cost of Economic Illiteracy [Remarks Delivered at California State University, San Diego, Calif.]," *Vital Speeches of the Day* 39 (August 15, 1973): 644–671; Vernon Louviere, "Economic Illiteracy and the Profit System," *Nation's Business* (October 1972): 17; Fones-Wolf, *Selling Free Enterprise,* 288–290.

11. Paul Davenport, "Former Arizona Governor Dead at 88," *Associated Press State & Local Wire,* August 26, 1998; Joseph Stocker, "Compulsory Free Enterprise: Brainwashing the Classrooms," *The Nation,* December 17, 1973, 653, quoting Arizona legislator Jim Skelly.

12. Stocker, "Compulsory Free Enterprise," 654, quoting materials authored by Weldon P. Shofstall.

13. Sheila Harty, *Hucksters in the Classroom: A Review of Industry Propaganda in Schools* (Washington, D.C.: Center for the Study of Responsive Law, 1979), 78. See also John P. Manzer, "What to Do (and Not to Do) When Johnny Can't Define Profit," *Wall Street Journal,* September 15, 1983, 30.

14. For earlier free-enterprise campaigns that were explicitly presented as economic education, see Bird, *Better Living,* 163–181, 183–184; Fones-Wolfe, *Selling Free Enterprise,* 189–217; Roland Marchand, *Creating the Corporate Soul: The Rise of Public Relations and Corporate Imagery in American Big Business* (Berkeley: University of California Press, 1998), 212–213, 295–301.

15. Barry M. Goldwater, "Business Faces the Fight of Its Life," *Nation's Business* (May 1974): 33.

16. See Burton Yale Pines, *Back to Basics* (New York: Morrow, 1982), esp. chaps. 1 and 2.

17. Priscilla Schwab, "Introducing Johnny and Mary to the World of Business," *Nation's Business* (January 1978): 57–58.

18. "Spreading Economic Education across the Country," *Nation's Business* (January 1978): 63–64.

19. Vernon Louviere, "Panorama of the Nation's Business: A Company's Salesman for Our Economic System," *Nation's Business* (February 1976): 82, quoting W. Richard Bryan of Goodyear Tire and Rubber Co.

20. Vernon Louviere, "Speaking up for the Free Enterprise System," *Nation's Business* (October 1976): 80.

21. Harold F. Boss, *How Green the Grazing: 75 Years at Southwestern Life, 1903–1978* (Dallas, Tex.: Taylor Publishing Company, 1978), 285. For a fuller historical account of Students in Free Enterprise, see Bethany E. Moreton, "The Soul of the Service Economy: Wal-Mart and the Making of Christian Free Enterprise, 1929–1994" (Ph.D. diss., Yale University, 2006), chaps. 5 and 6.

22. Boss, *How Green the Grazing,* 285.

23. Alsop, "Capitalism 101."

24. Robert Davis, quoted in King, "Corporations Back Campus Missionaries."

25. James J. Kilpatrick, "Why Students Are Hostile to Free Enterprise," *Nation's Business* (July 1975): 11–12; "Enterprise Square Teaches Economics," *Saturday Oklahoman & Times,* March 7, 1992, 10.

26. Schwab, "Introducing Johnny and Mary," 58–59.

27. "Foundations of a Better Society?" *Industry Week,* April 20, 1981, 49.

28. Henry E. Metzner and Edwin C. Sims, "Student Attitudes toward the Free Enterprise System," *Journal of Economic Education* 10 (Autumn 1978): 46–50.

29. Students in Free Enterprise, *Students in Free Enterprise 1980–81 National Competition* (Austin, Tex.: Students in Free Enterprise, 1981).

30. "Epsilon Psi Chapter 1611 Annual Activities Report," records of Phi Beta Lambda chapter 1611, University of the Ozarks, Clarksville, Ark. (1979), 33.

31. " 'Project Awareness' submitted for the Amoco Awards of Achievement in Business Advocacy," Records of Phi Beta Lambda chapter 1611, University of the Ozarks, Clarksville, Ark. (1979), 1.

32. "How a Company Changes Youngsters' Lives," *Nation's Business* (September 1972): 17.

33. Irving Kristol, "On 'Economic Education,'" *Wall Street Journal*, February 18, 1976, 20.

34. Though my intellectual debt to Michael Denning is too pervasive to tease out in every instance, I originally encountered this particular point, expressed in essentially these terms, in a 2002 lecture of his.

35. Jean Seligmann et al., "The Golden Passport," *Newsweek*, May 14, 1979, 110; "Courses That Lead to Jobs Are Taking Over on Campus," *U.S. News & World Report*, December 15, 1975, 50; Thomas D. Snyder, Alexandra G. Tan, and Charlene M. Hoffman, *Digest of Education Statistics 2003* (Washington, D.C.: National Center for Education Statistics, U.S. Department of Education Institute of Education Sciences, 2004), 316, table on 252; Thomas L. Wheelen, "Top Managements' Perspective of Business Education—a Preliminary Summary Report," *Academy of Management Proceedings* (1972): 289.

36. "Courses That Lead to Jobs," 50.

37. Jennifer Washburn, *University, Inc.: The Corporate Corruption of Higher Education* (New York: Basic Books, 2005), 57. See also the papers of the Working Group on Globalization and Culture, *Breaking Down the Ivory Tower: The University in the Creation of Another World*, 2005, www.yale.edu/laborculture/work_culture.html.

38. Merrill Sheils et al., "Bonus for Businessmen," *Newsweek*, June 7, 1976, 84; Carl M. Larson, "Management Assistance for the Small Businessman: A Joint Program of SBA and the University," *Journal of Small Business Management* 12 (1974): 6; "On the Way: A New Round of Help for Small Business," *U.S. News & World Report*, August 30, 1976, 38; "Spotlight on Small Business," *Nation's Business* (May 1973): 12. A parallel project, the Small Business Incubators, began in the same years but focused on the commercialization of technologies developed at major research universities.

39. SBA press release (May 1976), quoted on the Web site of the Association of Small Business Development Centers, www.asbdc-us.org (accessed October 11, 2006).

40. U.S. House, *Hearing before the Subcommittee on SBA and SBIC Authority and General Small Business Problems of the Committee on Small Business*, 96th Cong., 1st sess., 1979, 9–12. Quotations come from Congressman Neal Smith and from SBA Deputy Administrator William H. Mauk, respectively.

41. See www.asbdc-us.org (accessed October 11, 2006); Sheils et al., "Bonus for Businessmen." The Web site notes that by 2005, the SBDC Network commanded a $200 million budget, of which less than $85 million came from the federal government.

42. The metaphor is political economist Susan Strange's, elaborated in her *Casino Capitalism* (London: Basil Blackwell, 1986).

43. Roberta Graham, "Free Advice Pays Off for Small Business," *Nation's Business* (February 1979): 50.

44. Sheils et al., "Bonus for Businessmen."

45. Larson, "Management Assistance," 8–9.

46. "Center for Entrepreneurship," webs.wichita.edu (accessed June 22, 2006).

47. John A. Hornaday, "Research about Living Entrepreneurs," in *Encyclopedia of Entrepreneurship*, ed. Calvin A. Kent, Donald L. Sexton, and Karl A. Vesper (Englewood Cliffs, N.J.: Prentice-Hall, 1982), 30; John A. Walsh and Jerry F. White, "Converging on the Characteristics of Entrepreneurs," in *Frontiers of Entrepreneurship Research 1981: Proceedings of the 1981 Conference on Entrepreneurship at Babson College,* ed. Karl H. Vesper (Wellesley, Mass.: Babson College, 1981), 504.

48. Karl H. Vesper, *Entrepreneurship Education: A Bicentennial Compendium* (Milwaukee, Wisc.: Society for Entrepreneurship Research and Application, 1976), unpaginated.

49. Karl H. Vesper, *Entrepreneurship Education 1985* (Wellesley, Mass.: Center for Entrepreneurial Studies, Babson College, 1985), 220, 207.

50. Calvin A. Kent, "The Treatment of Entrepreneurship in Principles of Economics Textbooks," *Journal of Economic Education* 20 (Spring 1989): 611. Judging from his footnotes, Kent was influenced by the Institute of Economic Affairs, Britain's principal intellectual architect of Thatcherism. See Richard Cockett, *Thinking the Unthinkable: Think-Tanks and the Economic Counter-Revolution, 1931–1983* (London: Fontana Press, 1995).

51. Quoted in Vesper, *Entrepreneurship Education.*

52. Walsh and White, "Converging on the Characteristics of Entrepreneurs," 511. This veneration of a hero figure drew to some extent on the starring role that political economist Joseph A. Schumpeter and, later, management theorist Peter F. Drucker gave the entrepreneur in economic history. But the preoccupation with the entrepreneur's interior state was influenced by Harvard psychologist David C. McClelland,

who claimed to have isolated a measurable personality trait—*n* Ach, or the need for achievement—that explained all economic development from classical Greece and pre-Incan Peru to modern Japan. McClelland, *The Achieving Society* (Princeton, N.J.: D. van Nostrand, 1961).

53. Vesper, *Entrepreneurship Education.*

54. Donald M. Dible, *Up Your OWN Organization! A Handbook for the Employed, the Unemployed, and the Self-Employed on How to Start and Finance a New Business* (Santa Clara, Calif.: Entrepreneur Press, 1971). Subsequent editions dropped the reference to unemployment, and eventually replaced it with "entrepreneur."

55. Alsop, "Capitalism 101." In addition to this development on the Right explored here, Michael H. Carriere argues intriguingly that the very technophilia of the New Left itself often segued into an entrepreneurial faith in the free market and in the power of cybernetics to achieve freedom where social and political transformations had failed. Carriere, " 'Let the Machines Do It': The Global New Left, the 1960s, and the Promise of Technology," paper presented at the History of Capitalism in North America Graduate Student Conference, Harvard University, October 27, 2006.

56. Fellow veterans of the Yale Working Group on Globalization and Culture will recognize Michael Denning as the proximate source of this point.

57. Snyder, Tan, and Hoffman, *Digest of Education Statistics 2003*, 316, table on 252.

58. Carl P. Zeithaml and George H. Rice Jr., "Entrepreneurship/Small Business Education in American Universities," *Journal of Small Business Management* 25 (January 1987): 46–48; Pines, *Back to Basics*, 60.

59. Enterprise Square USA, press release (Oklahoma City, 1992); for an account of Enterprise Square, see Moreton, "The Soul of the Service Economy," 230–236.

60. Students in Free Enterprise, *National Conference Program* (Bolivar, Mo., 1984); Students in Free Enterprise, *All about Economic Freedom* [video recording] (1989); Students in Free Enterprise, "The Business Roundtable Halt the Deficit Awards $1,000 Each," *SIFE Lines* 5, no. 1 (Summer 1989): 27.

61. Students in Free Enterprise, "SIFE Has Record Year—Again!" *A Year in Review* (1991): 1.

62. Students in Free Enterprise, *Annual Report* (Springfield, Mo., 1989), 4.

63. Jaan Van Valkenburgh, " 'Hero,' Other Students Go to Bat for Business at Meet," *Commercial Appeal,* April 18, 1996, 9B.

4. Gender and America's Right Turn

The author wishes to thank the National Endowment for the Humanities and the Radcliffe Institute for Advanced Study at Harvard University for grants that supported this research.

1. Gloria Steinem, "Houston and History," in *Outrageous Acts and Everyday Rebellions* (New York: Holt, 1983): Gloria Steinem, "An Introductory Statement," in *What Women Want: From the Official Report to the President, the Congress and the People of the United States,* compiled by Caroline Bird and the Members and Staff of the National Commission on the Observance of International Women's Year (New York: Simon and Schuster, 1979), 10–17; National Commission on the Observance of International Women's Year, *The Spirit of Houston: The First National Women's Conference. An Official Report to the President, the Congress and the People of the United States,* ed. Mim Kelber (Washington, D.C.: U.S. Government Printing Office, 1978), 9–12, 170; Bella Abzug with Mim Kelber, *Gender Gap: Bella Abzug's Guide to Political Power for American Women* (Boston: Houghton Mifflin, 1984), 57.

2. Phyllis Schlafly, *Phyllis Schlafly Report,* September 1986, December 1977, http://www.eagleforum.org/psr/1986/sept86/psrsep86.html, http://www.eagleforum.org/psr; Marjorie J. Spruill, interview with Phyllis Schlafly, February 22, 2005.

3. *The Spirit of Houston;* see the extensive papers of the National Commission for Observance of IWY [hereafter referred to as the National Commission Papers], the Shelah Leader Collection, and the Records of the National Organization for Women (NOW), Schlesinger Library, Harvard University.

4. *The Spirit of Houston,* 9, 119–170.

5. Ibid.

6. Ibid., 9–11; National Commission on the Observance of International Women's Year, *"To Form a More Perfect Union"* . . . *Justice for American Women* (Washington, D.C.: U.S. Government Printing Office, 1976), esp. 117–136; Alice S. Rossi, *Feminists in Politics: A Panel Analysis of the First National Women's Conference* (New York: Academic Press, 1982), 4–34.

7. Rossi, *Feminists in Politics*, 4–34; *The Spirit of Houston*, 9–12.

8. *The Spirit of Houston*, 10, 11; Winifred D. Wandersee, *On the Move: American Women in the 1970s* (Boston: G.K. Hall, 1988), 175, 176; Sara M. Evans, *Tidal Wave: How Women Changed America at Century's End* (New York: The Free Press, 2003), 139–142; Rossi, *Feminists in Politics*, 31.

9. Steinem, "Introduction," in *What Women Want*, 10–17; *The Spirit of Houston*, quotation, 126; Wandersee, *On the Move*, 188; Jean O'Leary, letter to delegates, box 3, Marion Gressette Papers, South Carolina Political Collections, South Caroliniana Library, University of South Carolina, Columbia.

10. *The Spirit of Houston*, 166, 175–183; Evans, *Tidal Wave*, 50, 51, 248n94; Rossi, *Feminists in Politics*, 324, 325; *Daily Breakthrough* (November 18, 19, 20, 1977), special editions of the *Houston Breakthrough*, the Breakthrough Publishing Company, Houston, Tex., box 3, National Commission Papers.

11. For a sociologist's analysis of the group dynamics promoting at least temporary solidarity, see Rossi, *Feminists in Politics*, 324, 325.

12. *What Women Want*, 17, 83–178; *The Spirit of Houston*, 147–157, quotation 157; for the full text of the Plan, see *What Women Want*, 83–178, or *The Spirit of Houston*, 17–97.

13. Evans, *Tidal Wave*, 142.

14. Katherine Kish Sklar, "How Did the National Women's Conference in Houston in 1977 Shape a Feminist Agenda for the Future?" in *Women and Social Movements in the United States, 1600–2000*, online archive *Women and Social Movements, 1600–2000*, ed. Thomas Dublin and Kathryn Kish Sklar (Alexandria, Va.: Alexander Street Press, 1997–2006), http://www.binghamton.edu/womhist/ (accessed March 2005).

15. *Phyllis Schlafly Report*, December 1977; Rosemary Thomson, *The Price of Liberty* (Carol Stream, Ill.: Creation House, 1978), 94; Spruill, interview with Schlafly; *The Spirit of Houston*, 11, 112, 264–272.

16. *The Spirit of Houston*, 274, 275; on polls, see Jane J. Mansbridge, *Why We Lost the ERA* (Chicago: University of Chicago Press, 1986), 14–19; Rossi, *Feminists in Politics*.

17. Rossi, *Feminists in Politics*, 42, 43, 334–336.

18. Thomson, *The Price of Liberty*, esp. 7; Marjorie Spruill and Sara Farnsworth, interview with Dr. Cora Norman, Jackson, Miss., March

2001, in Spruill's possession; *Phyllis Schlafly Report,* August 1977; *Eagle Forum Newsletter,* August 1977; Spruill, interview with Schlafly; Sheryl Hansen, interview with Dr. and Mrs. Curtis Caine, February 28, 1993, Jackson, Miss., part of a series of interviews by Sheryl Hansen with participants in the Mississippi IWY conference, Mississippi Oral History Program of the University of Southern Mississippi, Hattiesburg; Elaine Donnelly, "What Women Wanted," *National Review Online,* June 7, 2004, http://www.nationalreview.com/comment/donnelly200406070944.asp

19. William C. Berman, *America's Right Turn: From Nixon to Clinton,* 2nd ed. (Baltimore: Johns Hopkins University Press, 1998); Dan T. Carter, *The Politics of Rage: George Wallace, the Origins of the New Conservatism, and the Transformation of American Politics* (Baton Rouge: Louisiana State University Press, 1995); Dan T. Carter, *From George Wallace to Newt Gingrich: Race in the Conservative Counterrevolution, 1963–1994* (Baton Rouge: Lousiana State University Press, 1996).

20. Carol Felsenthal, *The Sweetheart of the Silent Majority: The Biography of Phyllis Schlafly* (Garden City, N.Y.: Doubleday, 1981), 233–235; Thomson, *The Price of Liberty,* 12–15; Janet K. Boles, *The Politics of the Equal Rights Amendment: Conflict and the Decision Process* (New York: Longman, 1979), 53–56; Janet K. Boles, "Building Support for the ERA: A Case of 'Too Much, Too Late,'" *PS* 15 (Fall 1982): 573; Mansbridge, *Why We Lost the ERA.*

21. "A Matter of Simple Justice," the 1970 report of President Nixon's Task Force on Women's Rights and Responsibilities (Washington, D.C.: U.S. Government Printing Office, 1970); Thomson, *The Price of Liberty,* 13, 14.

22. *Phyllis Schlafly Report,* February 1972; Felsenthal, *The Sweetheart of the Silent Majority,* 239–241; Donald T. Critchlow, *Phyllis Schlafly and Grassroots Conservatism: A Woman's Crusade* (Princeton, N.J.: Princeton University Press, 2005), 217–221; Mansbridge, *Why We Lost the ERA,* 110, 283n55.

23. Thomson, *The Price of Liberty,* 47; Felsenthal, *The Sweetheart of the Silent Majority,* 179–197; Critchlow, *Phyllis Schlafly,* 137–162; Catherine E. Rymph, *Republican Women: Feminism and Conservatism from Suffrage through the Rise of the New Right* (Chapel Hill: University of North Carolina Press, 2006).

24. Thomson, *The Price of Liberty,* 56–57; Felsenthal, *The Sweetheart of the Silent Majority,* 277–281; Jerome L. Himmelstein, *To the Right:*

The Transformation of American Conservatism (Berkeley: University of California Press, 1990), 83, 117; William Martin, *With God on Our Side: The Rise of the Religious Right in America* (New York: Broadway Books, 1996); Critchlow, *Phyllis Schlafly;* Martha Sonntag Bradley, *Pedestals & Podiums: Utah Women, Religious Authority & Equal Rights* (Salt Lake City, Utah: Signature Books, 2005).

25. Though extremist groups including the Ku Klux Klan publicly endorsed antifeminist efforts during 1977, Schlafly, Rosemary Thomson, and others have heatedly denied connections with racist groups, especially the KKK. When asked by Spruill about the Klan's boasts of "controlling" the IWY conference in Mississippi, Schlafly adamantly denied that her allies sought Klan assistance or that they had any knowledge of their involvement and was proud of the support her efforts had attracted from among African Americans. She said that her policy had been to be open to all who wanted to join in the fight against ERA, regardless of their reasons. Spruill, interview with Schlafly.

26. On opposition to U.N. ties and "the international flavor" of the IWY program and fears that the Plan of Action would represent the desires of "a few fringe radical feminists, revolutionaries and internationalists," see "IWY Tax Dollars for Revolution," *The Mindszenty Report,* July 1977, box 3, Gressette Papers.

27. Thomson, *The Price of Liberty.* For example, see 118, where Thomson states that the aims of "secular humanism, progressive education, behavioral science, socialism, internationalism, communism, liberalism or feminism" are "diabolically synonymous" and are evidence that Satan is "alive and well on planet earth, urging its sisters to unite!"

28. *Phyllis Schlafly Report,* January 1976, May 1977; *Eagle Forum Newsletter,* March 1977; Susan M. Hartmann, *From Margin to Mainstream: American Women and Politics since 1960* (New York: Knopf, 1989), 137–141, 147; Felsenthal, *The Sweetheart of the Silent Majority,* 253.

29. *The Spirit of Houston,* 99–102; Thomson, *The Price of Liberty,* 92, 93; copies of material distributed by the IWY Citizens' Review Committee, box 3, Gressette Papers.

30. Thomson, *The Price of Liberty,* 92–94; for table showing action on the core resolutions and other information on the IWY state meetings, see *The Spirit of Houston,* 99–117.

31. Edmondson quotation in Carolyn Kortge, *Wichita Kansas Eagle & Beacon,* August 3, 1977, clipping in Briefing Book, National Women's

Conference, National Commission Papers; James J. Kilpatrick, "A Conservative View," "Bella's Troops Routed in Oklahoma," clipping, n.d., National Commission Papers.

32. "IWY Tax Dollars for Revolution," *The Mindszenty Report;* John M. Crewdson, "Mormon Turnout Overwhelms Women's Conference in Utah," *New York Times,* July 25, 1977, 27; *The Spirit of Houston,* 109; on the Mormon role in the IWY and ERA battles generally, see Bradley, *Pedestals & Podiums.*

33. See Sheryl Hansen, interview with Dr. Cora Norman, April 7, 1992, Jackson, Miss., vol. 432, Mississippi Oral History Program of the University of Southern Mississippi, Hattiesburg, Miss.; Spruill and Farnsworth, interview with Cora Norman; on Dallas Higgins, see "Mississippi IWY Conference Final Report, July 8–9, 1977," Jackson *Clarion-Ledger,* November 11, 1977, 1B, clipping in the Mississippi Department of Archives and History, Jackson, Miss.; Thomson, *The Price of Liberty,* 131; on George Higgins's claims, see Bob Schwatzman, "Klan Cardholder Wanted to Help," *Today,* Brevard County, Fla., July 18, 1977. In Houston, one Mississippi delegate stated that the conservatives present did not know one another before the IWY state conference and that they did not know until afterward that one of the delegates they elected on their slate was married to a Klansman. *Daily Breakthrough,* November 19, 1977, 27.

34. *The Spirit of Houston,* 112; Kay Mills, " 'Those Aren't Prayer Meetings They Hold on Sunday. Those Are Precinct Meetings . . . ,'" reprinted in the *Daily Breakthrough,* November 19, 1977.

35. See table with results of the state meetings, *The Spirit of Houston,* 114–115.

36. Ellen Cohn, "Mama Said There'd Be Days Like This," *The Village Voice,* July 11, 1977, NY folder 2, carton 5, National Commission Papers.

37. Ibid.

38. *The Spirit of Houston.*

39. "New Coalition Braces for Attacks against IWY," *Women Today* 7, no. 19 (September 19, 1977), Massachusetts Coordinating Committee for the Observance of International Women's Year Papers, Schlesinger Library, Harvard University; IWY Citizens' Review Committee, press releases, September 14 and October 28, 1977, Gressette Papers; Bella Abzug, letter to "Dear Coordinating Committee Chairs," National Commission Papers; Summary of IWY Executive Committee meetings, August 10, 11, 12, 1977, carton 1, Shelah Leader Papers.

40. Abzug to Fellow Commissioners, September 2, 1977, carton 1 folder, "September 15, 16 [1977]," Leader collection; *Eagle Forum Newsletter*, August 1977.

41. *The Spirit of Houston*, 112, 113, 119; Kortge, *Wichita Kansas Eagle & Beacon*, August 3, 1977.

42. Ellen Pratt Fout, " 'We Shall Go Forth': The Significance of the National Women's Conference, November 18–21, 1977" (M.A. thesis, University of Houston, 2000), 73–75.

43. "Mississippi IWY Conference Final Report," 1B.

44. Abzug, *Gender Gap*, 57; *The Spirit of Houston*, esp. 9–12; see, for example, discussion of the press relishing a "catfight," "In Perfumed Combat" (editorial), *Montgomery* [Ala.] *Independent*, July 15, 1977, National Commission Papers.

45. Thomson, *The Price of Liberty*, 138–150; *The Spirit of Houston*, 51, 162, 164, 168, 191.

46. Thomson, *The Price of Liberty*, esp. 7.

47. Dick Behm, "Antifeminism: New Conservative Force," *Ripon Forum* 13, no. 17 (September 1, 1977). By this time, conservative leader Richard Viguerie had built a "direct-mail fund-raising empire," the Viguerie Company, that had become the key fund-raising organization of the New Right. Himmelstein, *To the Right*, 81.

48. Donald Critchlow, "Mobilizing Women: The 'Social Issues,' " in *The Reagan Presidency: Pragmatic Conservatism and Its Legacies*, ed. W. Elliott Brownlee and Hugh Davis Graham (Lawrence: University Press of Kansas, 2003), 293–326; Critchlow, *Phyllis Schlafly*. Critchlow and historian Lisa McGirr also argue that too much emphasis has been placed on the role of intellectuals as opposed to the grassroots in creating the modern conservative movement. Lisa McGirr, *Suburban Warriors: The Origins of the New American Right* (Princeton, N.J.: Princeton University Press, 2001).

49. Hartmann, *From Margin to Mainstream*; Susan M. Hartmann, "Feminism, Public Policy, and the Carter Administration," in *The Carter Presidency: Policy Choices in the Post–New Deal Era*, ed. Gary M. Fink and Hugh Davis Graham (Lawrence: University Press of Kansas, 1998); Emily Walker Cook, "Women White House Advisors in the Carter Administration: Presidential Stalwarts or Feminist Advocates?" (Ph.D. diss., Vanderbilt University, 1995); Critchlow, "Mobilizing Women," 300, 321; Abzug, *Gender Gap*, 53–56, 62–75.

50. Betty Friedan, *The Second Stage,* with a new introduction (Cambridge, Mass.: Harvard University Press, 1998); Susan Faludi, *Backlash: The Undeclared War against American Women* (New York: Crown Publishers, 1991), 318–325.

51. Sklar, "How Did the National Women's Conference in Houston in 1977 Shape a Feminist Agenda for the Future?

52. Donnelly, "What Women Wanted"; Critchlow, *Phyllis Schlafly;* Rymph, *Republican Women,* 227–233; Abzug, *Gender Gap,* 81–82.

53. Abzug, *Gender Gap,* 60–63, 110–115.

5. Civil Rights and the Religious Right

The author would like to acknowledge Patrick Allitt, Matthew Dallek, Jonathan Prude, James Roark, and Benjamin Sasse, along with the editors, for their help in preparing this chapter.

1. Patrick Allitt, *Religion in America since 1945: A History* (New York: Columbia University Press, 2003), 154.

2. Viguerie quoted in Thomas Byrne Edsall and Mary D. Edsall, *Chain Reaction: The Impact of Race, Rights, and Taxes on American Politics* (New York: Norton, 1992), 132.

3. Weyrich quoted in Michael Cromartie, ed., *No Longer Exiles: The Religious New Right in American Politics* (Washington, D.C.: Ethics and Public Policy Center, 1993), 26.

4. U.S. Bureau of the Census, *Census of the Population: 1970,* vol. 1, *Characteristics of the Population,* part 26, Mississippi (Washington, D.C.: U.S. Government Printing Office, 1973), 85, 334; U.S. Bureau of the Census, *Census of the Population: 1940,* vol. 2, *Characteristics of the Population,* part 4, Minnesota–New Mexico (Washington, D.C.: U.S. Government Printing Office, 1943), 242.

5. *Norwood v. Harrison,* 93 S. Ct. 2807 (1973); U.S. Senate, Select Committee on Equal Educational Opportunity, 91st Cong., 2nd sess., *Equal Educational Opportunity,* Part 3D (Washington, D.C.: U.S. Government Printing Office, 1970), 2042.

6. *Green v. Kennedy,* 309 F. Supp. 1127 (1970), statistic on 1133.

7. *Coffey v. State Educational Finance Commission,* 296 F. Supp. 1389 (1969).

8. U.S. Senate, Hearing before the Subcommittee on Taxation and Debt Management Generally of the Committee on Finance, 96th Cong., 1st

sess., *Tax Exempt Status of Private Schools* (Washington, D.C.: U.S. Government Printing Office, 1979), 65.

9. Quoted in *Green v. Kennedy*, 309 F. Supp. 1127 (1970), quotation on 1135.

10. *New York Times*, January 14, 1970, 1; *Wall Street Journal*, January 14, 1970, 2.

11. Ehrlichman quoted in David Whitman, "Ronald Reagan and Tax Exemptions for Racist Schools," case no. 609.0, Case Studies in Public Policy and Management, John F. Kennedy School of Government, Harvard University, 7. For an abridged version of Whitman's article, see Martin Linsky, Jonathan Moore, Wendy O'Donnell, and David Whitman, *How the Press Affects Federal Policymaking: Six Case Studies* (New York: Norton, 1986), 254–305. All page references cited herein are to the Kennedy School of Government case study.

12. *Christian Science Monitor*, January 9, 1970, 17.

13. See Clarke Reed to W. W. Gresham Jr., January 20, 1970, folder 1969–1970 Schools—Southern (January–February), box F-11, series 6, Mississippi Republican Party, Special Collections, Mitchell Memorial Library, Mississippi State University, Starkville.

14. John Ehrlichman, handwritten notes of Oval Office Meetings, January 9, 1970, folder 1/9/70 notes, box 1, Ehrlichman Papers, Hoover Archives, Stanford University, Stanford, Calif.

15. Whitman, "Ronald Reagan and Tax Exemptions for Racist Schools," 8; Dan T. Carter, *The Politics of Rage: George Wallace, the Origins of the New Conservatism, and the Transformation of American Politics* (Baton Rouge: Louisiana State University Press, 1995), 387–388.

16. *Wall Street Journal*, December 17, 1973, 1. For a critique of the Briarcrest schools, see the testimony of Kenneth Dean before the 1978 IRS Hearings in Martin P. Claussen and Evelyn Bills Claussen, eds., *The Voice of Christian and Jewish Dissenters in America: U.S. Internal Revenue Service Hearings on Proposed "Discrimination" Tax Controls over Christian, Jewish, and Secular Private Schools, December 5, 6, 7, 8, 1978* (Washington, D.C.: Piedmont Press, 1982), 67–73.

17. For more on the Lamar Society, see H. Brandt Ayers and Thomas H. Naylor, eds., *You Can't Eat Magnolias* (New York: McGraw-Hill, 1972); Thomas Naylor, "The L.Q.C. Lamar Society," *New South* 25, no. 3 (1970): 21–25.

18. Brief review of *The Schools That Fear Built*, in *Social Forces* 56 (December 1977): 753; David Nevin and Robert E. Bills, *The Schools That*

Fear Built: Segregationist Academies in the South (Washington, D.C.: Acropolis Books, 1976), 88; *New York Times,* January 7, 1970, 30.

19. For a survey of southern private schools from the late 1960s, see U.S. Senate, Select Committee on Equal Educational Opportunity, 91st Cong., 2nd sess., *Equal Educational Opportunity,* part 3A (Washington, D.C.: U.S. Government Printing Office, 1970), 1196–1197.

20. Nevin and Bills, *The Schools That Fear Built,* 1, 2.

21. Peter Skerry, "Christian Schools versus the IRS," *Public Interest* 61 (Fall 1980): 30–31; Virginia Davis Nordin and William Lloyd Turner, "More Than Segregation Academies: The Growing Protestant Fundamentalist Schools," *Phi Delta Kappan* 61 (February 1980): 392. Also see "Are the New Fundamentalist Schools Racist Havens or Moral Alternatives?" *Phi Delta Kappan* 61 (June 1980): 724–725.

22. United States Commission on Civil Rights, *The Federal Civil Rights Enforcement Effort—1974, vol. III: To Ensure Equal Educational Opportunity: A Report* (Washington, D.C.: U.S. Government Printing Office, 1975), 142–197.

23. Rev. Proc. 75-50, 1975-2 C.B. 587.

24. Rev. Rul. 75-231, 1975-1 C.B. 158.

25. Joint Committee on Taxation, *Background Relating to the Effect of Racially Discriminatory Policies on the Tax-Exempt Status of Private Schools* (Washington, D.C.: U.S. Government Printing Office, 1982), 4.

26. Jim Lyons to Louis Nunez, memo, May 11, 1978, reprinted in U.S. House, Hearings before the Subcommittee on Oversight of the Committee on Ways and Means, 96th Congress, 1st sess., *Tax-Exempt Status of Private Schools* (Washington, D.C.: U.S. Government Printing Office, 1979), 239–251 (the seven Mississippi academies are listed on 248–249; IRS Commissioner Kurtz quoted on 5); *Washington Post,* May 23, 1978, 4.

27. Internal Revenue Service, news release, August 21, 1978, reprinted in U.S. House, *Tax-Exempt Status of Private Schools,* 20–37, quotation on 32.

28. IRS official quoted in Skerry, "Christian Schools versus the IRS," 19.

29. Allitt, *Religion in America,* 186.

30. For a transcript of the IRS hearings, see Claussen and Claussen, *The Voice of Christian and Jewish Dissenters in America;* Robert C. Liebman and Robert Wuthnow, *The New Christian Right: Mobilization and Legitimation* (Hawthorne, N.Y.: Aldine Publishing Company,

1983), 60; Benjamin Sasse, "Federal Bureaucrat as a Common Enemy" (unpublished paper in author's possession), 3, 32.

31. U.S. Senate, Hearing before the Subcommittee on Taxation and Debt Management Generally of the Committee on Finance, 96th Cong., 1st sess., *Tax-Exempt Status of Private Schools* (Washington, D.C.: U.S. Government Printing Office, 1979), 44.

32. Ibid., 119.

33. *Congressional Quarterly Almanac, 96th Congress, 1st Session,* vol. 35 (Washington, D.C.: Congressional Quarterly, 1979), 199–202; *Congressional Quarterly Almanac, 97th Congress, 2nd Session,* vol. 38 (Washington, D.C.: Congressional Quarterly, 1982), 397.

34. For examples of Helms's contributions to the *Citizen,* see "Northern Racial Violence Exposes Basic Hypocrisy of 'Liberal Views,' " *Citizen* (November 1964): 21–23; "Whatever Became of the 'Checks and Balances,' " *Citizen* (May 1965): 2, 22; "LBJ: Architect of Anarchy?" *Citizen* (September 1965): 20–21; "Guidelines Author on the Griddle," *Citizen* (December 1966): 8–9.

35. Platform quotation cited in Whitman, "Ronald Reagan and Tax Exemptions for Racist Schools," 24; Liebman and Wuthnow, *The New Christian Right,* 60–61; Reagan quoted in Whitman, "Ronald Reagan and Tax Exemptions for Racist Schools," 25; *New York Times,* January 31, 1980, 8B.

36. Joseph Crespino, *In Search of Another Country: Mississippi and the Conservative Counterrevolution* (Princeton, N.J.: Princeton University Press, 2007), 261–263; Aaron Haberman, "Into the Wilderness: Ronald Reagan, Bob Jones University, and the Political Education of the Christian Right," *Historian* 67, no. 2 (2005): 234–253.

37. John D. Skrentny, *The Minority Rights Revolution* (Cambridge, Mass.: Belknap Press of Harvard University Press, 2002), 4.

6. The Decade of the Neighborhood

1. "Brownstoners' Fair Attended by 2000," *New York Times,* October 28, 1973, 120.

2. *Plan for New York City 1969: A Proposal: I. Critical Issues* (New York: Department of City Planning, 1969), 142; Shirley Bradway Laska and Daphne Spain, eds., *Back to the City: Issues in Neighborhood Renovation* (New York: Pregamon Press, 1980); for a history of the brownstone revitalization movement in Brooklyn, see Suleiman

Osman, "The Birth of Postmodern New York: Gentrification, Postindustrialization and Race in South Brooklyn, 1950–1980" (Ph.D. diss., Harvard University, 2006).

3. J. Thomas Black, Allan Borut, and Robert Dubinsky, *Private-Market Housing Renovation in Older Urban Areas* (Washington D.C.: Urban Land Institute, 1977), 1, 7–37.

4. "A Half-Million Street Trees and More on the Way," *New York Times,* August 15, 1971, R1; Osman, "The Birth of Postmodern New York," 333–384.

5. "Neighborhood Action Moves into the 80's," *Los Angeles Times,* December 30, 1979, D5; "Activist Neighborhood Groups Are Becoming a New Political Force," *New York Times,* June 18, 1979, A1; Harry Boyte, "Neighborhood Power—A Term Representing a New Constituency Entering National Political Life," *New York Times,* August 19, 1979, E23; for a description of the "neighborhood revolt," see John H. Mollenkopf, *The Contested City* (Princeton, N.J.: Princeton University Press, 1983), 180–212; the "neighborhood movement" is also described in Jon C. Teaford, *The Rough Road to Renaissance: Urban Revitalization in America, 1940–1985* (Baltimore: Johns Hopkins University Press, 1990), 240–252; David Morris and Karl Hess, *Neighborhood Power: The New Localism* (Boston: Beacon Press, 1975).

6. Thomas J. Sugrue, *The Origins of the Urban Crisis: Race and Inequality in Postwar Detroit* (Princeton, N.J.: Princeton University Press, 1996); Arnold R. Hirsch, *Making the Second Ghetto: Race and Housing in Chicago, 1940–1960* (Cambridge: Cambridge University Press, 1983); John T. Tumbler, *A Social History of Economic Decline: Business, Politics, and Work in Trenton* (New Brunswick, N.J.: Rutgers University Press, 1989).

7. Teaford, *The Rough Road to Renaissance,* 203–213; William Julius Wilson, *The Truly Disadvantaged: The Inner City, the Underclass, and Public Policy* (Chicago: University of Chicago Press, 1987), 22–26; "Murder Wave of the 1970's Appears to Ebb in Cities," *New York Times,* January 11, 1976, 1; "Crime Fear Levels Off, Polls Find," *New York Times,* December 18, 1977, 45.

8. Boyte, "Neighborhood Power."

9. John Louis Flateau, "Black Brooklyn: The Politics of Ethnicity, Class, and Gender" (Ph.D. diss., City University of New York, 2005), 47–55; John Hull Mollenkopf, *A Phoenix in the Ashes: The Rise and Fall of the Koch Coalition in New York City Politics* (Princeton, N.J.: Princeton

University Press, 1992), 89–92; Craig Steven Wilder, *A Covenant with Color: Race and Social Power in Brooklyn* (New York: Columbia University Press, 2000), 235–239; "Head of Operation Breadbasket Says He Opposes Mrs. Chisholm," *New York Times,* January 27, 1972, 22; "Minutes of the Steering Committee of the National Action Council Meeting," April 11, 1964, Papers of the Congress of Racial Equality, reel 1, section 1, Microform Reading Room, Butler Library, Columbia University; for the shift of black power from activism to electoral politics in the 1970s, see Matthew J. Countryman, *Up South: Civil Rights and Black Power in Philadelphia* (Philadelphia: University of Pennsylvania Press, 2006).

10. Teaford, *The Rough Road to Renaissance,* 192–199; Jonathan Reider, *Canarsie: The Jews and Italians of Brooklyn against Liberalism* (Cambridge, Mass.: Harvard University, 1985); for descriptions of antibusing as a form of "reactionary populism," see Ronald P. Formisano, *Boston against Busing: Race, Class and Ethnicity in the 1960s and 1970s* (Chapel Hill: University of North Carolina Press, 1991), 172–173, and Matthew D. Lassiter, *The Silent Majority: Suburban Politics in the Sunbelt South* (Princeton, N.J.: Princeton University Press, 2006), 148–174.

11. Calvin Trillin, "The Bubble Gum Store," *The New Yorker,* July 21, 1975; Vance Packard, *A Nation of Strangers* (New York: David McKay, 1972), quoted in Joy and Paul Wilkes, *You Don't Have to Be Rich to Own a Brownstone* (New York: Quadrangle Books, 1973), vii–xii.

12. Harry C. Boyte, *The Backyard Revolution: Understanding the New Citizen's Movement* (Philadelphia: Temple University Press, 1980), 2; "Urban Settlers: With Sweat and Money, Affluent Families 'Unslum' a Community," *Wall Street Journal,* October 29, 1971, 1.

13. "They Fought a Highway and Formed a Congress," *Christian Science Monitor,* September 9, 1977, 16; Boyte, *The Backyard Revolution,* 69.

14. For more on the imagery of the "old machine" and "new machine" in the rhetoric of postwar neighborhood reformers, see Osman, "The Birth of Postmodern New York," 215–216; Mollenkopf, *The Contested City,* 181–190.

15. "A New Politics via the Neighborhood," *Social Policy* (October 1979): 2.

16. "A Nation of Neighborhoods: Series Explores 'New Localism,'" *Christian Science Monitor,* September 9, 1977, 1.

17. Polls quoted in Boyte, *The Backyard Revolution,* 3–5.

18. Osman, "The Birth of Postmodern New York," 95, 128–129.

19. Jane Jacobs, *The Death and Life of Great American Cities* (New York: Random House, 1961); Herbert Gans, *The Urban Villagers: Group and Class in the Life of Italian-Americans* (New York: Free Press of Glencoe, 1962); Osman, "The Birth of Postmodern New York," 297–332.

20. "Rising Out of the Rubble Green Things Are Growing among the City's Canyons," *New York Times,* June 20, 1976; Osman, "The Birth of Postmodern New York," 361–362, 370.

21. Osman, "The Birth of Postmodern New York," 321–322. The most radical expression of the 1970s desire to reinhabit an organic inner city was Philadelphia's back-to-nature/back-to-the-city sect, MOVE; see John Anderson and Hilary Hevenor, *Burning Down the House: MOVE and the Tragedy of Philadelphia* (New York: Norton, 1987); see also Lawrence Buell, *Writing for an Endangered World: Literature, Culture, and Environment in the U.S. and Beyond* (Cambridge, Mass.: Harvard University Press, 2001), 125–128. For the role of the neighborhood and ancestor in black fiction and thought, see Toni Morrison, "City Limits, Village Values: Concepts of the Neighborhood in Black Fiction," in *Literature & the Urban Experience: Essays on the City and Literature,* ed. Michael C. Jaye and Ann Chalmers Watts (New Brunswick, N.J.: Rutgers University Press, 1981), 39–43.

22. "They Fought a Highway and Formed a Congress," 15; "Brooklyniana" was coined by Walt Whitman to describe the everyday goings-on of 1860s Brooklyn. I use it here and elsewhere in the same vein as "Victoriana" or "Americana" to describe a strand of Brooklyn nostalgia that developed in the 1970s; Walt Whitman, "Brooklyniana," in *The Uncollected Poetry and Prose of Walt Whitman,* ed. Emory Holloway (Garden City, N.Y.: Doubleday, 1921), 2:222–321; Reider, *Canarsie,* 90–94; Teaford, *The Rough Road to Renaissance,* 246–248; founded as part of the "War on Poverty" in 1964, VISTA (Volunteers in Service to America) enlisted volunteers to serve in poor communities throughout the United States.

23. "Activist Neighborhood Groups Are Becoming a New Political Force"; Rem Koolhaas, *Delirious New York: A Retroactive Manifesto for Manhattan* (New York: Oxford University Press, 1978); Douglass Yates, *The Ungovernable City: The Politics of Urban Problems and Policy Making* (Cambridge, Mass.: MIT Press, 1977).

24. "Lindsay Picks Housing Task Force," *New York Times*, March 27, 1965; "Lindsay Names 21 Top Officials of New Housing Superagency," *New York Post*, November 28, 1967, 14; "Lindsay Creates Agency to Direct Fight on Slums," *New York Times*, November 23, 1966; "Three Little City Halls Helping Thousands Fight City Hall as Opposition Mounts in the Council," *New York Times*, June 9, 1967; Charles R. Morris, *The Cost of Good Intentions: New York City and the Liberal Experiment, 1960–1975* (New York: Norton, 1980), 37–38, 46–55; for the conflicting agenda of the Great Society, see Sidney M. Milkis, "Lyndon Johnson, the Great Society, and the 'Twilight' of the Modern Presidency," in *The Great Society and the High Tide of Liberalism*, ed. Sidney M. Milkis and Jerome M. Mileur (Amherst: University of Massachusetts Press, 2005), 1–37.

25. Teaford, *The Rough Road to Renaissance*, 232–236; "Public Sector Failing to Close Housing Gap," *New York Times*, March 14, 1971, 1; "City Must Reduce Its Housing Plans," *New York Times*, December 14, 1970, 1; Norman I. Fainstein and Susan S. Fainstein, "Governing Regimes and the Political Economy of Development in New York City, 1946–1984," in *Power, Culture, and Place: Essays on New York City*, ed. John Mollenkopf (New York: Russell Sage Foundation, 1988), 178–184; George Steinlieb and James W. Hughes, "Housing in the United States: An Overview," in *America's Housing: Prospects and Problems* (New Brunswick, N.J.: Rutgers University Press, 1980), 24; "Congress Changes Its Busing Tune," *Wall Street Journal*, October 7, 1975, 24; Lassiter, *The Silent Majority*, 308–318.

26. "Citibank Is Planning to Commit $10 Million to Mortgage Program," *New York Times*, November 22, 1977; "A Detailed Study Charges 'Redlining' by Major Savings Bank in Brooklyn," *New York Times*, December 6, 1976, 37; "The Long Redline in Brooklyn," *New York Post*, October 5, 1977, 31; "Redline Fever: How People Are Beating the Banks," *The Village Voice*, March 13, 1978, 1; "Foes of Redlining Target 3 More Areas," *New York Post*, July 8, 1978, 8.

27. "How a Community Won the Redlining Drive," *Christian Science Monitor*, October 14, 1977, 16; Boyte, *The Backyard Revolution*, 4.

28. Osman, "The Birth of Postmodern New York," 410–411; Boyte, *The Backyard Revolution*, 161–163; David R. Colburn, "Running for Office: African-American Mayors from 1967 to 1996," in *African-American Mayors: Race, Politics, and the American City*, ed. David

R. Colburn and Jeffrey S. Adler (Chicago: University of Illinois Press, 2001), 36–40.

29. "Homesteaders Combating Urban Blight," *New York Times*, September 16, 1973, 1; "Planning Unit Introduces Neighborhood 'Miniplans,'" *New York Times*, June 26, 1974, 89; "Zuccotti, Planning Unit Head, Ranks High with Beame," *New York Times*, November 29, 1974, 41; "Why City Is Switching from Master Plan to 'Miniplan'," *New York Times*, June 27, 1974; Fainstein and Fainstein, "Governing Regimes and the Political Economy of Development in New York City, 1946–1984," 183–184; David P. Varady, *Neighborhood Upgrading: A Realistic Assessment* (Albany: State University of New York Press, 1986), 37–50.

30. Osman, "The Birth of Postmodern New York," 382–383; Black, Borut, and Dubinsky, *Private-Market Housing Renovation*, 1; Teaford, *The Rough Road to Renaissance*, 251–252.

31. Osman, "The Birth of Postmodern New York," 26–28; Richard Florida, *The Rise of the Creative Class: And How It's Transforming Work, Community Leisure and Everyday Life* (New York: Perseus Books, 2002).

32. Coined by British sociologist Ruth Glass to describe upgrading neighborhoods in London in 1964, the word *gentrification* did not come into popular usage until the late 1970s.

33. "Displacement Report to the Gowanus-Boerum Hill Community," unpublished booklet, August 1980, Brooklyn Collection, Brooklyn Public Library.

34. Nan Ellin, *Postmodern Urbanism* (Cambridge, Mass.: Blackwell, 1996); Michael Sorkin, ed., *Variations on a Theme Park: The New American City and the End of Public Space* (New York: Hill and Wang, 1992); Mollenkopf, *A Phoenix in the Ashes*.

35. Osman, "The Birth of Postmodern New York," 448.

7. Cultural Politics and the Singer/Songwriters of the 1970s

1. Lester Bangs, "James Taylor Marked for Death," reprinted in *Psychotic Reactions and Carburetor Dung* (New York: Vintage Books, 1988), 53–81. The quoted material appears on 71–72. Originally published in *Who Put the Bomp* (Winter/Spring 1971).

2. Lyrics are from James Taylor, "Sweet Baby James," *Sweet Baby James*, Warner Brothers Records, 1970; and Jackson Browne, "Sing My Songs

to Me," *For Everyman,* Elektra/Asylum Records, 1973. Though this was one of Browne's earliest songs, dating back to the late 1960s, it did not appear on an album until *For Everyman,* which appeared at the height of the singer/songwriter movement, when its sentiment of self-discovery resonated with the "Me Decade" ethic.

3. Reebee Garofalo, *Rockin' Out: Popular Music in the U.S.A.,* 3rd ed. (Upper Saddle River, N.J.: Pearson Prentice Hall, 2005), 221.

4. Ibid., 210–214.

5. Ibid., 238–247; David P. Szatmary, *Rockin' in Time: A Social History of Rock-and-Roll,* 6th ed. (Upper Saddle River, N.J.: Pearson Prentice Hall, 2006), 222–226.

6. Garofalo, *Rockin' Out,* 214–220.

7. The Weir quote appears in Alexander Bloom and Wini Breines, eds., *Takin' It to the Streets: A Sixties Reader* (New York: Oxford University Press, 1995) 296. Cooper is quoted in Szatmary, *Rockin' in Time,* 233.

8. Szatmary, *Rockin' in Time,* 221.

9. Garofalo, *Rockin' Out,* 200.

10. "Frontline: The Way the Music Died," PBS Home Video, 2004. Originally aired May 27, 2004.

11. Steve Chapple and Reebee Garofalo, *Rock 'n' Roll Is Here to Pay: The History and Politics of the Music Industry* (Chicago: Nelson-Hall, 1977), 201–205.

12. Ibid., 205–208, 292.

13. On Dylan's influence on Browne, see Anthony DeCurtis, "Jackson Browne," *Rolling Stone* 20th anniversary issue, November 5–December 12, 1987, 157–160; and Mark Bego, *Jackson Browne: His Life and Music* (New York: Citadel Press, 2005), 19–20. Stephen Holden, "The Evolution of the Singer-Songwriter," in *The Rolling Stone Illustrated History of Rock & Roll,* ed. Anthony DeCurtis and Holly George Warren (New York: Random House, 1992), 480–491, provides a deft overview of the movement. The quote appears on 482.

14. Steve Pond, "Jackson Browne Adapts," *Rolling Stone,* September 15, 1983, 33–39.

15. "Berklee Beat: James Taylor Comes to Class," *Berklee Today* (Summer 2000), www.berklee.edu/bt/ (accessed February 21, 2006).

16. "Words and Music—Joni Mitchell and Morrissey," *Joni Mitchell Library,* jonimitchell.com/library/view.cfm?id=678 (accessed February 21, 2006). Original interview took place on October 18, 1996.

17. "James Taylor: One Man's Family of Rock," *Time,* March 1, 1971, 45–53.

18. Quotes are from Stephen Holden, review of *No Secrets, Rolling Stone,* January 4, 1973, 64; and Garofalo, *Rockin' Out,* 223.

19. Michele Kort, *Soul Picnic: The Music and Passion of Laura Nyro* (New York: St. Martin's Press, 2002).

20. "Russ Kunkel," *Drummerworld,* www.drummerworld.com/drummers/ Russ_Kunkel.html (accessed March 7, 2006).

21. Paul Nelson, "Jackson Browne: This Wheel's on Fire," *Rolling Stone,* March 9, 1978, 11–12.

22. Lester Bangs, "James Taylor: One Man Dog," reprinted in *Psychotic Reactions and Carburetor Dung* (New York: Vintage Books, 1988), 114–115. Originally published in *Creem,* February 1973.

23. Robert Christgau, *Any Old Way You Choose It: Rock and Other Pop Music 1967–1973* (Baltimore: Penguin Books, 1973), 210–213.

24. Rich Wiseman, "Jackson Browne Sings for Utopia," *Rolling Stone,* September 9, 1976, 13.

25. "Taylor at Midnight," *The New Yorker,* November 25, 1972, 37–38.

26. Christgau, *Any Old Way You Choose It,* 211, 214.

27. Bangs, "James Taylor: One Man Dog," 114.

28. Robert Christgau, "Carly Simon as Mistress of Schlock," in *Any Old Way You Choose It: Rock and Other Pop Music 1967–1973* (Baltimore: Penguin Books, 1973), 291–294.

29. Christgau, *Any Old Way You Choose It,* 210–213.

30. Stephen Davis, "Joni Mitchell's *For the Roses:* It's Good for a Hole in the Heart," *Rolling Stone,* January 4, 1973, 60.

31. Jackson Browne, "The Pretender," *The Pretender,* Asylum Records, 1976.

32. See Joe Klein and Dave Marsh, "Rock and Politics," *Rolling Stone,* September 9, 1976, 30–35.

33. Wiseman, "Jackson Browne Sings for Utopia," 13.

34. *No Nukes: The MUSE Concerts for a Non-Nuclear Future,* Elektra/ Asylum Records, 1979. The Simon statement is included in the accompanying book, Harvey Wasserman, ed., *The MUSE Record Book* (New York: Musicians United for Safe Energy, 1979), 11.

35. Kurt Loder, "James Taylor Plays Benefits for Anderson Campaign," *Rolling Stone,* July 10, 1980, 16.

36. An informative sampling of the singer/songwriters' engagement with politics can be found on the following Web sites: www.jacksonbrowne

.com; www.caroleking.com; www.jonimitchell.com; www.james-tay lor.com.

8. Financing the Counterrevolution

Passages in this chapter are reprinted from chapter five of O'Connor, Alice. *Social Science for What?* copyright 2007 Russell Sage Foundation, 112 East 64th Street, New York, NY 10021. Reprinted with permission.

1. F.O.R.D. pamphlet, included as attachment in Report no. 012797, Ford Foundation Archives (hereafter FFA), New York.
2. Kai Bird, *The Chairman: John J. McCloy and the Making of the American Establishment* (New York: Simon and Schuster, 1992), 436–440.
3. Richard Magat to McGeorge Bundy, December 23, 1969, Office Files of Richard Magat, FFA, box 6, folder 54.
4. Alfred A. May to Allen Merrell, Ford Motor Company, January 1970; Richard Magat, "Highly Confidential" Report, March 12, 1970, both in Report no. 012797, FFA.
5. "UnAmerican Causes Get Foundation Funds," *Hollywood Citizen-News,* January 5, 1970, in Report no. 012797, FFA.
6. Henry Ford II to M.R.H. Davies, March 13, 1970, in Report no. 012797, FFA.
7. Charles P. Moore Jr. to McGeorge Bundy, September 10, 1970, Report no. 010894, FFA.
8. Patrick Buchanan, "The Forgotten Americans," media analysis prepared in Summer 1969, Papers of H.R. Haldeman, box 207, Nixon Papers, National Archives, Washington, D.C.
9. McGeorge Bundy, quoted in Kai Bird, *The Color of Truth: McGeorge Bundy and William Bundy, Brothers in Arms: A Biography* (New York: Simon and Schuster, 1998), 393.
10. The quote is from New York *Daily News* columnist John O'Donnell, December 21, 1954, in Rene A. Wormser, *Foundations: Their Power and Influence* (New York: Devin-Adair, 1958), vii.
11. The discussion that follows draws on the more fully developed analysis in Alice O'Connor, *Social Science for What? Philanthropy and the Social Question in a World Turned Rightside Up* (New York: Russell Sage Foundation, 2007).
12. Irving Kristol, "Business and the New Class," *Wall Street Journal,* May 19, 1975.

13. William E. Simon, *A Time for Truth* (New York: Reader's Digest Press, 1978), 230.

14. On the Powell memo, see David A. Hollinger, "Money and Academic Freedom a Half-Century after McCarthyism: Universities amid the Force Fields of Capital," in *Unfettered Expression: Freedom in American Intellectual Life,* ed. Peggie J. Hollingsworth (Ann Arbor: University of Michigan Press, 2000), 161–184; and Oliver A. Houck, "With Charity for All," *Yale Law Journal* 93 (1984): 1457–1460.

15. Lewis F. Powell Jr., "Confidential Memorandum, Attack of Free Enterprise System," August 23, 1971, reprinted in Chamber of Commerce, *Washington Report,* and on the Web site http://www.media transparency.org.

16. Simon, *A Time for Truth,* 228–231.

17. Walter Goodman, "Irving Kristol: Patron Saint of the New Right," *New York Times Magazine,* December 6, 1981, 90.

18. The editorial page recognized as much in "Grants and Groans," *Wall Street Journal,* January 14, 1977, 10.

19. Simon, *A Time for Truth,* 231.

20. Powell, "Confidential Memorandum," 15.

21. Simon, *A Time for Truth,* 238.

22. Irving Kristol, "On Corporate Philanthropy," *Wall Street Journal,* March 21, 1977, 18.

23. John Miller, *The Gift of Freedom: How the John M. Olin Foundation Changed America* (San Francisco: Encounter Books, 2006), 188–189; Alice O'Connor, interview with Olin Foundation Executive Director James Piereson, February 2004.

24. Olin quoted in *New York Times* obituary, September 10, 1982, D16. On the Grantmakers Roundtable, see Miller, *The Gift of Freedom,* 132; Alice O'Connor, interview with James Piereson; Alice O'Connor, interview with Adam Meyerson, Executive Director of the Philanthropy Roundtable, February 2006.

25. "Simon: Preaching the Word for Olin," *New York Times,* July 16, 1978, F1.

26. For figures and annual breakdowns of the foundation's endowment and expenditures since 1982, see Miller, *The Gift of Freedom,* 209; Alice O'Connor, interview with Michael Joyce, June 2004.

27. Joyce and Lenkowsky quoted in Bernard Weinraub, "Foundations Assist Conservative Cause," *New York Times,* January 20, 1981, A25.

28. James Piereson, "The Conservative Foundation Movement—Past and Future," speech delivered to a meeting of the State Policy Network, Chicago, April 29, 2004. The phrase "from protest to politics" is from social democrat and civil rights movement activist Bayard Rustin, who used it in a famously controversial article to urge the movement to shift to coalition-building with labor and other Democratic Party constituencies in the wake of major civil rights victories. Bayard Rustin, "From Protest to Politics: The Future of the Civil Rights Movement," *Commentary* (February 1965).

9. The White Ethnic Strategy

1. Quoted in Gerald S. Strober and Deborah Strober, *Nixon: An Oral History of His Presidency* (New York: HarperCollins, 1994), 82.
2. Jason A. Kaufman, *For the Common Good? American Civic Life and the Golden Age of Fraternity* (New York: Oxford University Press, 2002).
3. Louis L. Gerson, *The Hyphenate in Recent American Politics and Diplomacy* (Lawrence: University of Kansas Press, 1964).
4. Michael Novak, *The Rise of the Unmeltable Ethnics* (New York: Macmillan, 1972); Murray Friedman, ed., *Overcoming Middle-Class Rage* (Philadelphia: Westminster Press, 1971); Andrew M. Greeley, *Why Can't They Be Like Us? America's White Ethnic Groups* (New York: E.P. Dutton, 1971); Orlando Patterson, *Ethnic Chauvinism: The Reactionary Impulse* (New York: Stein and Day, 1977); Gerson, *The Hyphenate in Recent American Politics and Diplomacy.*
5. Nathan Glazer and Daniel Patrick Moynihan, *Beyond the Melting Pot: The Negroes, Puerto Ricans, Jews, Italians and Irish of New York City,* 2nd ed. (Cambridge, Mass.: M.I.T. Press, 1970); Roger Waldinger, *Still the Promised City? African Americans and New Immigrants in Postindustrial New York* (Cambridge, Mass.: Harvard University Press, 1996).
6. Richard D. Alba, *Ethnic Identity: The Transformation of White America* (New Haven, Conn.: Yale University Press, 1990), offers an excellent summary of these trends.
7. Novak, *The Rise of the Unmeltable Ethnics,* 39; Donna R. Gabaccia, *We Are What We Eat: Ethnic Food and the Making of Americans* (Cambridge, Mass.: Harvard University Press, 1998); Matthew Frye Jacobson, *Roots Too: White Ethnic Revival in Post–Civil Rights America* (Cambridge, Mass.: Harvard University Press, 2006).

8. Andrew M. Greeley, *Ethnicity in the United States: A Preliminary Reconnaissance* (New York: Wiley, 1974).

9. Franklin D. Roosevelt, "The President Condemns Discharging Loyal Aliens from Jobs," January 2, 1942, in *Public Papers and Addresses of Franklin D. Roosevelt, 1942* (New York: Harper and Brothers, 1950), 5–6; Richard W. Steele, " 'No Racials': Discrimination against Ethnics in American Defense Industry, 1940–42," *Labor History* 32 (1991): 66–90; Philip Gleason, "Americans All: World War II and the Shaping of American Identity," *The Review of Politics* 43 (1981): 483–518; Gary Gerstle, *American Crucible: Race and Nation in the Twentieth Century* (Princeton, N.J.: Princeton University Press, 2001).

10. See Thomas J. Sugrue, *Sweet Land of Liberty: The Unfinished Struggle for Racial Equality in the North* (forthcoming).

11. Stokely Carmichael and Charles V. Hamilton, *Black Power: The Politics of Liberation* (New York: Random House, 1967), 44–45.

12. *Newsweek,* October 6, 1969, 29.

13. Arthur Mann, *The One and the Many: Reflections on the American Identity* (Chicago: University of Chicago Press, 1979), 22.

14. Barbara Mikulski, "Who Speaks for Ethnic America?" *New York Times,* September 29, 1970, 43.

15. Pete Hamill, "The Revolt of the White Lower-Middle Class," in *The White Majority: Between Poverty and Affluence,* ed. Louise Kapp Howe (New York: Random House, 1970), 13–14.

16. "The Troubled American: A Special Report on the White Majority," *Newsweek,* October 6, 1969, 65; more generally, see Michael Flamm, *Law and Order: Street Crime, Civil Unrest, and the Crisis of Liberalism in the 1960s* (New York: Columbia University Press, 2004), and Philip Jenkins, *Decade of Nightmares: The End of the Sixties and the Making of Eighties America* (New York: Oxford University Press, 2006).

17. Hamill, "The Revolt of the White Lower-Middle Class," 13–14.

18. Novak, *The Rise of the Unmeltable Ethnics,* 71–72. For an astute analysis of Novak and race, see Jacobson, *Roots Too,* 187–191.

19. Quoted in Perry L. Weed, *The White Ethnic Movement and Ethnic Politics* (New York: Praeger, 1973), 19–20. See also Arthur Mann, *The One and the Many* (Chicago: University of Chicago Press, 1979), 20, 25. On the relationship between ethnics and blacks, also see Hamill, "The Revolt of the White Lower Middle Class," and Andrew Hacker, "Is There a Republican Majority?" in *The White Majority,* 10–22 and 263–278, respectively.

20. Weed, *The White Ethnic Movement,* chap. 3.
21. David R. Colburn and George E. Pozzetta, "Race, Ethnicity and the Evolution of Political Legitimacy," in *The Sixties: From Memory to History,* ed. David Farber (Chapel Hill: University of North Carolina Press, 1994), 119–148, quote on 132.
22. Geno Baroni, "Ethnicity and Public Policy," in *Pieces of a Dream: The Ethnic Worker's Crisis with America,* ed. Michael Wenk, S.M. Tomasi, and Geno Baroni (New York: Center for Migration Studies, 1972), 1–12.
23. Weed, *The White Ethnic Movement,* 27, 32, 118. Also see *Newsweek,* December 21, 1971, on Baroni's activities.
24. Vincent J. Trapani to Stephen Shulman, April 21, 1967, in folder: Research EEO-1, Papers of Chairman Stephen Shulman, box 10, EEOC Papers, National Archives.
25. Mary Patrice Erdmans, *Opposite Poles: Immigrants and Ethnics in Polish Chicago, 1976–1996* (University Park: Pennsylvania State University Press, 1998), 49.
26. Russell Barta, "Minority Report: The Representation of Poles, Italians, Latins and Blacks in the Executive Suites of Chicago's Largest Corporations" (n.d. [1973 or 1974]), in *Civil Rights during the Nixon Administration, 1969–1973,* ed. Hugh Davis Graham (Bethesda, Md.: University Publications of America, 1989), part I, reel 19, frames 493–496.
27. Brief of the Polish American Congress, the National Advocates Society, and the National Medical and Dental Association as Amici Curiae, reprinted in *Regents of the University of California v. Allan Bakke: Complete Case Record,* vol. 2 (Englewood, Colo.: Information Handling Services, 1978).
28. See the testimony of Weldon J. Rougeau, U.S. Commission on Civil Rights, *Consultations on the Affirmative Action Statement of the U.S. Commission on Civil Rights,* vol. 2: *Proceedings, February 10 and March 10–11, 1981* (Washington, D.C.: U.S. Government Printing Office, 1982), 85.
29. *Civil Rights Issues of Euro-Ethnic Americans in the United States: Opportunities and Challenges, A Consultation Sponsored by the U.S. Commission on Civil Rights,* Chicago, December 3, 1979 (Washington, D.C.: U.S. Government Printing Office, 1980); U.S. Commission on Civil Rights, *Consultations on the Affirmative Action Statement of the U.S. Commission on Civil Rights,* vol. 2.

30. *Congressional Record,* December 15, 1969, 39:062–063.

31. Hearings before the Special Subcommittee on Education of the Committee on Education and Labor, U.S. House, 93rd Cong., 2nd sess., part 2A, Civil Rights Obligations, 1974, 25–28.

32. Ibid., 238–239. Buckley made similar arguments on the Senate floor. See Philip Gleason's discussion in *Speaking of Diversity: Language and Ethnicity in Twentieth-Century America* (Baltimore: Johns Hopkins University Press, 1992), chap. 4, especially 106.

33. House Joint Resolution 983, *Congressional Record,* November 13, 1969, 34:165.

34. *Congressional Record,* November 21, 1969, 35:435–436.

35. *Congressional Quarterly Weekly Report,* July 22, 1972, 1837. See the discussion in Nathan Glazer, *Ethnic Dilemmas: 1964–1982* (Cambridge, Mass.: Harvard University Press, 1983), 135–136.

36. Judith Herman, ed., *The Schools and Group Identity: Educating for a New Pluralism* (New York: Institute on Pluralism and Group Identity of the American Jewish Committee, 1974), 8.

37. Quoted in Noel Epstein, *Language, Ethnicity and the Schools: Policy Alternatives for Bilingual-Bicultural Education* (Washington, D.C.: George Washington University Institute for Educational Leadership, 1977), 38–39. Some ethnic groups found more success at the local or state level. For example, state legislatures created Polish American studies programs in higher education institutions in Connecticut, Massachusetts, Michigan, and Wisconsin. See Stanislaus A. Blejwas, "Polonia and Politics," in *Polish Americans and Their History,* ed. John J. Bukowczyk (Pittsburgh: University of Pittsburgh Press, 1996), 121–151, 139.

38. Novak, *The Rise of the Unmeltable Ethnics,* 55.

39. John D. Skrentny, *The Minority Rights Revolution* (Cambridge, Mass.: Belknap Press of Harvard University Press, 2002), chap. 5.

40. Memo from H.R. Haldeman to Mr. Dent, October 31, 1969, paraphrasing Nixon, in *Civil Rights during the Nixon Administration,* reel 2, frame 129; Paul Frymer and John D. Skrentny, "Coalition-Building and the Politics of Electoral Capture during the Nixon Administration: African Americans, Labor, Latinos," *Studies in American Political Development* 12 (1998): 131–161, quote on 151.

41. Memo from Patrick J. Buchanan to the president, November 10, 1972, in *From: The President: Richard Nixon's Secret Files,* ed. Bruce Oudes (New York: Harper and Row, 1989), 562.

42. Memo for the president from Harry S. Dent, October 13, 1969, in folder: Middle Americans, Dent, SMOF, Papers of Harry S. Dent, box 8, NPMP, National Archives.

43. Memo from H.R. Haldeman to Mr. Dent, October 31, 1969, paraphrasing Nixon, in *Civil Rights during the Nixon Administration*, reel 2, frame 129.

44. Memo to the president from Secretary of Labor Shultz, June 26, 1969, in *Civil Rights during the Nixon Administration*, part I, reel 2, frame 14.

45. Jefferson Cowie, "Nixon's Class Struggle: Romancing the New Right Worker, 1969–1973," *Labor History* 43 (August 2002): 257–283.

46. Robert Mason, *Richard Nixon and the Quest for a New Majority* (Chapel Hill: University of North Carolina Press, 2004), 73.

47. Hugh Davis Graham, *The Civil Rights Era* (New York: Oxford University Press, 1990), 342–243. "Goals and timetables" referred to contractors' good-faith promises to hire numerical ranges of particular minority employees by specified time periods.

48. *Federal Register* 36:250 (December 29, 1971), 25:165.

49. Skrentny, *The Minority Rights Revolution*.

50. Mason, *Richard Nixon and the Quest for a New Majority*, 168.

51. Confidential Memo for Mr. Colson from H.R. Haldeman, September 8, 1970, in folder: CF LA-7 Unions [1969–1970], WHSF, Confidential Files, box 38, NPMP, National Archives; Memorandum for H.R. Haldeman from Charles Colson, September 14, 1970, in Folder: LA-7 Labor Management Relations [1969–1970], WHSF, Confidential Files, box 38, NPMP, National Archives.

52. Untitled, undated report, in folder: Ethnics, WHSF, SMOF, Papers of Charles Colson, box 62, NPMP, National Archives.

53. Ibid.

54. Cowie finds a similar preference for symbolism over substance in Nixonian labor politics See Cowie, "Nixon's Class Struggle," 279. Nixon's advisers often mixed their appeals to labor, ethnics, and Catholics; see Skrentny, *The Minority Rights Revolution*, chap. 9.

55. Mason, *Richard Nixon and the Quest for a New Majority*, 168–169; "Remarks at the Dedication of the American Museum of Immigration on Liberty Island," September 26, 1972, and "Statement about the Dedication of the American Museum of Immigration," September 26, 1972, in *Public Papers of the Presidents of the United States: Richard M. Nixon, 1971* (Washington, D.C.: U.S. Government Printing Office, 1972), 913–916; Memo for Susan Porter from Michael Balzano,

February 21, 1973, in folder: Events-Speaking Engagements, WHCF, SMOF, Papers of Michael P. Balzano, box 5, NPMP, National Archives. In July of 1970, Nixon aide Dwight Chapin sought a study of the ethnic groups in the key states to determine special events or dates that should be exploited. "For example," Chapin continued, "in the State of Illinois, if there is a big Polish holiday between now and election day we would program someone in for that particular event." Memo for Murray Chotiner and Harry Dent from Dwight L. Chapin, July 25, 1970, in *Civil Rights during the Nixon Administration,* part I, reel 2, frame 865: "Republican figures attended thirteen separate ethnic events in Chicago alone." On ethnic lobbying for government jobs, see Letter from Laszlo Pasztor to Harry Dent, July 31, 1970; and Letter from Harry Dent to Laszlo Pasztor, August 10, 1970, in folder: Nationalities and Minorities [1 of 2], WHSF, SMOF, Papers of Harry S. Dent, box 9, NPMP, National Archives; Laszlo Pasztor to Harry Dent, March 19, 1970, in folder: 1970 Nationalities and Minorities [2 of 2], WHSF, SMOF, Papers of Harry S. Dent 1969–1970, box 9, NPMP, National Archives; and Memo from Tom Lias to Harry Dent, June 1, 1970, in folder: 1970 Nationalities and Minorities [2 of 2], WHSF, SMOF, Papers of Harry S. Dent 1969–1970, box 9, NPMP, National Archives.

56. Confidential Memo for Mr. Colson from H.R. Haldeman, September 8, 1970, in folder: CF LA-7 Unions [1969–1970], WHSF, Confidential Files, box 38, NPMP, National Archives; more generally, see Cowie, "Nixon's Class Struggle," and Judith Stein, *Running Steel, Running America: Race, Economic Policy, and the Decline of Liberalism* (Chapel Hill: University of North Carolina Press, 1998).

57. Frymer and Skrentny, "Coalition-Building and the Politics of Electoral Capture during the Nixon Administration."

10. The Conservative Struggle and the Energy Crisis

1. John Updike, *Rabbit Is Rich* (New York: Knopf, 1981), 3.
2. David Vogel, *Fluctuating Fortunes: The Political Power of Business in America* (New York: Basic Books, 1989), 54, 114.
3. David Howard Davis, *Energy Politics,* 3rd ed. (New York: St. Martin's Press, 1982), 83–84.
4. "Gas Fever," *Time,* February 18, 1974, 35.
5. Energy Meeting, November 7, 1973, Nixon Papers, President's Meetings File, box 93, National Archives, College Park, Md.

6. News Summary, February 4, 1974, Nixon Papers, box 71; Al Richman, "The Polls: Public Attitudes toward the Energy Crisis," *Public Opinion Quarterly* 43, no. 4 (Winter 1979): 576–585.

7. John McGlaughlin to Alexander Haig, November 14, 1973, Nixon Papers, Chief of Staff, Interstaff Communications, box 10, Maryland.

8. William Safire, "Do Something!" *New York Times,* February 14, 1974.

9. Richard Vietor, *Energy Policy in America since 1945: A Study of Business-Government Relations* (Cambridge: Cambridge University Press, 1984).

10. Roy Ash to Richard Nixon, February 11 and 15, 1974, Nixon Papers, President's Handwriting, box 26; Roy Ash, Memorandum for the President, February 12, 1974, William Simon Papers, Federal Energy Office, Lafayette College, folder 29.

11. Judy Bachrach, "William Simon, The Energetic Czar," *Washington Post,* January 13, 1974, 1, 2; Cabinet Meeting, February 21, 1974, Nixon Papers, President's Meetings File, box 93.

12. William Simon to Alexander Haig, n.d., Nixon Papers, Energy Policy Office, box 1.

13. Linda Charlton, "Simon Announces Stand-By System on 'Gas' Rationing," *New York Times,* December 28, 1973, 1; William Simon, *A Time for Truth* (New York: Reader's Digest Press, 1978), 53.

14. "Growing an Energetic Monster," *St. Louis Globe Democrat,* William Simon Papers, Clipping file, box 22.

15. "One State's Response to Gasoline Panic," *U.S. News & World Report,* February 4, 1974, 16; "Do-It-Yourself Rationing," *Economist,* February 16, 1974, 50–51; News Summary, February 6, 1974, Nixon Papers, News Summaries, box 71; "Byrne Announces Mandatory Plan of 'Gas' Rationing," *New York Times,* February 9, 1974, 1.

16. Vietor, *Energy Policy in America since 1945.*

11. Turnabout Years

1. Robert H. Zieger and Gilbert J. Gall, *American Workers, American Unions: The Twentieth Century* (Baltimore: Johns Hopkins University Press, 2002), 209–212, 216; Joseph A. McCartin, "Bringing the State's Workers in: Time to Rectify an Imbalanced US Labor Historiography," *Labor History* 47, no. 1 (February 2006): 73–94.

2. Francis Ryan, "Everyone Royalty: AFSCME, Municipal Workers and Urban Power in Philadelphia, 1921–1983" (Ph.D. diss., University of

Pennsylvania, 2003); Joseph C. Slater, *Public Workers: Government Employee Unions, the Law, and the State, 1900–1962* (Ithaca, N.Y.: ILR Press, 2004); Richard J. Murphy and Morris Sackman, eds., *The Crisis in Public Employee Relations in the Decade of the 1970s* (Washington, D.C.: Bureau of National Affairs, 1970); Zieger and Gall, *American Workers.*

3. Aaron Brenner, "Striking against the State: The Postal Wildcat of 1970," *Labor's Heritage* 7, no. 4 (1996): 4–27; Joseph A. McCartin, " 'Fire the Hell out of Them': Sanitation Workers' Struggles and the Normalization of the Striker Replacement Strategy in the 1970s," *Labor: Studies in the Working-Class History of the Americas* 2, no. 3 (Fall 2005): 67–71.

4. Joshua Freeman, *Working-Class New York: Life and Labor since World War II* (New York: New Press, 2000); Joan Turner Beifuss, *At the River I Stand: Memphis, the 1968 Strike, and Martin Luther King* (Brooklyn, N.Y.: Carlson Publishing, 1989).

5. *National Public Employee Relations Act,* H.R. 18972, August 13, 1970, box 75, file 16, AFSCME President's Office, Jerry Wurf Collection, Walter Reuther Library, Wayne State University, Detroit, Mich.; *Government Employee Relations Report* [hereafter *GERR*], June 25, 1973, B2; *Wall Street Journal,* August 6, 1974; Ralph J. Flynn, *Public Work, Public Workers* (Washington, D.C.: New Republic Book Company, 1975); Richard N. Billings and John Greenya, *Power to the Public Worker* (New York: Robert B. Luce, 1974). On the origins of NPERA, see Joseph A. McCartin, "A Wagner Act for Public Sector Workers," forthcoming in *Journal of American History.*

6. Freeman, *Working-Class New York;* "The Crisis in 'Stink City,' " *Newsweek,* July 14, 1975.

7. See McCartin, "Fire the Hell out of Them," 79–81; "Cities in Peril," *U.S. News & World Report,* April 7, 1975.

8. *New York Times,* July 1, 2, 3, 4, 8, 1975; *Philadelphia Inquirer,* July 2, 3, 1975; *Seattle Times,* June 24, 1975.

9. *GERR,* December 18, 1978, 25.

10. Young quoted in *GERR,* October 6, 1975, Z1–Z5; Joseph A. McCartin, interview with Ken Young, November 30, 2001, Silver Spring, Md., tape recording in author's possession.

11. *Maryland v. Wirtz,* 392 U.S. 183 (1968); Neal R. Pierce, "Major Impact Expected from Decision on Labor Act," *National Journal,* May 17, 1975, 740–745.

12. Harry A. Blackmun, Memo on [Cases] 74-878, 74-879, April 15, 1975, and conference notes on 74-878 and 74-879, March 5, 1976, folder 5, box 217, Harry A. Blackmun Papers, Manuscript Division, Library of Congress. On the legal history of labor's long and unsuccessful effort to pass a public sector Wagner Act, see McCartin, "A Wagner Act for Public Sector Workers."

13. Joseph A. McCartin, interview with David Y. Denholm, January 28, 2004, tape recording in author's possession; Sylvester Petro, *The Labor Policy of a Free Society* (New York: Ronald Press Company, 1957); Sylvester Petro, "Sovereignty and Compulsory Public-Sector Bargaining." *Wake Forest Law Review* 10 (March 1974): 25–165.

14. Public Sector Research Council, *Public Sector Bargaining and Strikes* (Vienna, Va.: Public Service Research Council, 1982).

15. Ralph de Toledano, *Let Our Cities Burn* (New Rochelle, N.Y.: Arlington House, 1975), 33, 42.

16. *National Right to Work Newsletter,* August 28, 1975; *GERR,* July 28, 1975, F1–F5.

17. See the following issues of *GERR:* August 25, 1975, A-8, A-9; March 15, 1976, A-10; October 23, 1978, A6; October 13, 1975, B-4. Kirkland quoted in *GERR,* November 3, 1975, A8.

18. On labor and Carter, see Taylor Dark, "Organized Labor and the Carter Administration: The Origins of Conflict," and Gary M. Fink, "Fragile Alliance: Jimmy Carter and the American Labor Movement," both in *The Presidency and Domestic Policies of Jimmy Carter,* ed. Herbert D. Rosenbaum and Alexej Ugrinsky (Westport, Conn.: Greenwood Press, 1994), 761–782 and 783–803, respectively.

19. *Wall Street Journal,* April 28, 1977; *Washington Post,* April 30, May 23, and May 26, 1977; *GERR,* May 23, 1977, 5; Joseph A. McCartin, interview with William Clay, June 22, 2006, tape recording in author's possession.

20. Carter quoted in *GERR,* March 6, 1978, 37; August 14, 1978, 9; September 18, 1978, 3.

21. McCartin, "Fire the Hell out of Them"; Michael Spear, "Lessons to Be Learned: The New York City Municipal Unions, the 1970s Fiscal Crisis, and New York City at a Crossroads after September 11," *International Labor and Working-Class History* 62 (2002): 89–95.

22. Freeman, *Working-Class New York;* Randolph H. Boehm and Dan C. Heldman, *Public Employees, Unions, and the Erosion of Civic Trust:*

A Study of San Francisco in the 1970s (Frederick, Md.: Aletheia Books, University Publications of America, 1982).

23. "Why So Many Strikes by Public Workers," *U.S. News & World Report,* August 7, 1978, 65; Nicholas Von Hoffman, "The Last Days of the Labor Movement," *Harper's Magazine* (December 1978): 22.

24. *Washington Post,* March 20, 1979.

25. McCartin, "Fire the Hell out of Them"; Willis J. Nordlund, *Silent Skies: The Air Traffic Controllers' Strike* (Westport, Conn.: Praeger, 1998); Arthur B. Shostak and David Skocik, *The Air Controllers' Controversy: Lessons from the PATCO Strike* (New York: Human Sciences Press, 1986).

12. Détente and Its Discontents

1. "Kissinger: An Interview with Oriana Fallaci," *New Republic,* December 16, 1972, 21. For a fuller description of this interview, and the wide attention it received, see Oriana Fallaci, *Interview with History,* trans. John Shepley (Boston: Houghton Mifflin, 1976), 17–44.

2. Yitzhak Rabin with the assistance of Eithan Haber, *Yitzhak Rabin mesocheach im manhigim ve-rashey medinot* [Yitzhak Rabin Converses with Leaders and Heads of State] (Giva'atayim, Israel: Revivim, 1984). My research assistant, Gil Ribak, translated these passages from the Hebrew original.

3. See Odd Arne Westad, *The Global Cold War: Third World Interventions and the Making of Our Times* (Cambridge: Cambridge University Press, 2005), 207–287; Jeremi Suri, *Power and Protest: Global Revolution and the Rise of Détente* (Cambridge, Mass.: Harvard University Press, 2003), esp. 258–259.

4. Memorandum of Conversation between Henry Kissinger and a group of Fellows from the Harvard Center for International Affairs, December 7, 1971, Digital National Security Archive Document Database, http://nsarchive.chadwyck.com (accessed July 26, 2006). See also Suri, *Power and Protest,* 164–258.

5. Handwritten diary entry, April 17, 1968, Papers of Michael Stewart, Number 8/1/5, Churchill Archives Center, Churchill College, Cambridge, England [hereafter Stewart Papers].

6. Handwritten diary entry, April 29, 1968, Stewart Papers.

7. Henry Kissinger, *White House Years* (Boston: Little, Brown, 1979), 755. See also Margaret Macmillan, *Nixon and Mao: The Week That Changed the World* (New York: Random House, 2007).

8. Anatoly Dobrynin, *In Confidence: Moscow's Ambassador to America's Six Cold War Presidents* (New York: Random House, 1995), 225.

9. See Raymond L. Garthoff, *Détente and Confrontation: American–Soviet Relations from Nixon to Reagan*, rev. ed. (Washington, D.C.: Brookings Institution, 1994), 325–359.

10. "Basic Principles of Relations between the United States of America and the Union of Soviet Socialist Republics," May 29, 1972, reprinted in *The U.S. Department of State Bulletin* 66 (June 26, 1972): 898–899.

11. Henry Kissinger, News Conference, Kiev, May 29, 1972, reprinted in *The U.S. Department of State Bulletin* 66 (June 26, 1972): 890–897.

12. See Suri, *Power and Protest*, 256–258.

13. See Jeffrey Kimball, *Nixon's Vietnam War* (Lawrence: University Press of Kansas, 1998), esp. 119–123; Jeffrey Kimball, ed., *The Vietnam War Files: Uncovering the Secret History of Nixon-Era Strategy* (Lawrence: University Press of Kansas, 2004), 61–76.

14. See Jeremi Suri, *Henry Kissinger and the American Century* (Cambridge, Mass.: Belknap Press of Harvard University Press, 2007), chap. 5.

15. Richard Nixon, Radio and Television Address, January 23, 1973, http://www.vietnamwar.com/peacewithhonor.htm (accessed March 23, 2006).

16. Former American ambassador to South Vietnam Henry Cabot Lodge Jr. congratulated Kissinger on "the miracles which you have wrought." See Henry Cabot Lodge Jr. to Henry Kissinger, July 9, 1974, reel 9, part 1, Papers of Henry Cabot Lodge II, Massachusetts Historical Society, Boston.

17. See Henry Kissinger, *Years of Renewal* (New York: Simon and Schuster, 1999), 520–546; Robert Schulzinger, *A Time for War: The United States and Vietnam, 1941–1975* (New York: Oxford University Press, 1997), 305–327.

18. See Suri, *Henry Kissinger and the American Century,* chap. 5.

19. Margaret E. Keck and Kathryn Sikkink, *Activists beyond Borders* (Ithaca, N.Y.: Cornell University Press, 1998), 89–90.

20. Ibid., 89–92; Paul Heath Hoeffel and Peter Kornbluh, "The War at Home: Chile's Legacy in the United States," *NACLA Report on the Americas* 17 (September–October 1983): 27–39; Steve J. Stern, *Remembering Pinochet's Chile: On the Eve of London 1998* (Durham, N.C.: Duke University Press, 2004), xxiv–xxv.

21. Kathryn Sikkink, *Mixed Signals: U.S. Human Rights Policy in Latin America* (Ithaca, N.Y.: Cornell University Press, 2004), 48–76.

22. See *Covert Action in Chile,* Staff Report of the Select Committee to Study Government Operations with Respect to Intelligence Activities, U.S. Senate (Washington, D.C.: U.S. Government Printing Office, 1975); *Alleged Assassination Plots Involving Foreign Leaders,* Interim Report of the Select Committee to Study Government Operations with Respect to Intelligence Activities, U.S. Senate (Washington, D.C.: U.S. Government Printing Office, 1975).

23. Kissinger, *Years of Renewal,* 307.

24. *La rapport de Luxembourg (rapport Davignon),* available at www.ellopos.net/politics/davignon.htm (accessed July 8, 2005). With one exception, I have used the English translation of the Davignon Report found in David de Giustino, *A Reader in European Integration* (London: Longman, 1996), 196–199. The text of the Davignon Report in de Giustino's volume translates "les droits de l'homme" literally as "the rights of man." I have translated this phrase as the more recognized and accurate English term "human rights."

25. Transcript of Henry Kissinger's telephone conversation with Jerrold Schecter, March 22, 1974, Henry A. Kissinger Telephone Conversation Transcripts, Richard Nixon Presidential Materials Project, National Archives, College Park, Md.

26. See http://www.hri.org/docs/Helsinki75.html#H4.5 (accessed March 21, 2006).

27. Handwritten text of Ronald Reagan's radio address, taped November 30, 1976, reprinted in Kiron K. Skinner, Annelise Anderson, and Martin Anderson, eds., *Reagan in His Own Hand: The Writings of Ronald Reagan That Reveal His Revolutionary Vision for America* (New York: Simon and Schuster, 2001), 134–135.

28. Handwritten text of Reagan's radio address, taped October 10, 1978, in Skinner, Anderson, and Anderson, *Reagan in His Own Hand,* 94–95.

29. See John Lewis Gaddis, *Strategies of Containment: A Critical Appraisal of American National Security Policy during the Cold War,* rev. ed.

(New York: Oxford University Press, 2005), 349–377; Jeremi Suri, "Explaining the End of the Cold War: A New Historical Consensus?" *Journal of Cold War Studies* 4 (Fall 2002): 60–92.

30. Henry Kissinger, *Diplomacy* (New York: Simon and Schuster, 1994), 766.

31. See Suri, *Henry Kissinger and the American Century,* chap. 4.

32. For more on Kissinger's legacy in the Middle East, and its relevance for contemporary foreign policy, see Suri, *Henry Kissinger and the American Century,* chap. 6.

13. Carter's Nicaragua and Other Democratic Quagmires

1. Gaddis Smith, *Morality, Reason, and Power: American Diplomacy in the Carter Years* (New York: Hill and Wang, 1986), 28. For further examples of campaign statements in this vein, see 29–30.

2. Remarks to People of Other Nations on Assuming Office, January 20, 1977, in *Public Papers of the Presidents of the United States: Jimmy Carter, 1977,* vol. 1 (Washington, D.C.: U.S. Government Printing Office, 1977), 4.

3. Commencement Address, University of Notre Dame, May 22, 1977, in *Public Papers of the Presidents of the United States: Jimmy Carter, 1977,* vol. 1, 954–957.

4. Letter, Conservative Congressional Members to Carter, September 22, 1978, folder CO 114, 1/1/78–12/31/78, box CO-46, White House Central File—Countries, Jimmy Carter Library, Atlanta.

5. Robert A. Pastor, *Condemned to Repetition: The United States and Nicaragua* (Princeton, N.J.: Princeton University Press, 1987), 4–5.

6. Ibid., 58. For a detailed list of the members of the Group of Twelve, see Holly Sklar, *Washington's War on Nicaragua* (Boston: South End Press, 1988), 11–12.

7. *New York Times,* December 26, 1977, 22.

8. *New York Times,* February 5, 1978, 3.

9. *New York Times,* March 5, 1978, 14.

10. Walter LaFeber, *Inevitable Revolutions: The United States in Central America,* 2nd ed. (New York: Norton, 1993), 229.

11. Pastor, *Condemned to Repetition,* 66–71. The letter text, edited for space, appears in Sklar, *Washington's War on Nicaragua,* 15.

12. Memo, Vance to Carter, Undated, folder Serial Xs—[9/78–12/78], box 36, Donated Historical Material—Brzezinski, Jimmy Carter Library.

13. Interview with the President, September 22, 1978, in *Public Papers of the Presidents of the United States: Jimmy Carter, 1978*, vol. 2 (Washington, D.C.: U.S. Government Printing Office, 1979), 1599.

14. Sklar, *Washington's War on Nicaragua*, 19.

15. Pastor, *Condemned to Repetition*, 116.

16. Letter, Murphy to Carter, January 22, 1979, folder CO 114, 1/1/79–6/30/79, box CO-46, White House Central File—Countries, Jimmy Carter Library.

17. *New York Times*, January 24, 1979, 2.

18. Letter, Cranston et al. to Carter, February 9, 1979, folder CO 114, 1/1/79–6/30/79, box CO-46, White House Central File—Countries, Jimmy Carter Library.

19. Memo, Pastor to Brzezinski et al., June 8, 1979, folder Pastor, Robert—1989–1994, Vertical File, Jimmy Carter Library.

20. On Vance, see *New York Times*, June 22, 1979, 8, and LaFeber, *Inevitable Revolutions*, 234. On Brzezinski, see Pastor, *Condemned to Repetition*, 147–148.

21. See Pastor, *Condemned to Repetition*, 170–171, and Sklar, *Washington's War on Nicaragua*, 32.

22. *New York Times*, July 11, 1979, 20.

23. President's News Conference, July 25, 1979, in *Public Papers of the Presidents of the United States: Jimmy Carter, 1979*, vol. 2 (Washington, D.C.: U.S. Government Printing Office, 1980), 1307.

14. Conservatives, Carter, and the Politics of National Security

1. Rosalynn Carter, *First Lady from Plains* (New York: Fawcett Gold Metal, 1984), 298.

2. Joshua Muravchik, "Our Worst Ex-President," *Commentary* (February 2007).

3. James Mann, *Rise of the Vulcans: The History of Bush's War Cabinet* (New York: Viking, 2004), 73–75.

4. Jay Winik, *On the Brink: The Dramatic, Behind-the-Scenes Saga of the Reagan Era and the Men and Women Who Won the Cold War* (New York: Simon and Schuster, 1996), 111.

5. William Stueck, "Placing Jimmy Carter's Foreign Policy," in *The Carter Presidency: Policy Choices in the Post–New Deal Era*, ed. Gary M. Fink and Hugh Davis Graham (Lawrence: University of Kansas Press, 1998), 245–248.

6. Jimmy Carter, "University of Notre Dame: Address at Commencement Exercises," May 22, 1977, in *Public Papers of the Presidents of the United States: Jimmy Carter, 1977*, vol. 1 (Washington, D.C.: U.S. Government Printing Office, 1977), 956.

7. Coalition for a Democratic Majority to President Carter, May 14, 1977, Lyndon Johnson Presidential Library (Austin, Tex.), Papers of Peter Rosenblatt, box 49, File: Open Letter to Carter.

8. Steven F. Hayward, *The Age of Reagan: The Fall of the Old Liberal Order 1964–1980* (Roseville, Calif.: Forum, 2001), 536–537.

9. Joshua Muravchik, *The Uncertain Crusade: Jimmy Carter and the Dilemmas of Human Rights Policy* (Lanham, Md.: Hamilton Press, 1986), 161–195.

10. Memorandum of Conversation, February 1, 1977, Carter Library, NSA, Brzezinski Material, Subject File, box 34, File: Memocons, President 2/77.

11. Jessica Tuchman Matthews to Zbigniew Brzezinski, July 7, 1978, Carter Library, White House Central File, Subject File, Human Rights, box HU-1, File: 7/1/78–8/31/78.

12. Peter Beinart, *The Good Fight: Why Liberals—and Only Liberals—Can Win the War on Terror and Make America Great Again* (New York: HarperCollins, 2006), 58–59.

13. Julian E. Zelizer, *On Capitol Hill: The Struggle to Reform Congress and Its Consequences, 1948–2000* (New York: Cambridge University Press, 2004).

14. Rachel Bronson, *Thicker Than Oil: America's Uneasy Partnership with Saudi Arabia* (New York: Oxford University Press, 2006), 134.

15. Zbigniew Brzezinksi, *Power and Principle: Memoirs of the National Security Adviser* (New York: Farrar, Straus, Giroux, 1983), 189.

16. Landon Butler to Hamilton Jordan, March 17, 1977, Carter Library, Office of Chief of Staff, box 37, File: SALT, 1977.

17. Hamilton Jordan to President Carter, June 28, 1977, Carter Library, Hamilton Jordan Papers, box 34, File: Foreign Policy/Domestic Politics Memo 6/77.

18. David Skidmore, *Reversing Course: Carter's Foreign Policy, Domestic Politics, and the Failure of Reform* (Nashville: Vanderbilt University Press, 1996), 117.

19. J. Michael Hogan, *The Panama Canal in American Politics: Domestic Advocacy and the Evolution of Policy* (Carbondale: Southern Illinois University Press, 1986), 114–131.

20. Richard A. Viguerie, *The New Right: We're Ready to Lead* (Falls Church, Va.: Viguerie Company, 1981), 70–71.

21. Patrick Caddell, "A Memorandum on Current Public Attitudes on SALT," Carter Library, Office of Chief of Staff, box 37, File: SALT 1979.

22. Dan Tate to Frank Moore, November 18, 1977, Carter Library, Office of Chief of Staff, box 37, File: SALT, 1977.

23. Frank Moore and Hamilton Jordan to the President, 1979, Carter Library, Office of Congressional Liaison, box 230, File: SALT II Memo, 7/30/79–8/17/79.

24. Frank Moore to President Carter, July 7, 1978, Carter Library, Hamilton Jordan Papers, box 34, File: Comprehensive Test Ban Treaty, SALT, 1978.

25. "What Chance Now of Selling SALT to the Senate?" *The Economist*, November 18, 1978, 19.

26. Tip O'Neill with William Novak, *Man of the House: The Life and Political Memoirs of Speaker Tip O'Neill* (New York: Random House, 1987), 308.

27. Gaddis Smith, *Morality, Reason, and Power: American Diplomacy in the Carter Years* (New York: Hill and Wang, 1986), 9.

28. Ibid., 115.

29. Philip Jenkins, *Decade of Nightmares: The End of the Sixties and the Making of Eighties America* (New York: Oxford University Press, 2006), 156–157.

30. David D. Newsom, *The Soviet Brigade in Cuba: A Study in Political Diplomacy* (Bloomington: Indiana University Press, 1987), 16, 40.

31. Jimmy Carter, "Address to the Nation on Soviet Combat Troops in Cuba and the Strategic Arms Limitation Treaty," October 1, 1979, in *Public Papers of the Presidents of the United States: Jimmy Carter, 1979*, vol. 2 (Washington, D.C.: U.S. Government Printing Office, 1980), 1806.

32. Albert R. Hunt, "Carter Apparently Didn't Boost Chances for Passage of SALT with Cuban Speech," *Wall Street Journal*, October 3, 1979.

33. Hedley Donovan to Zbigniew Brzezinski and Lloyd Cutler, September 27, 1979, Carter Library, NSA, Brzezinski Material, box 16, File: Cuba Soviet Brigade (Meetings) 9/79.

34. David Farber, *Taken Hostage: The Iran Hostage Crisis and America's Encounter with Radical Islam* (Princeton, N.J.: Princeton University Press, 2005), 5, 187.

35. Robert D. Schulzinger, *U.S. Diplomacy since 1900,* 5th ed. (New York: Oxford University Press, 2002), 329.

36. For the best history of terrorism in the 1970s, see Timothy Naftali, *Blind Spot: The Secret History of American Counterterrorism* (New York: Basic Books, 2005), 1–115.

37. See Wattenberg letters from January 1980 in Johnson Library, Papers of Peter Rosenblatt, box 59, File: White House Meeting.

38. Jimmy Carter, *Keeping Faith: Memoirs of a President* (New York: Bantam Books, 1982), 473.

39. David S. Broder, "Bipartisan Support Wanes for Carter's Iran Policy," *Washington Post,* January 3, 1980.

40. Jimmy Carter, "Annual Message to Congress," January 21, 1980, in *Public Papers of the Presidents of the United States: Jimmy Carter, 1980–1981,* vol. 1 (Washington, D.C.: U.S. Government Printing Office, 1981), 164.

41. Les Francis to Frank Moore, June 11, 1979, Carter Library, Office of Congressional Liaison, box 228, File: Registration and the Draft.

42. ABC Evening News, Reference 62358, January 24, 1980, Vanderbilt Television Archives.

43. Marshall Brement to Zbigniew Brzezinski, January 10, 1980, Carter Library, Brzezinski Material, Subject File, box 48, File: Olympics 6/79–2/80.

44. William Dyess to the Deputy Secretary of State, March 21, 1980, Carter Library, Office of the Press Secretary, box 66, File: Olympic Boycott 1/80.

45. Lloyd Cutler, interview with Marie Allen, March 2, 1981, Carter Library, Exit Interview Collection, 7–8.

46. Tip O'Neill, John Brademas, Clement Zablocki, Jim Wright, John Rhodes, and William Broomfield to U.S. Olympic Committee, April 1, 1980, Carter Library, NSA, Brzezinski Material, Subject File, box 48, File: Olympics 6/79–2/80.

47. Patrick Caddell to Les Francis, May 26, 1980, Carter Library, Office of Chief of State, box 77, File: Campaign Strategy—Caddell.

48. Kiron S. Skinner, Annelise Anderson, and Martin Anderson, *Reagan: A Life in Letters* (New York: Free Press, 2003), 400.

49. Thomas B. Edsall, *Building Red America: The Conservative Coalition and the Drive for Permanent Power* (New York: Basic Books, 2006), 50–52.

Epilogue

1. Center for American Progress, "Stem Cells Figure Prominently in 2006 Election," http://www.americanprogress.org/issues/2006/11/stem_cell _election.html.
2. Richard Viguerie, *Conservatives Betrayed* (Los Angeles: Bonus Books, 2006).
3. Karen Tumulty, "How the Right Went Wrong," *Time*, March 26, 2007, 26–35.
4. Ralph Reed, quoted in ibid., 29.

Contributors

Paul Boyer is Merle Curti Professor of History Emeritus at the University of Wisconsin–Madison.

Derek N. Buckaloo is Assistant Professor of History at Coe College in Cedar Rapids, Iowa.

Joseph Crespino is Assistant Professor of History at Emory University.

Meg Jacobs is Associate Professor of History at the Massachusetts Institute of Technology.

Matthew D. Lassiter is Associate Professor of History at the University of Michigan.

Bradford Martin is Associate Professor of History at Bryant University in Smithfield, Rhode Island.

Joseph A. McCartin is Associate Professor of History at Georgetown University.

Bethany E. Moreton is Assistant Professor of History and Women's Studies at the University of Georgia.

Alice O'Connor is Associate Professor of History at the University of California, Santa Barbara.

Suleiman Osman is Assistant Professor in American Studies at George Washington University.

Bruce J. Schulman is Professor of History at Boston University.

John D. Skrentny is Professor of Sociology at the University of California, San Diego.

Marjorie J. Spruill is Professor of History at the University of South Carolina.

Thomas J. Sugrue is Kahn Professor of History and Sociology at the University of Pennsylvania.

Jeremi Suri is Professor of History at the University of Wisconsin–Madison.

Julian E. Zelizer is Professor of History and Public Affairs at Princeton University.

Index